Tree Tops Residential I
Overton - Timber Hil
Lyme Regis
Dorset
DT7 3HQ
Tel: 01297 44 38 21

Property of Tree Tops Residential Care Home.

NB :- PLEASE DO NOT REMOVE FROM TREE TOPS.

Bought for Activities purposes.

AA

Francis Frith's

English Country Houses

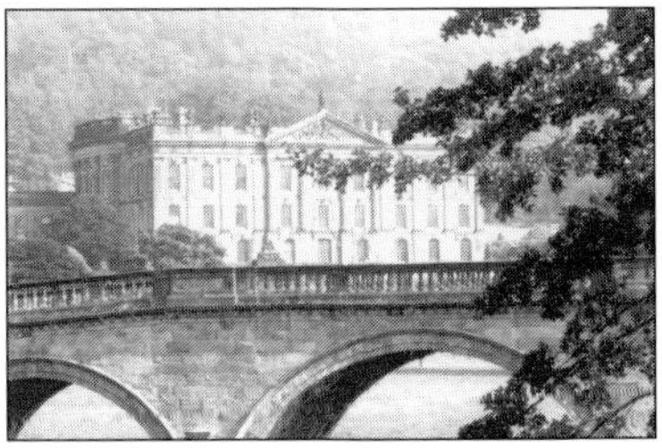

PHOTOGRAPHIC MEMORIES

Francis Frith's
ENGLISH COUNTRY HOUSES

Martin Dunning

FRITH BOOK Co

First published in the United Kingdom in 2000 by
Frith Book Company Ltd

British Library Cataloguing in Publication Data

English Country Houses
Martin Dunning
ISBN 1-85937-161-2

Frith Book Company Ltd
Frith's Barn, Teffont,
Salisbury, Wiltshire SP3 5QP
Tel: +44 (0) 1722 716 376
Email: info@frithbook.co.uk
www.frithbook.co.uk

Printed and bound in Great Britain

Front Cover: Romsey, Broadlands 1898 42110

AS WITH ANY HISTORICAL DATABASE THE FRITH ARCHIVE IS CONSTANTLY BEING CORRECTED AND IMPROVED AND THE PUBLISHERS WOULD WELCOME INFORMATION ON OMISSIONS OR INACCURACIES

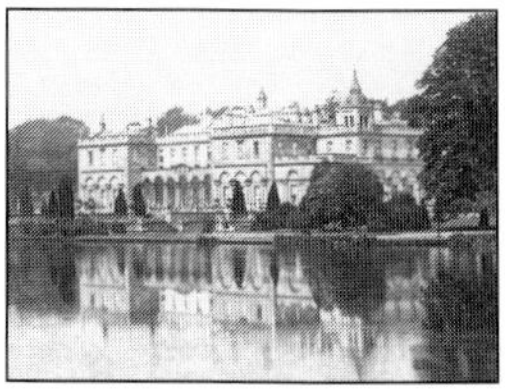

Contents

Francis Frith: *Victorian Pioneer*

Francis Frith, Victorian founder of the world-famous photographic archive, was a complex man. A devout Quaker and a highly successful Victorian businessman, he was both philosophic by nature and pioneering in outlook.

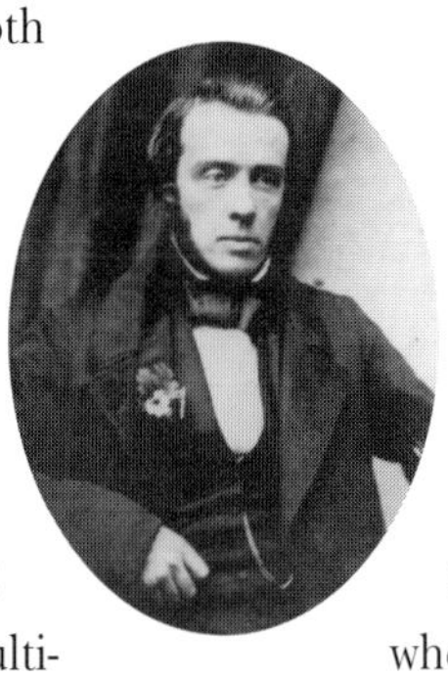

By 1855 Francis Frith had already established a wholesale grocery business in Liverpool, and sold it for the astonishing sum of £200,000, which is the equivalent today of over £15,000,000. Now a multi-millionaire, he was able to indulge his passion for travel. As a child he had pored over travel books written by early explorers, and his fancy and imagination had been stirred by family holidays to the sublime mountain regions of Wales and Scotland. 'What a land of spirit-stirring and enriching scenes and places!' he had written. He was to return to these scenes of grandeur in later years to 'recapture the thousands of vivid and tender memories', but with a different purpose. Now in his thirties, and captivated by the new science of photography, Frith set out on a series of pioneering journeys to the Nile regions that occupied him from 1856 until 1860.

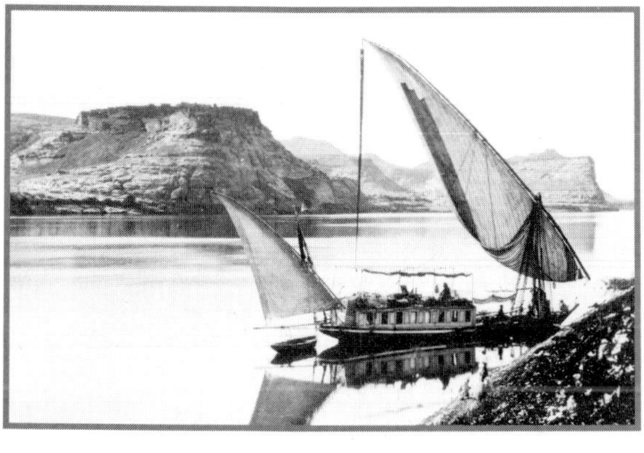

Intrigue and Adventure

He took with him on his travels a specially-designed wicker carriage that acted as both dark-room and sleeping chamber. These far-flung journeys were packed with intrigue and adventure. In his life story, written when he was sixty-three, Frith tells of being held captive by bandits, and of fighting 'an awful midnight battle to the very point of surrender with a deadly pack of hungry, wild dogs'. Sporting flowing Arab costume, Frith arrived at Akaba by camel seventy years before Lawrence, where he encountered 'desert princes and rival sheikhs, blazing with jewel-hilted swords'.

During these extraordinary adventures he was assiduously exploring the desert regions bordering the Nile and patiently recording the antiquities and peoples with his camera. He was the first photographer to venture beyond the sixth cataract. Africa was still the mysterious 'Dark Continent', and Stanley and Livingstone's historic meeting was a decade into the future. The conditions for picture taking confound belief. He laboured for hours in his wicker dark-room in the sweltering heat of the desert, while the volatile chemicals fizzed dangerously in their trays. Often he was forced to work in remote tombs and caves where conditions were cooler. Back in London he exhibited his photographs and was 'rapturously cheered' by members of the Royal Society. His reputation as a photographer was made overnight. An eminent modern historian has likened their impact on the population of the time to that on our own generation of the first photographs taken on the surface of the moon.

Venture of a Life-Time

Characteristically, Frith quickly spotted the opportunity to create a new business as a specialist publisher of photographs. He lived in an era of immense and sometimes violent change. For the poor in the early part of Victoria's reign work was a drudge and the hours long, and people had precious little free time to enjoy themselves. Most had no transport other than a cart or gig at their disposal, and had not travelled far beyond the boundaries of their own town or village.

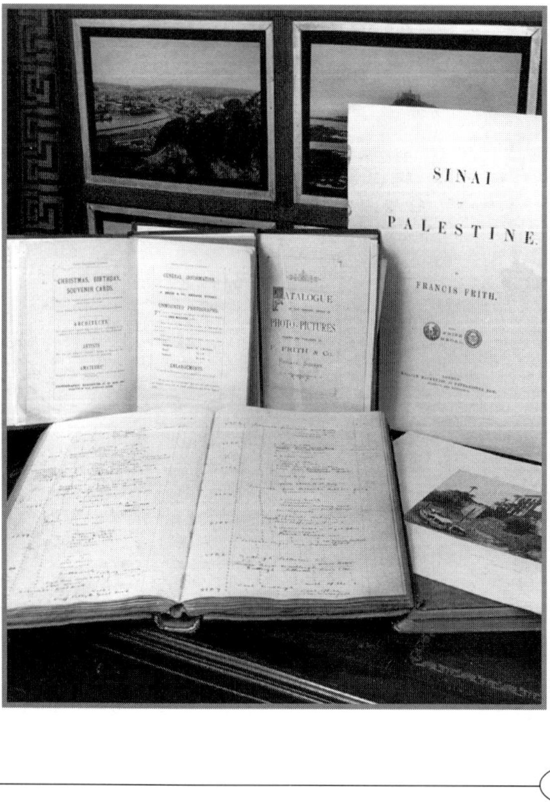

However, by the 1870s, the railways had threaded their way across the country, and Bank Holidays and half-day Saturdays had been made obligatory by Act of Parliament. All of a sudden the ordinary working man and his family were able to enjoy days out and see a little more of the world.

With characteristic business acumen, Francis Frith foresaw that these new tourists would enjoy having souvenirs to commemorate their days out. In 1860 he married Mary Ann Rosling and set out with the intention of photographing every city, town and village in Britain. For the next thirty years he travelled the country by train and by pony and trap, producing fine photographs of seaside resorts and beauty spots that were keenly bought by millions of Victorians. These prints were painstakingly pasted into family albums and pored over during the dark nights of winter, rekindling precious memories of summer excursions.

The Rise of Frith & Co

Frith's studio was soon supplying retail shops all over the country. To meet the demand he gathered about him a small team of photographers, and published the work of independent artist-photographers of the calibre of Roger Fenton and Francis Bedford. In order to gain some understanding of the scale of Frith's business one only has to look at the catalogue issued by Frith & Co in 1886: it runs to some 670 pages, listing not only many thousands of views of the British Isles but also many photographs of most European countries, and China, Japan, the USA and Canada – note the sample page shown above

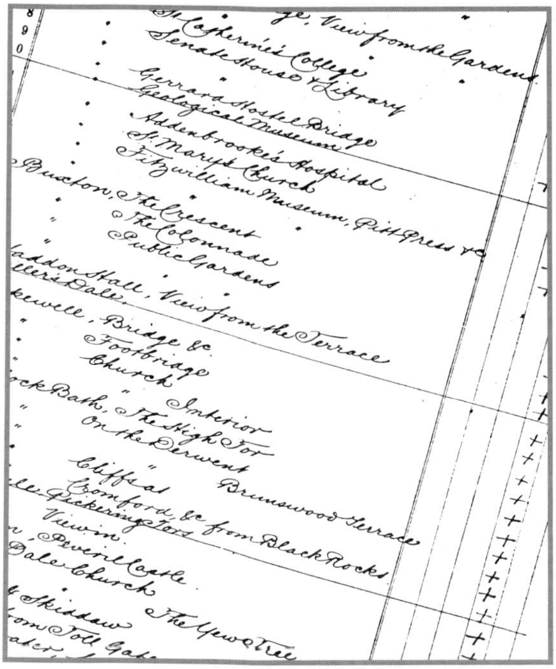

from the hand-written *Frith & Co* ledgers detailing pictures taken. By 1890 Frith had created the greatest specialist photographic publishing company in the world, with over 2,000 outlets – more than the combined number that Boots and WH Smith have today! The picture on the right shows the *Frith & Co* display board at Ingleton in the Yorkshire Dales. Beautifully constructed with mahogany frame and gilt inserts, it could display up to a dozen local scenes.

Postcard Bonanza

The ever-popular holiday postcard we know today took many years to develop. In 1870 the Post Office issued the first plain cards, with a pre-printed stamp on one face. In 1894 they allowed other publishers' cards to be sent through the mail with an attached adhesive halfpenny stamp. Demand grew rapidly, and in 1895 a new size of postcard was permitted called the court card, but there was little room for illustration. In 1899, a year after Frith's death, a new card measuring 5.5 x 3.5 inches became the standard format, but it was not until 1902 that the divided back came into being, with address and message on one face and a full-size illustration on the other. *Frith & Co* were in the vanguard of postcard development, and Frith's sons Eustace and Cyril continued their father's monumental task, expanding the number of views offered to the public and recording more and more places in Britain, as the coasts and countryside were opened up to mass travel.

Francis Frith died in 1898 at his villa in Cannes, his great project still growing. The archive he created continued in business for another seventy years. By 1970 it contained over a third of a million pictures of 7,000 cities, towns and villages. The massive photographic record Frith has left to us stands as a living monument to a special and very remarkable man.

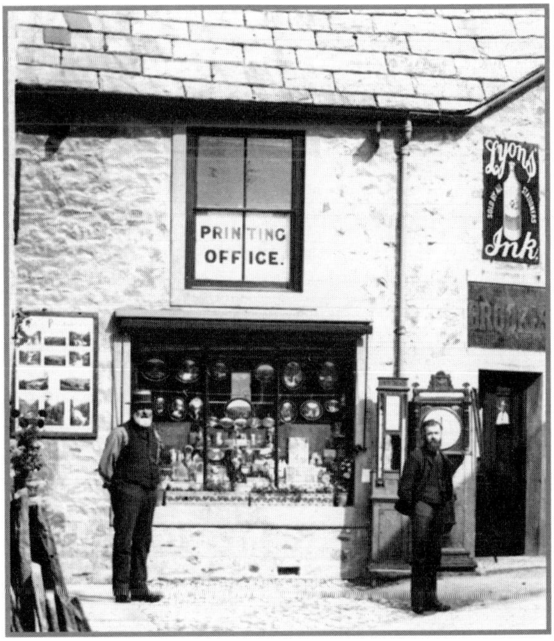

Frith's Archive: *A Unique Legacy*

Francis Frith's legacy to us today is of immense significance and value, for the magnificent archive of evocative photographs he created provides a unique record of change in 7,000 cities, towns and villages throughout Britain over a century and more. Frith and his fellow studio photographers revisited locations many times down the years to update their views, compiling for us an enthralling and colourful pageant of British life and character.

We tend to think of Frith's sepia views of Britain as nostalgic, for most of us use them to conjure up memories of places in our own lives with which we have family associations. It often makes us forget that to Francis Frith they were records of daily life as it was actually being lived in the cities, towns and villages of his day. The Victorian age was one of great and often bewildering change for ordinary people, and

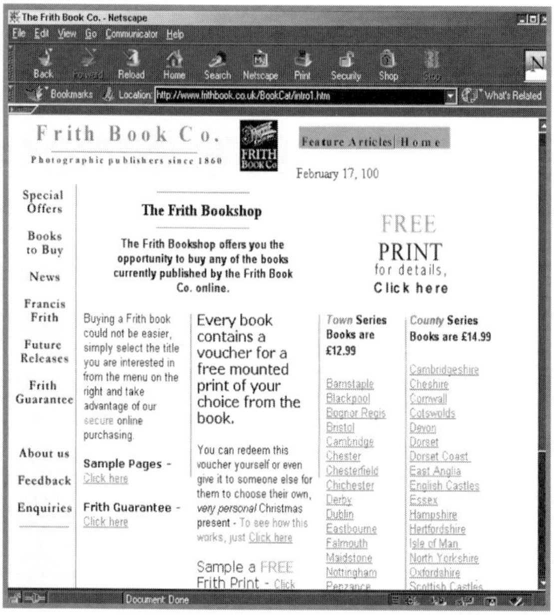

See Frith at www. frithbook.co.uk

though the pictures evoke an impression of slower times, life was as busy and hectic as it is today.

We are fortunate that Frith was a photographer of the people, dedicated to recording the minutiae of everyday life. For it is this sheer wealth of visual data, the painstaking chronicle of changes in dress, transport, street layouts, buildings, housing, engineering and landscape that captivates us so much today. His remarkable images offer us a powerful link with the past and with the lives of our ancestors.

Today's Technology

Computers have now made it possible for Frith's many thousands of images to be accessed almost instantly. In the Frith archive today, each photograph is carefully 'digitised' then stored on a CD Rom. Frith archivists can locate a single photograph amongst thousands within seconds. Views can be catalogued and sorted under a variety of categories of place and content to the immediate benefit of researchers.

Inexpensive reference prints can be created for them at the touch of a mouse button, and a wide range of books and other printed materials assembled and published for a wider, more general readership - in the next twelve months over a hundred Frith local history titles will be published! The day-to-day workings of the archive are very different from how they were in Francis Frith's time: imagine the herculean task of sorting through eleven tons of glass negatives as Frith had to do to locate a particular sequence of pictures! Yet the archive still prides itself on maintaining the same high standards of excellence laid down by Francis Frith, including the painstaking cataloguing and indexing of every view.

It is curious to reflect on how the internet now allows researchers in America and elsewhere greater instant access to the archive than Frith himself ever enjoyed. Many thousands of individual views can be called up on screen within seconds on one of the Frith internet sites, enabling people living continents away to revisit the streets of their ancestral home town, or view places in Britain where they have enjoyed holidays. Many overseas researchers welcome the chance to view special theme selections, such as transport, sports, costume and ancient monuments.

We are certain that Francis Frith would have heartily approved of these modern developments in imaging techniques, for he himself was always working at the very limits of Victorian photographic technology.

The Value of the Archive Today

Because of the benefits brought by the computer, Frith's images are increasingly studied by social historians, by researchers into genealogy and ancestory, by architects, town planners, and by teachers and schoolchildren involved in local history projects.

In addition, the archive offers every one of us an opportunity to examine the places where we and our families have lived and worked down the years. Highly successful in Frith's own era, the archive is now, a century and more on, entering a new phase of popularity.

The Past in Tune with the Future

Historians consider the Francis Frith Collection to be of prime national importance. It is the only archive of its kind remaining in private ownership and has been valued at a million pounds. However, this figure is now rapidly increasing as digital technology enables more and more people around the world to enjoy its benefits.

Francis Frith's archive is now housed in an historic timber barn in the beautiful village of Teffont in Wiltshire. Its founder would not recognize the archive office as it is today. In place of the many thousands of dusty boxes containing glass plate negatives and an all-pervading odour of photographic chemicals, there are now ranks of computer screens. He would be amazed to watch his images travelling round the world at unimaginable speeds through network and internet lines.

The archive's future is both bright and exciting. Francis Frith, with his unshakeable belief in making photographs available to the greatest number of people, would undoubtedly approve of what is being done today with his lifetime's work. His photographs, depicting our shared past, are now bringing pleasure and enlightenment to millions around the world a century and more after his death.

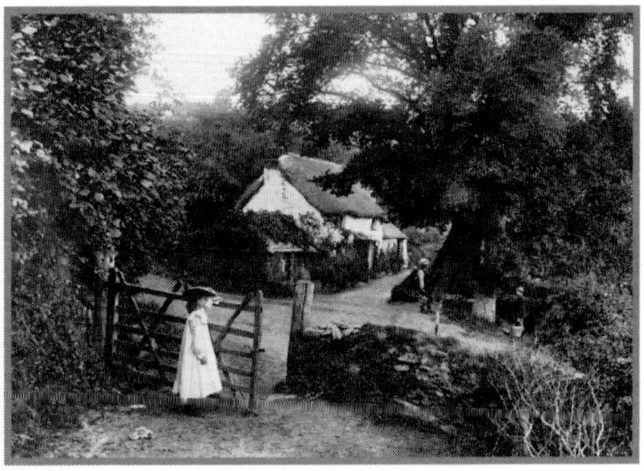

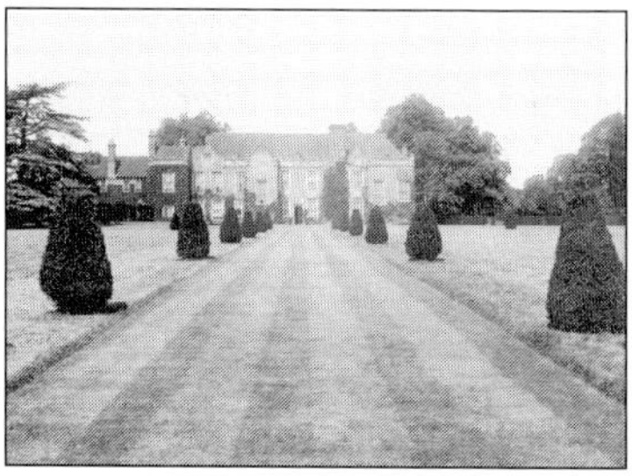

ENGLISH COUNTRY HOUSES
An Introduction

AN ENGLISHMAN'S HOME is his castle, says the old proverb. And a castle provides security and expresses status. Security and status - these two words go some way to explain the evolution of the English country house. Security is a primal need, one going back to man's dawn. Even a cave provides shelter from the weather, safety from wolves and bears, and a refuge from enemies. But caves are in short supply, particularly in the east of England, and caves may not be situated near running water or hunting grounds, so it was quite natural that somewhere in the mists of time man decided to create his own security by building his own home at a site that suited his way of life.

Early houses were no more than a ring of stones surmounted by a thatched or peat roof held up by branches and resting on a central pole. The addition of a wooden palisade, surrounding a hut or perhaps a group of homes, met the requirements of security, while at the same time making a statement: 'this is my land'. And the bigger your house and the stronger your palisade, because you happened to be an important chief or a successful hunter, the louder you were saying 'this is my land' and the higher your status.

Today's adage is that the three things most important in a house are location, location and location; this modern proverb is regularly trotted out by pundits and estate agents, who believe that they are passing on some new-found wisdom. In fact, location has always been a prime consideration; in addition to factors like running

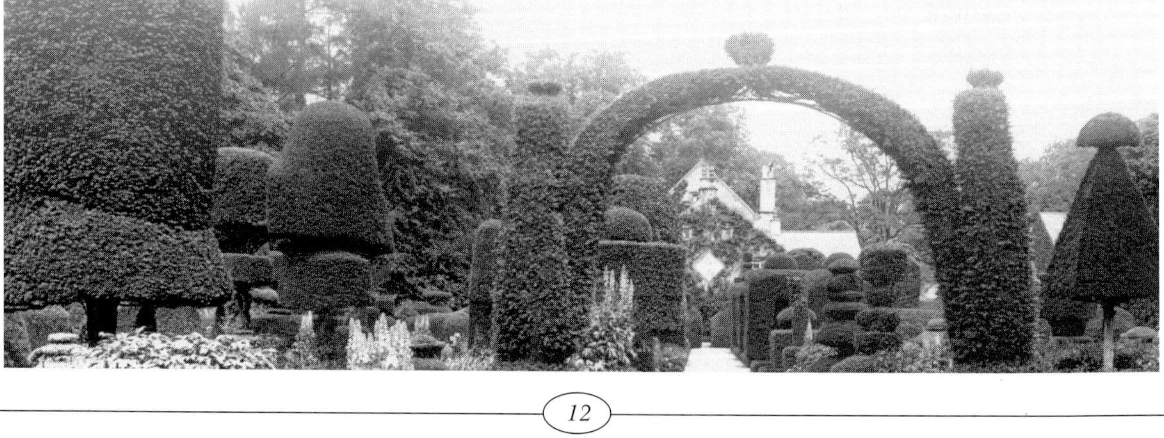

water and hunting grounds, sites tended to be chosen because they were easy to defend (security again) or because they were near some natural line of communication such as a river. Thus a house like Boughton Monchelsea Place, high on its hill above the Weald in Kent, would have been secure against attackers, while Cotehele in Cornwall, on the bank of the broad estuary of the Tamar, was easily accessible by boat in days when a road journey was a major undertaking.

Looking at English country houses today, however, it is not always easy to see their raison d'être. At Boughton Monchelsea, the castellated parapet appears more for decoration than defence, and the windows are too large to defend easily. This reveals another part of the story. The house was built on the site of an earlier fortified mansion, and may have been occupied for centuries before that. Many houses have this long hidden history - Yorkshire's Hovingham Hall, for instance, was built on an old Roman site - and what we see today is the tip of the iceberg.

The oldest buildings in this book date from the 14th century, but over the centuries extension, alteration and demolition have changed the face of Clevedon Court, for example, a fate it shares with many other houses. Some have a 17th-century wing here and a Tudor gatehouse there, while others may have a Victorian bay window perched incongruously on an Elizabethan gable.

By the turn of the 15th century, England had become a safer place to live. The Wars of the Roses were over, and the long reign of Henry VII had brought peace and prosperity. Freed from considerations of security, and with money to indulge their tastes, the powerful and wealthy ushered in a golden age of house building. In this they were aided by Henry VIII's break with Rome and the subsequent Dissolution of the Monasteries. Prime sites, hitherto occupied by priories and abbeys, were given to favourites of the King or bought for a pittance; at least twenty of the houses in this book were built on the site of a religious foundation, while others, such as Knole, were acquired by the king as a result of his battles with the church.

The first true Renaissance house in England, Longleat, dates from this time. Classically proportioned, with tiers of enormous windows and a symmetry unprecedented in English architecture, it was a far cry from previous fortified houses, and its construction owed more to status than security. Status was undoubtedly a major motivation for Cardinal Wolsey when he built Hampton Court Palace - its 1,000 rooms, and the enormous workforce employed during the five years it took to build, made an emphatic statement about the man who had risen from humble beginnings to become Lord Chancellor of England. Politics and intrigue were never very far away in Henry VIII's time, and some houses, often by pure chance, played a pivotal role in English

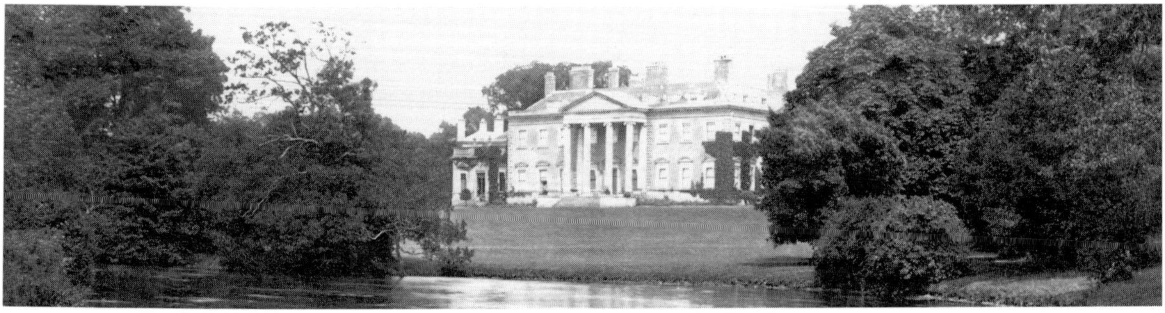

history. What would the outcome have been if Henry had never met Anne Boleyn at Sutton Place? Perhaps Britain would still be a Catholic country, in which case the bloody history of Ireland would have been completely different.

With the building of the great houses, a new profession emerged - that of the architect. Few English architects are known before the 17th century (Robert Smythson, who worked on Longleat and Wollaton Hall, is an exception), but the ideas of the Italian Renaissance architect Andrea Palladio eventually made their way across the channel, brought by a young landscape painter and stage designer by the name of Inigo Jones. Jones's influence was enormous - he introduced the simplicity, proportion and lack of ornamentation that was to remain the hallmark of English country houses for most of the 17th century, and which we can see in houses like Wilton and Syon.

Many great names were to follow in Jones's footsteps, but progress was interrupted in the mid 17th century by the outbreak of the Civil War. The owners of many houses, such as Compton Wynyates and Lathom House, found themselves wishing that when designing their properties they had concentrated less on decoration and more on fortification, for they were unable to hold out against the Parliamentarian troops that besieged them. Royalist sympathisers sheltered fugitives - notably at Boscobel House, where Charles II hid in the famous oak tree - and paid for it, often paying large fines to ensure continued ownership. Others, like the Earl of Pembroke at Wilton, saw which way the wind was blowing and threw in their lot with the Parliamentarian side, thus saving their houses from a sacking.

With the Restoration of the monarchy in 1660, the landed and wealthy could continue building monuments to their status; one of the most impressive of these is Chatsworth House, built at the turn of the century by William Talman for the first Duke of Devonshire. Soon after, Sir John Vanbrugh embarked on Blenheim Palace for the Duke of Marlborough, a job that eventually passed to Nicholas Hawksmoor, a disciple of Christopher Wren and an exponent of the English Baroque of which Blenheim is such a good example.

Two names have become indelibly associated with developments in the mid 18th century: Lancelot 'Capability' Brown and Robert Adam. Brown was the first landscape gardener. He earned his nickname from his habit, on first seeing a garden or park, of saying 'I see great capability of improvement here'. And improve them he did, with a carefully-contrived informality designed to set off the architecture of the house in question. Castle Ashby, Chatsworth and Syon House are among the many estates on which he worked, and he even dabbled in architecture at Corsham Court and Broadlands. Adam developed a neo-classical style that preserved the balance and proportion of

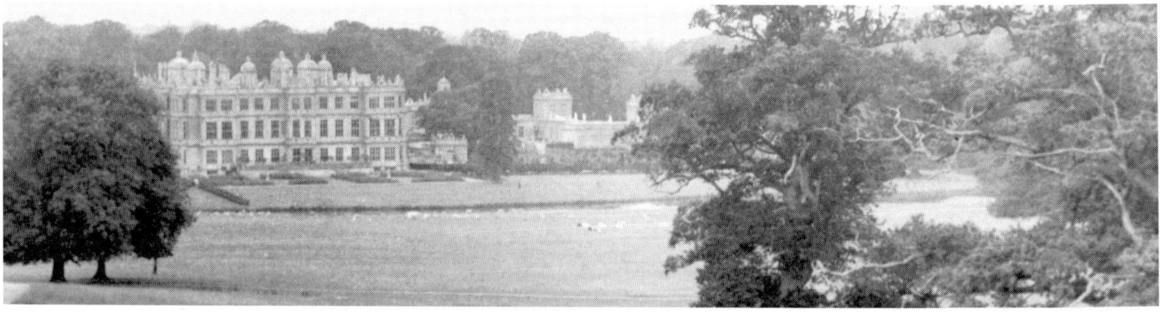

the Palladian but enlivened it with decoration and ornamentation. He is particularly known for his magnificent interiors, including that at Harewood House, where his intention that a room should be 'all of a piece' is brilliantly demonstrated.

While the 18th century produced houses celebrated as superb expressions of power, wealth and creativity - Seaton Delaval Hall, Harewood House, and Blenheim Palace, for instance - it also produced less celebrated and ambitious but nonetheless beautiful buildings. Priory House in Bodmin is a fine example of an unassuming yet handsome and perfectly-proportioned private house, and around the country minor landowners were constructing little gems such as Beaminster Manor.

The man who bore the standard for classical architecture into the 19th century was Sir Charles Barry. His adaptations of Greek and Roman themes won him many followers and commissions, among them Cliveden House and the south front of Harewood House, but he is best known as the designer of the Houses of Parliament. His collaborator on this massive project was Augustus Welby Pugin, who designed much of the decorative detail. Pugin was high priest of the other major school of architecture of the time - the Victorian Gothic Revival. Nothing could have contrasted more with the relative restraint of the neo-classicists than Victorian Gothic with its pointed arches, buttresses and tracery windows. Architects like Anthony Salvin, who designed Harlaxton Hall and Hodnet Hall, indulged in extravagant displays which were intended once again to express the status of the owners, if not (arguably) their tastes. Knebworth House, with its fantastic collection of gargoyles, decorated chimneys and almost minaret-like pinnacles is perhaps the extreme of the Gothic Revival.

And here our tour of English country houses ends. After the 19th century very few great houses were built; the social upheavals of two world wars pressed change on the mansion-owning classes, and not all were able to adapt. Financial pressures caused the decline which claimed victims such as Clumber House, demolished in the 1930s, while others had no option but to hand over their properties to the National Trust, which had the means to cover the enormous costs of running and maintaining these huge houses. Some, better managed than the rest, stayed in private hands, and still house the descendants of the original builders.

Whether in public or private hands, English country houses, from the perfect little medieval manor of Cotehele on the banks of the Tamar to the Gothic splendour of Knebworth, represent much of the greatest art and design accomplished in this country, and also constitute a record in stone, brick, glass and timber, of the nation's history.

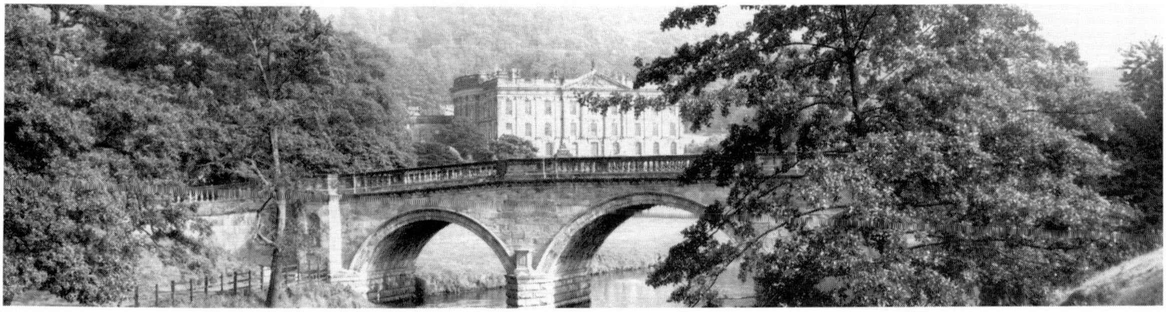

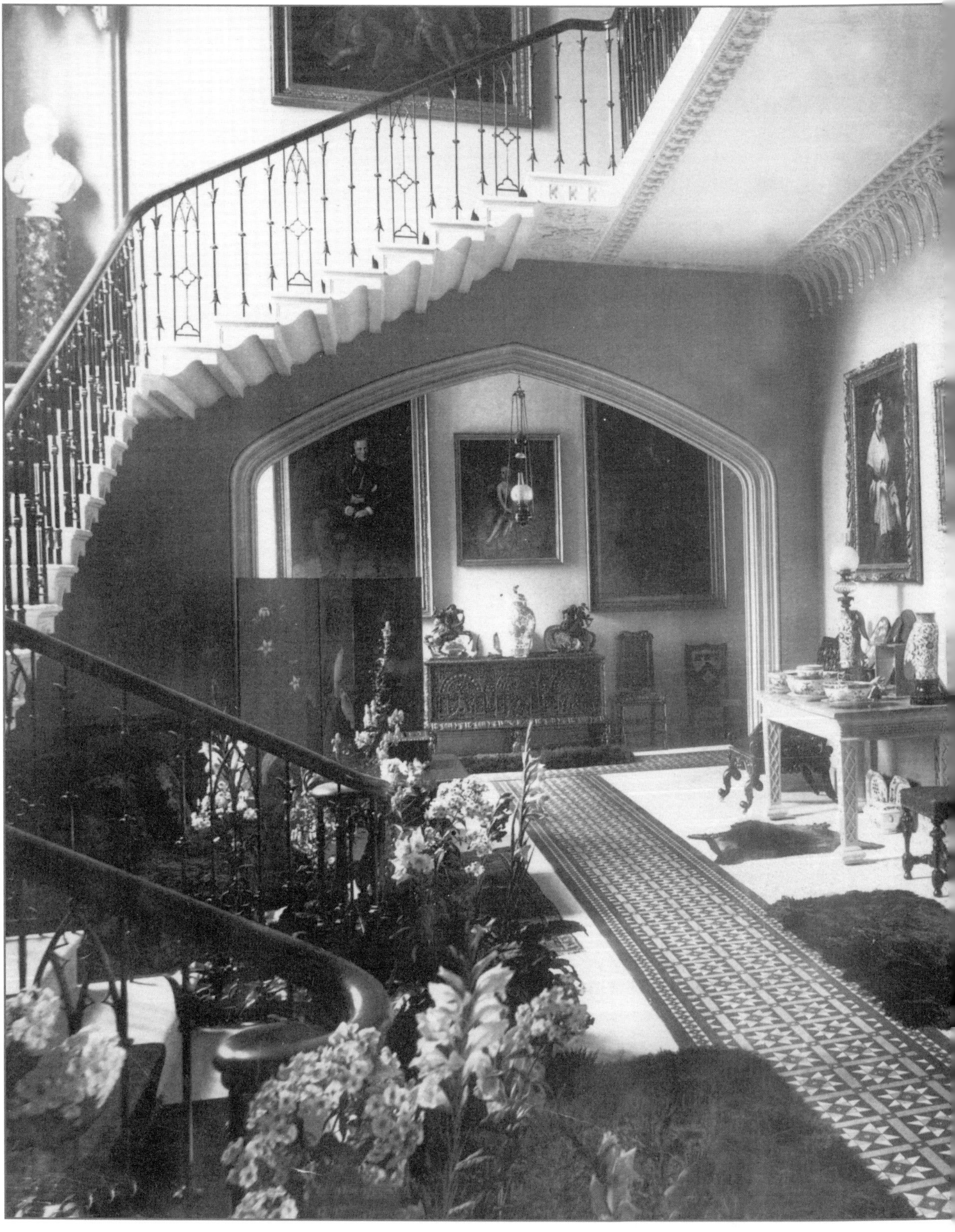

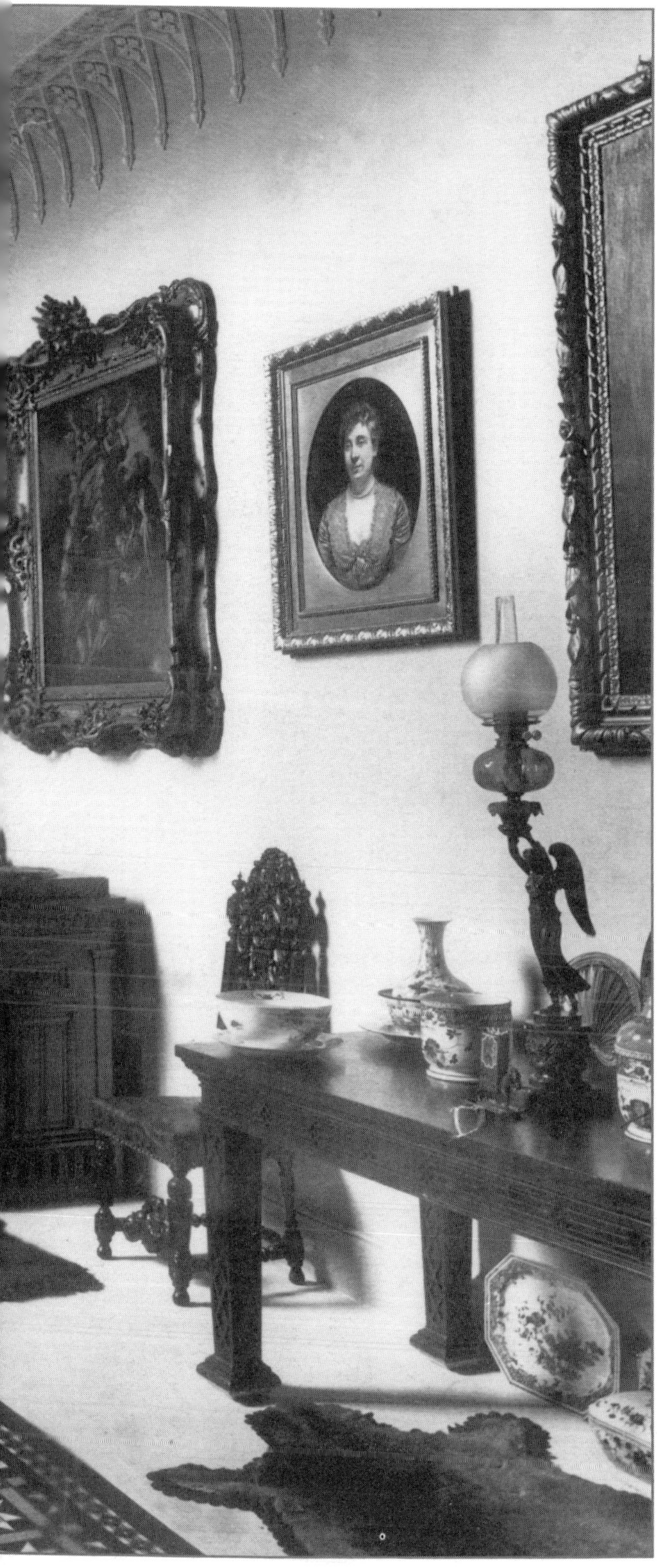

The South West

▼ **PADSTOW, PRIDEAUX PLACE 1903** 49951
Home of the Prideaux-Brune family since 1592 when it was built by Nicholas Prideaux, Prideaux Place is built in an E-plan from local stone. It overlooks the oldest deer park in Britain, first recorded in AD 435.

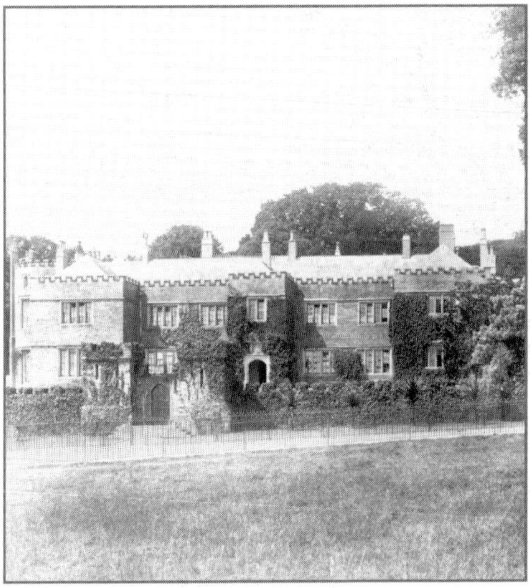

◄ **PADSTOW, PRIDEAUX PLACE, THE HALL 1888** 21206
The finest room at Prideaux Place, the Staircase Hall has wonderful carved plaster cornices and ceilings in the Georgian Gothic style. The staircase is unusual in that it is cantilevered throughout, with no pillars to support it.

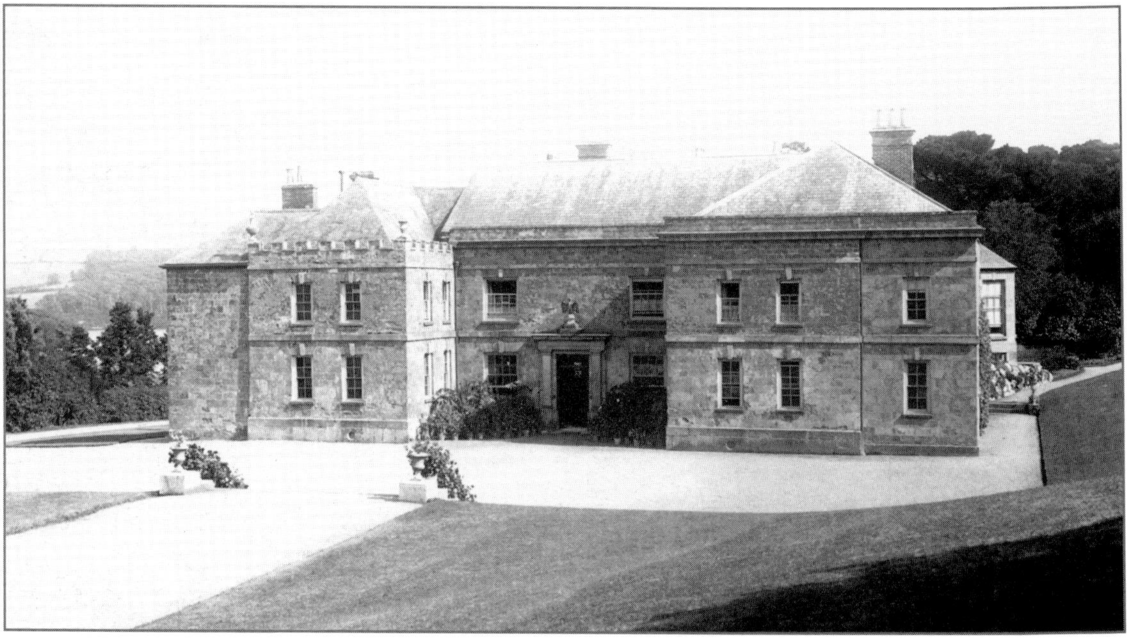

Helston, Godolphin Hall 1895 36194

This is a house with a history. Charles II visited here when he was Prince of Wales, and the royal connection continued during the Civil War when the Godolphin family fought on the losing Royalist side. The house declined after the family died out in the 18th century, but it has been restored since the 1930s by new owners.

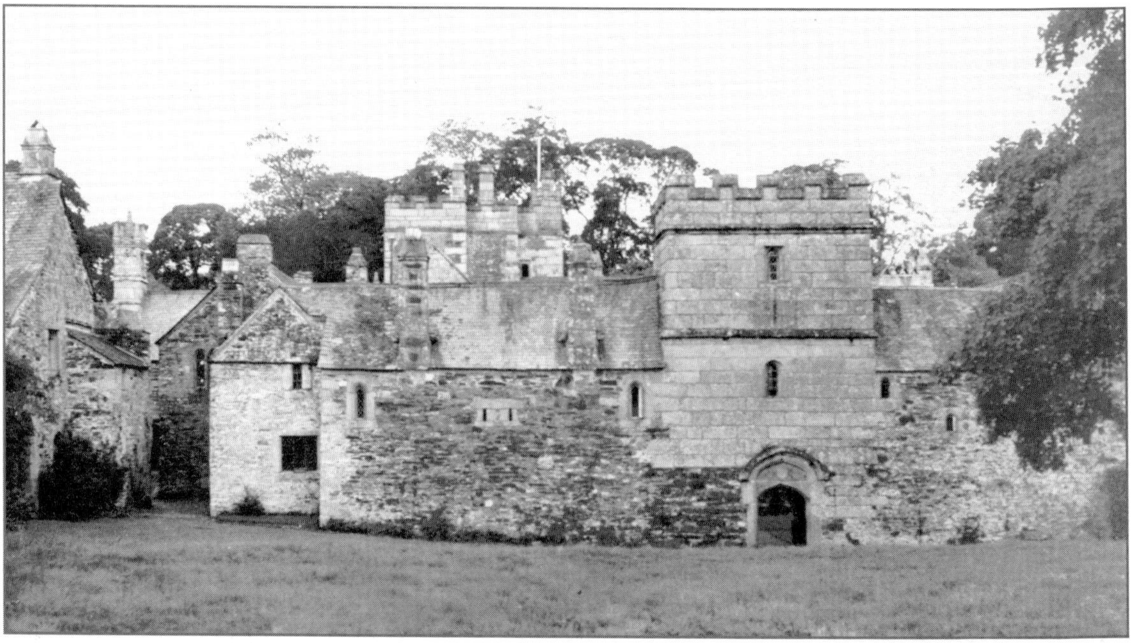

Calstock, Cotehele House c1960 C9041

On an idyllic site on the bank of the River Tamar, Cotehele is probably the best example of a fortified medieval manor house in the country. Built by the Edgecumbe family, it became their second seat when they built Mount Edgecumbe in the 17th century; the family's concentration on their new home saved Cotehele from too much alteration.

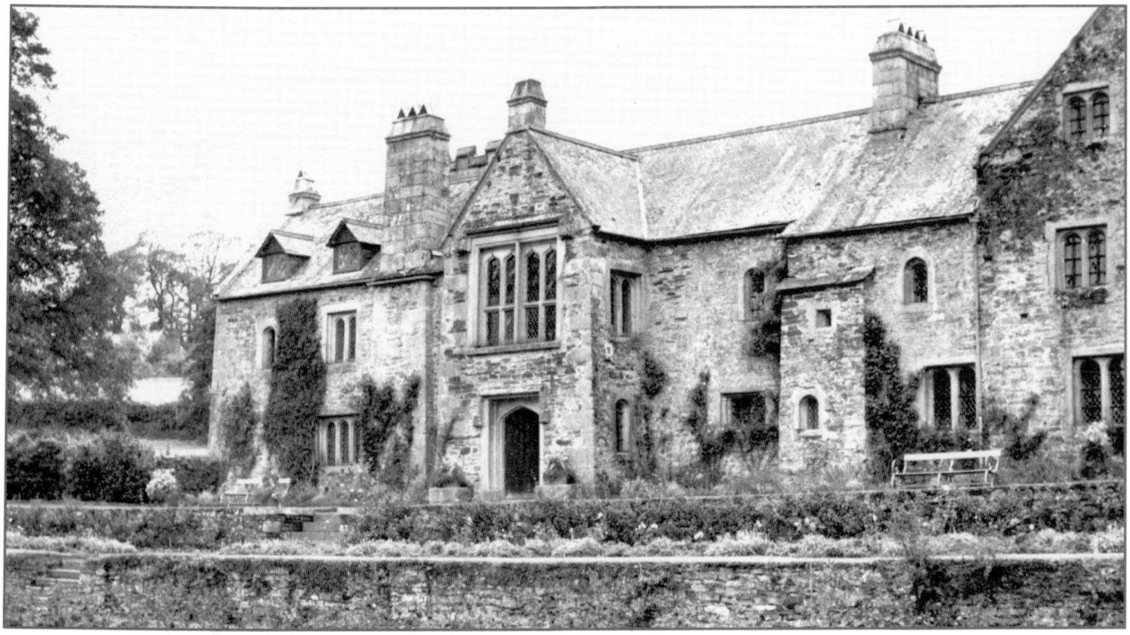

Calstock, Cotehele House c1955 C8050
Although medieval, the house was extended in Tudor times when Sir Piers Edgecumbe built the Great Hall. The Chapel clock dates from 1480, and is one of the oldest in the country. Cotehele is also home to the 'Shamrock', the last of the Tamar sailing barges, which used to ply the river carrying everything from tin to potatoes.

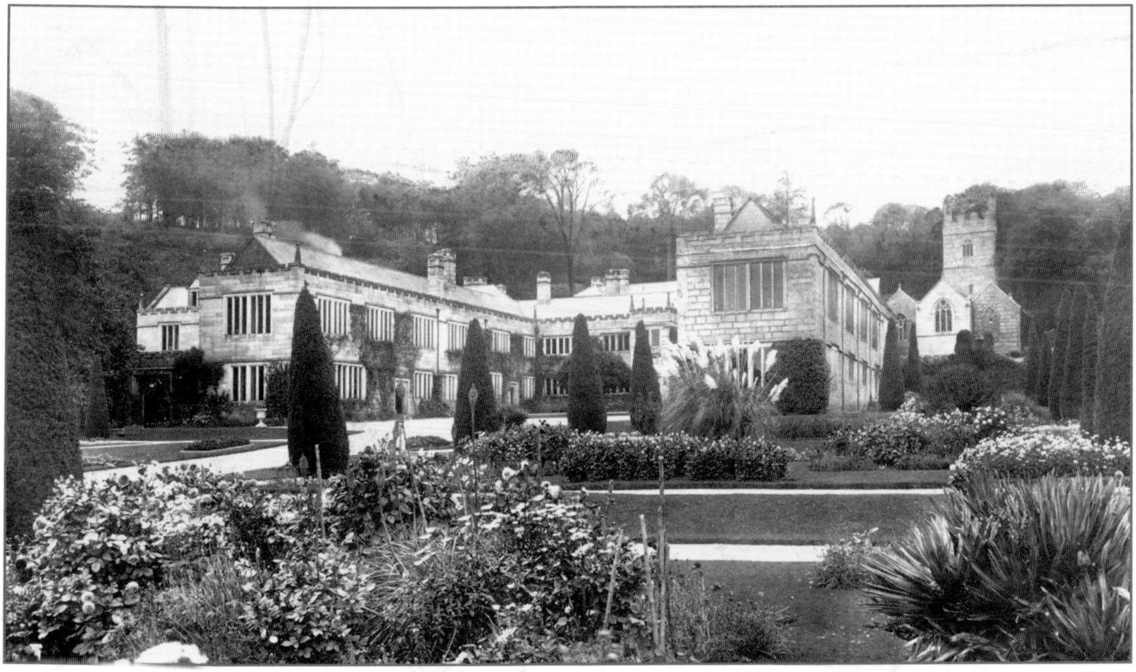

Bodmin, Lanhydrock 1897 40589
Completed in 1642 for Lord Robartes, Lanhydrock suffered a disastrous fire in 1881. Most of the house had to be rebuilt, but one of the survivors of the blaze was the magnificent Long Gallery with its extraordinary plaster ceiling.

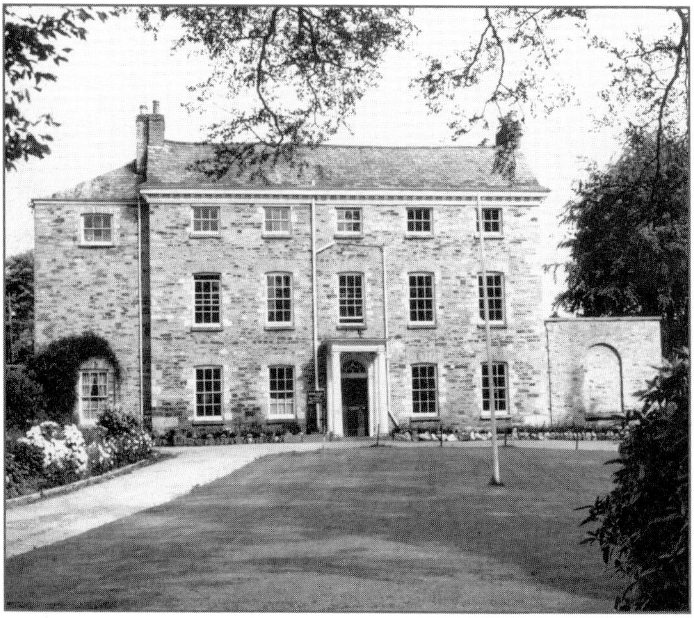

BODMIN, PRIORY HOUSE c1955 B129043

BODMIN

Priory House c1955

Priory House stands on the site of a 12th-century Augustinian priory, which was dismantled during the Reformation. This handsome house, built for William Pennington in 1790 from local stone with granite dressings, passed through a succession of owners before becoming the municipal offices in 1948.

NEWTON ABBOT

Bradley Manor House 1890

Bradley Manor occupies a magnificent site in the steep, thickly wooded valley of the River Lemon, a tributary of the Teign. Built in the 15th century, it has survived largely unaltered except for a few additions such as the Victorian bay window above the arched doorway.

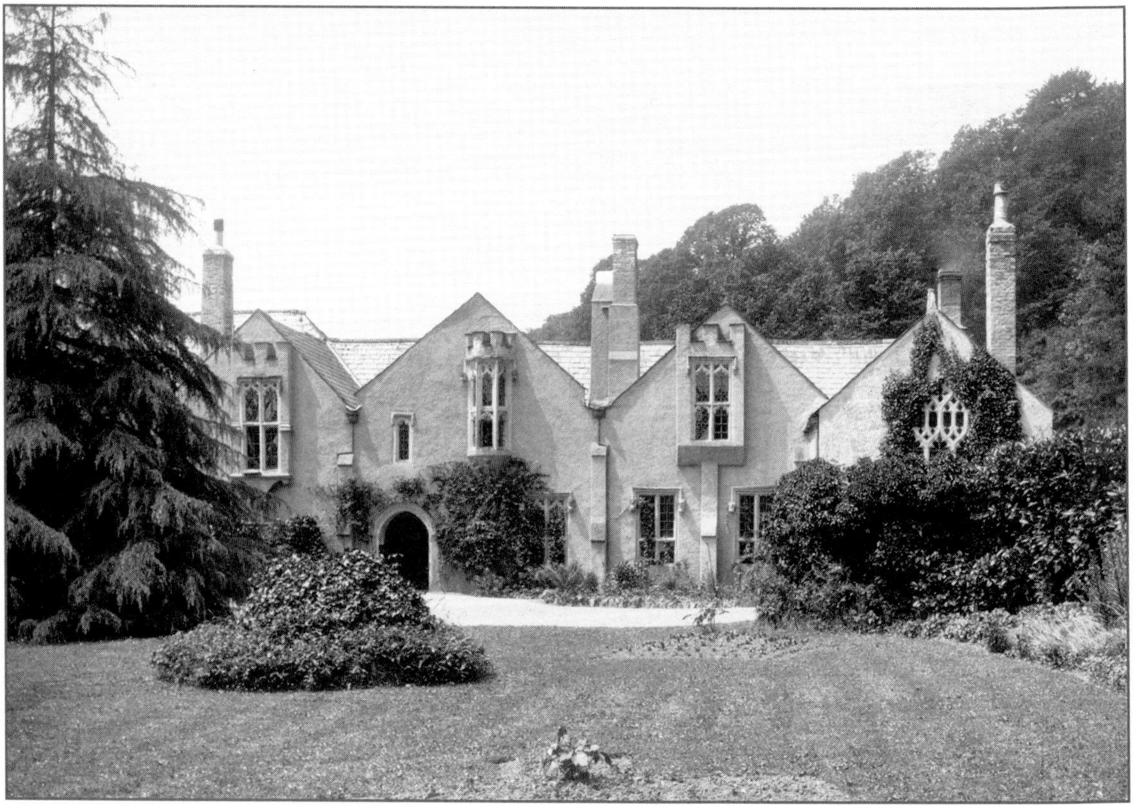

NEWTON ABBOT, BRADLEY MANOR HOUSE 1890 25436

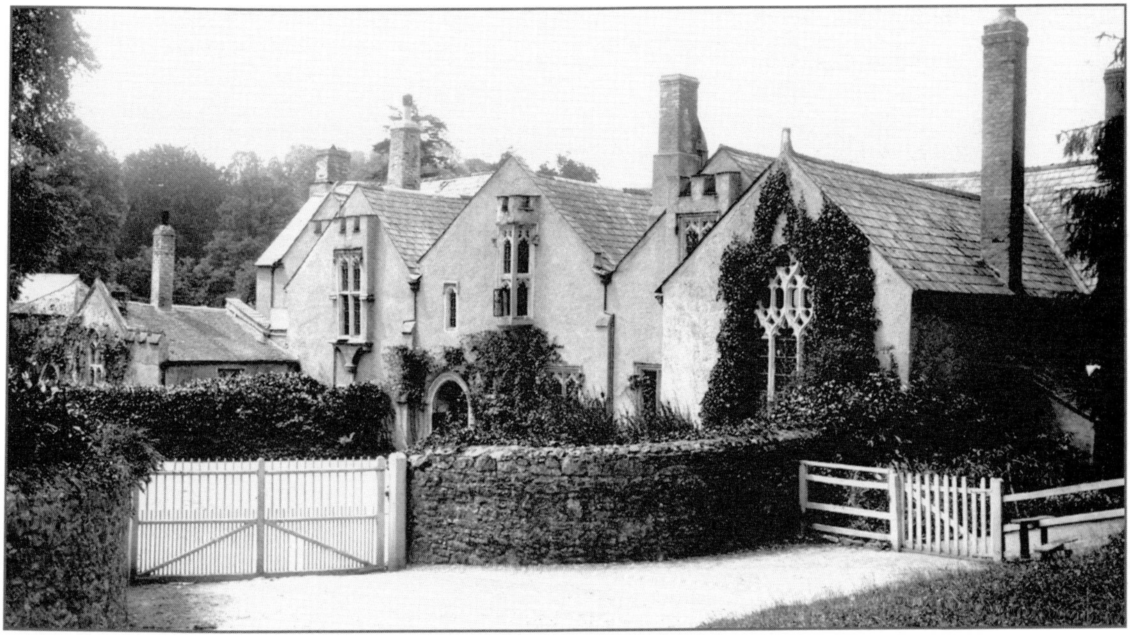

Newton Abbot, Bradley Manor House 1890 25435
Here we see the house from another angle, giving a better view of Bradley Manor's attractive roofline. The chapel (left) was added soon after the building of the house; it has a barrel roof. Now a National Trust property, Bradley Manor is occupied by the Woolner family.

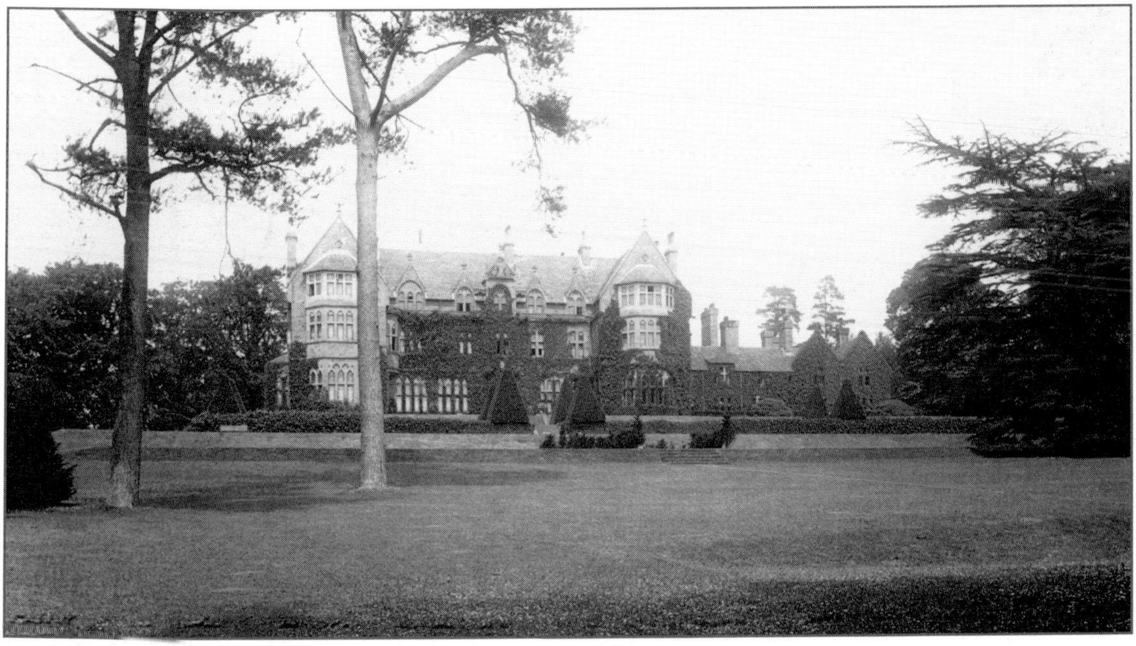

Tiverton, Knightshayes Court 1896 38057
A National Trust property since 1973, Knightshayes Court was built for John Heathcote-Amory MP. His father, also MP for Tiverton, was an inventor and industrialist who invented one of the first lace making machines in 1809. Built in the 1870s, Knightshayes was designed by William Burges, and the interior was decorated by J D Crace.

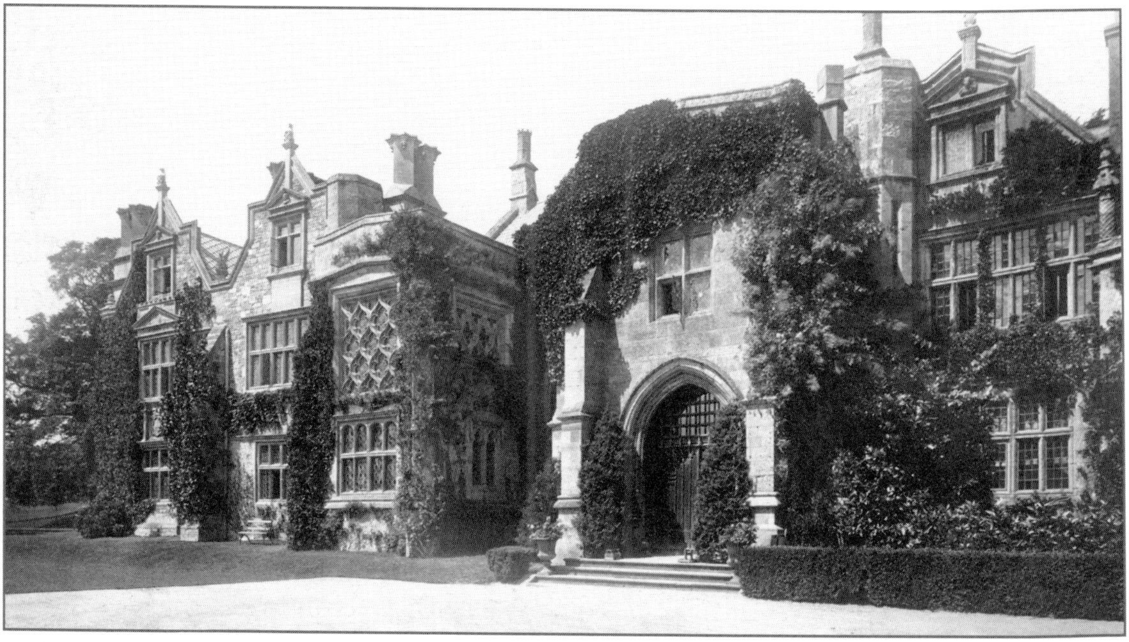

Clevedon, Clevedon Court 1892 31266

Originally built for Sir John de Clevedon in 1320, Clevedon has had its share of alteration. The west wing (on the left corner), added by the city architect of Bath C E Davis in 1882, is no longer standing. The National Trust acquired the property in 1961.

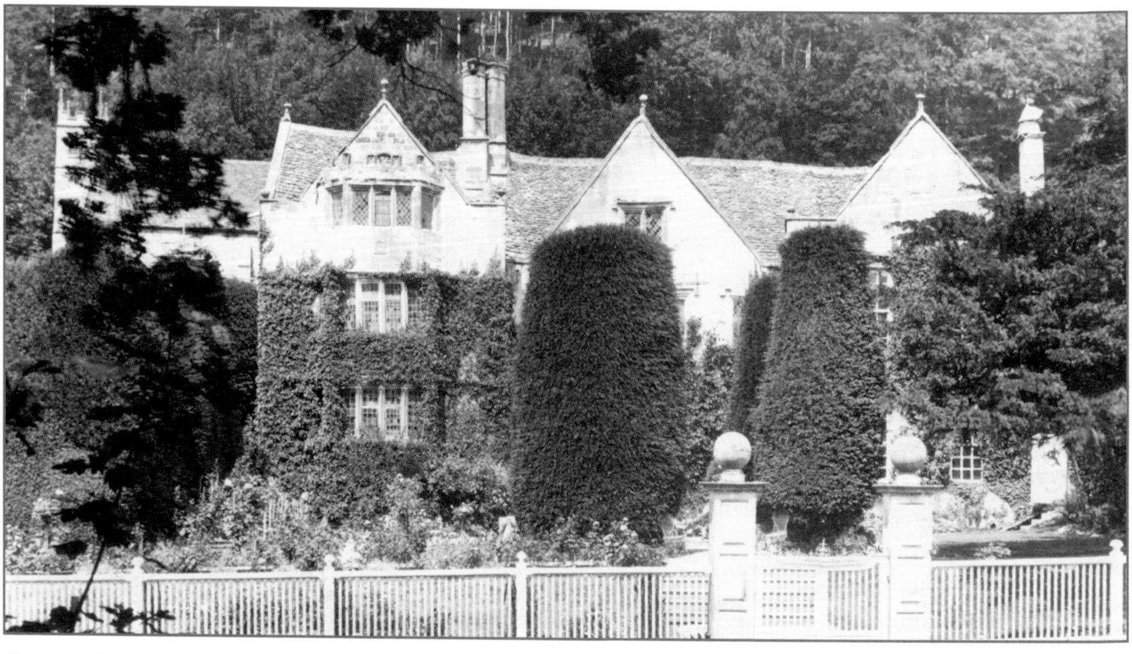

Owlpen, The Manor House 1900 45544

Owlpen, like many English country houses, is the product of centuries of addition and rebuilding. First constructed in the 15th century, it was enlarged in 1540, and in 1666 the West Wing (left, with ivy and bay windows) was built. The East Wing was rebuilt in 1720 - its age is betrayed by the sash windows peeping out from behind the trees.

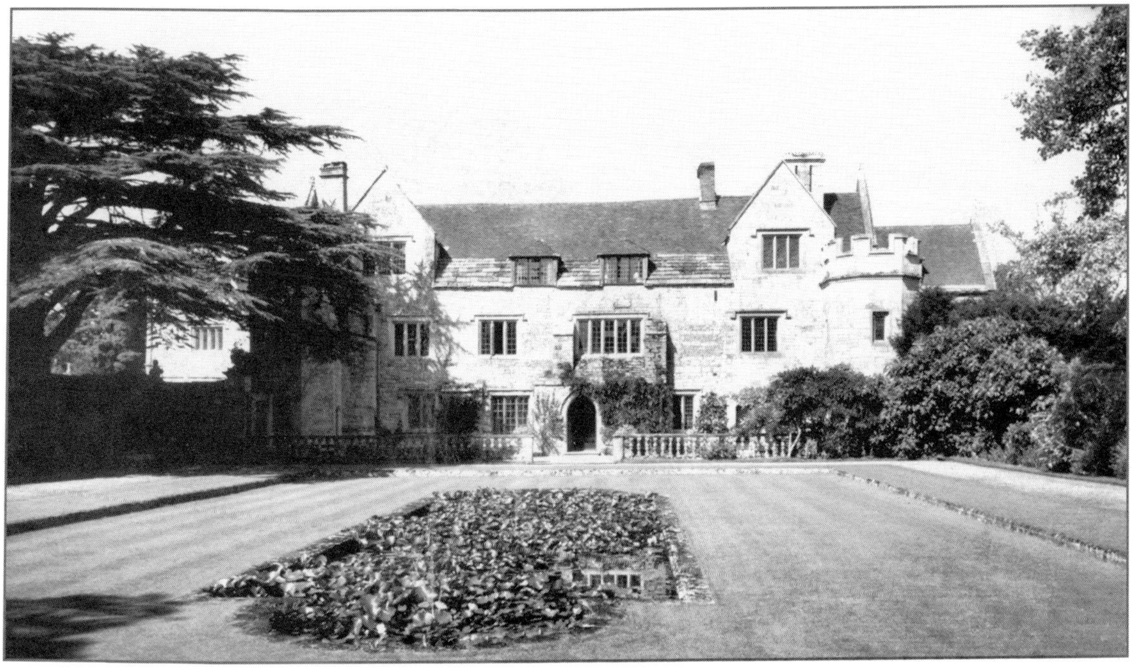

PUDDLETOWN, ATHELHAMPTON HALL C1955 A198001

A medieval manor house, Athelhampton was built in 1485 by Sir William Martyn, who became Lord Mayor of London in 1493. The Great Hall is particularly fine, with a timber roof, minstrels' gallery and brass chandelier.

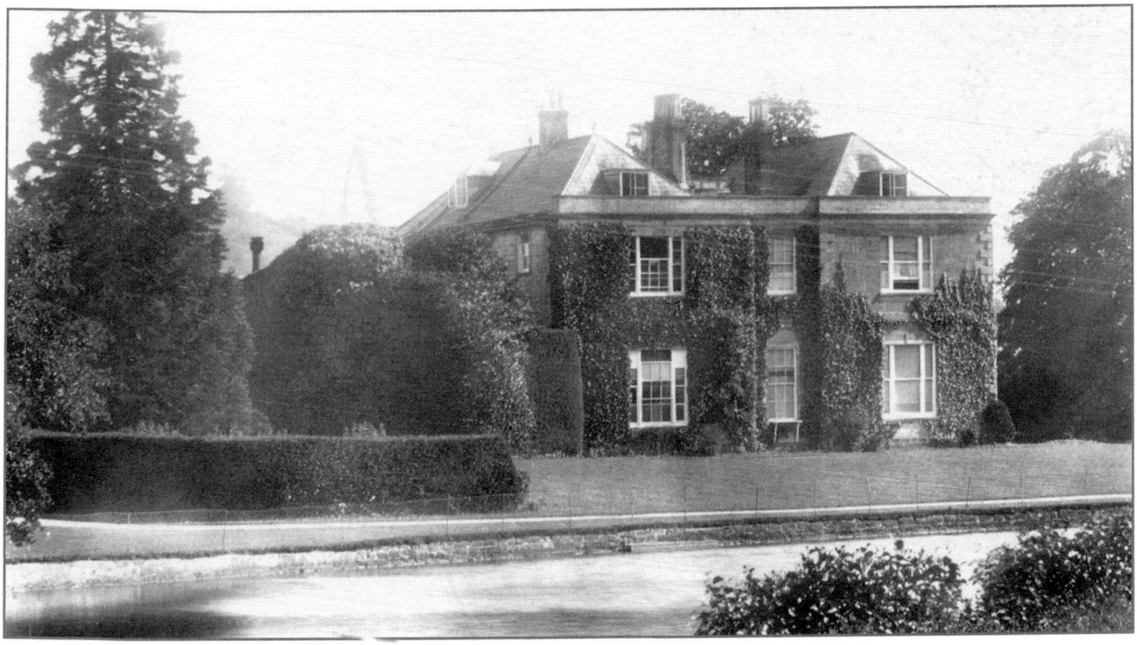

BEAMINSTER, THE MANOR HOUSE 1902 48434

The stables are late 17th-century, but the house itself dates from the late 18th century and was remodelled in the early 19th century. For many years Beaminster Manor was the home of the Cox family, who first settled there in 1767; Mary Cox, the last of the line, died in 1906.

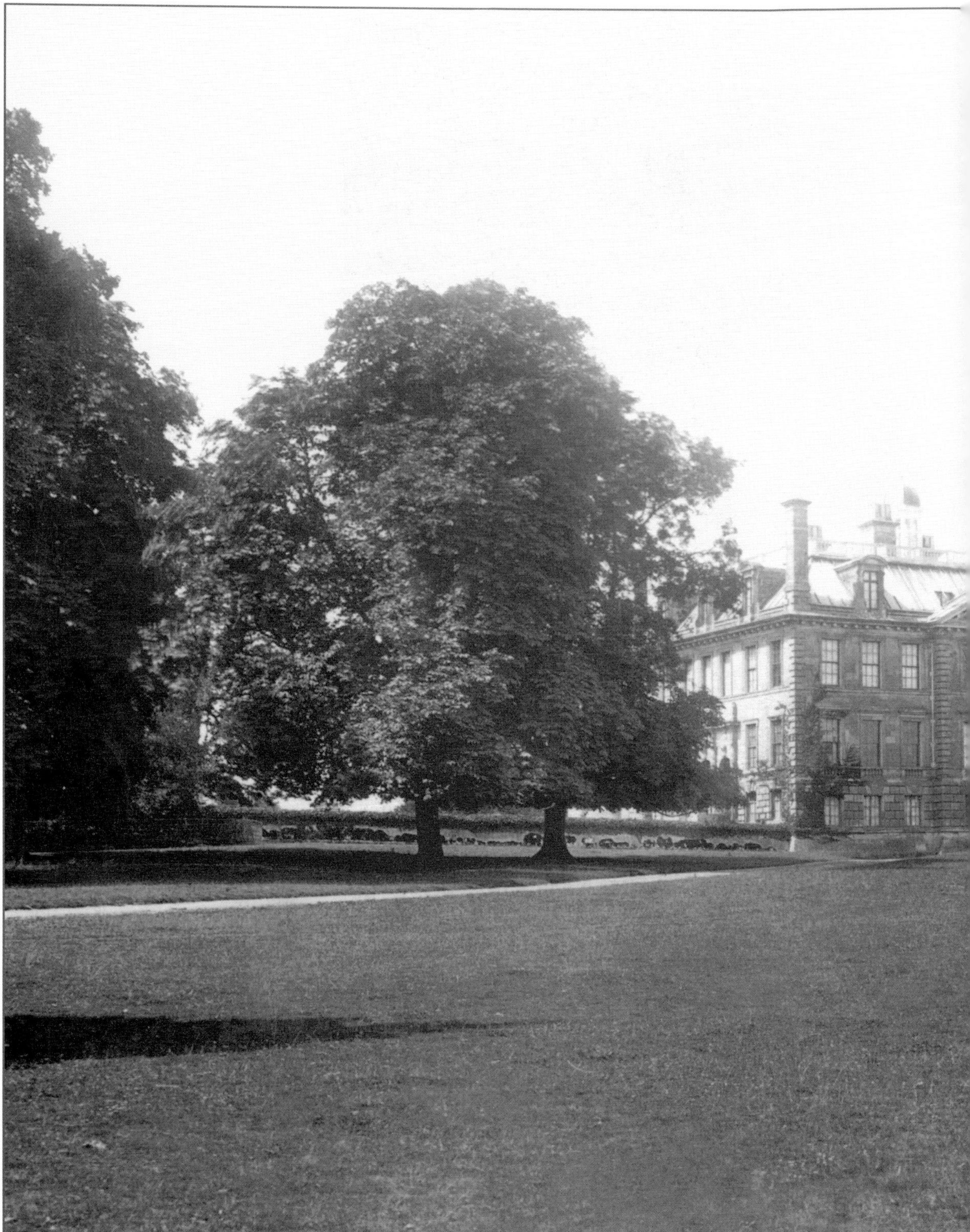

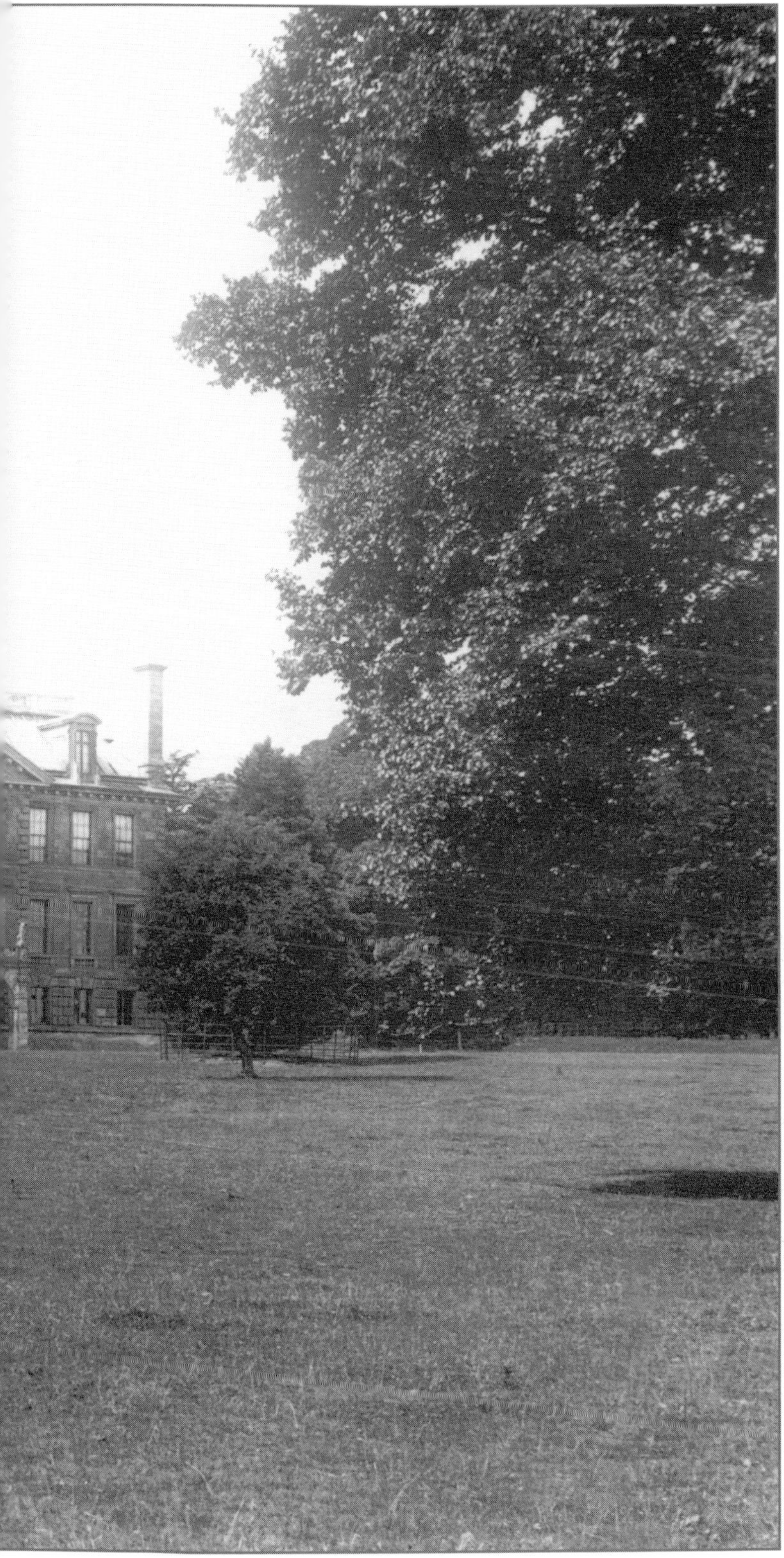

WIMBORNE
KINGSTON LACY 1899 43720
Set in magnificent parkland, Kingston Lacy was built in Chilmark stone and designed by Sir Roger Pratt for the Bankes family; they owned it until 1982, when it was left to the National Trust by Mr H J R Bankes.

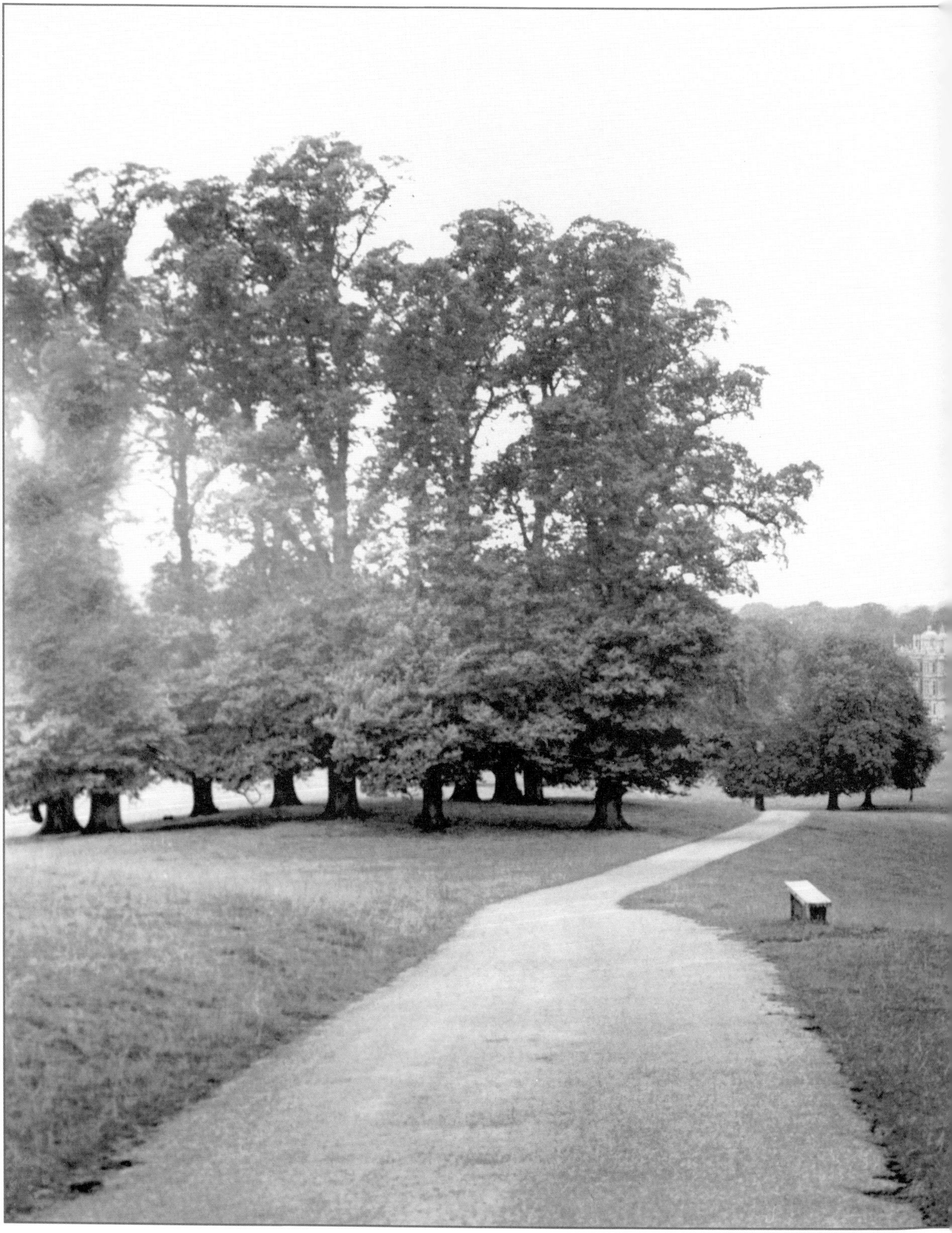

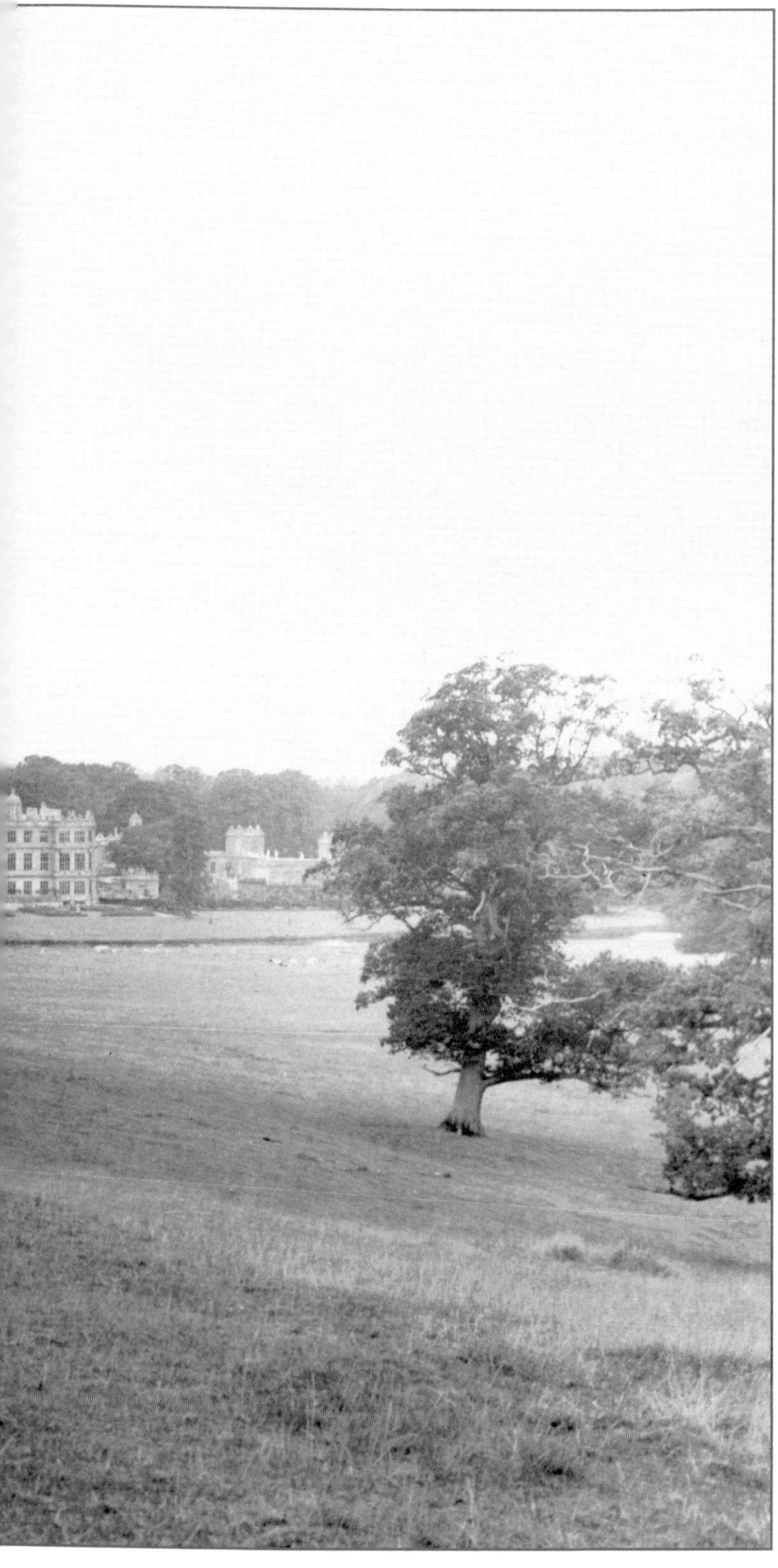

WARMINSTER
LONGLEAT C1965 L190027
The relative peace and stability of the reign of Henry VII meant that less emphasis was put on fortification and more on decoration; hence Longleat's acres of windows, which gave plenty of light, but would have been difficult to defend. The gardens are by Capability Brown.

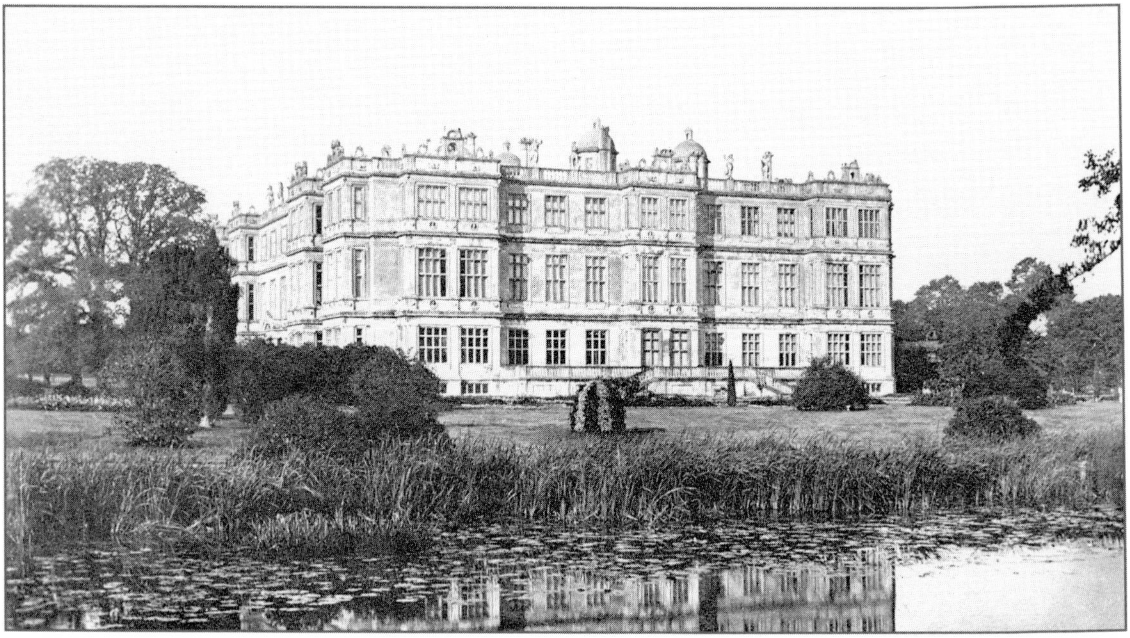

Warminster, Longleat 1907 58850a
Ancestral home of the Marquesses of Bath, and sometimes described as the first true Renaissance house in England, Longleat was built by Sir John Thynne between 1547 and 1580. He bought the land, on which an Augustinian Priory had stood, for £53; the building costs were £8,016 13s 6d.

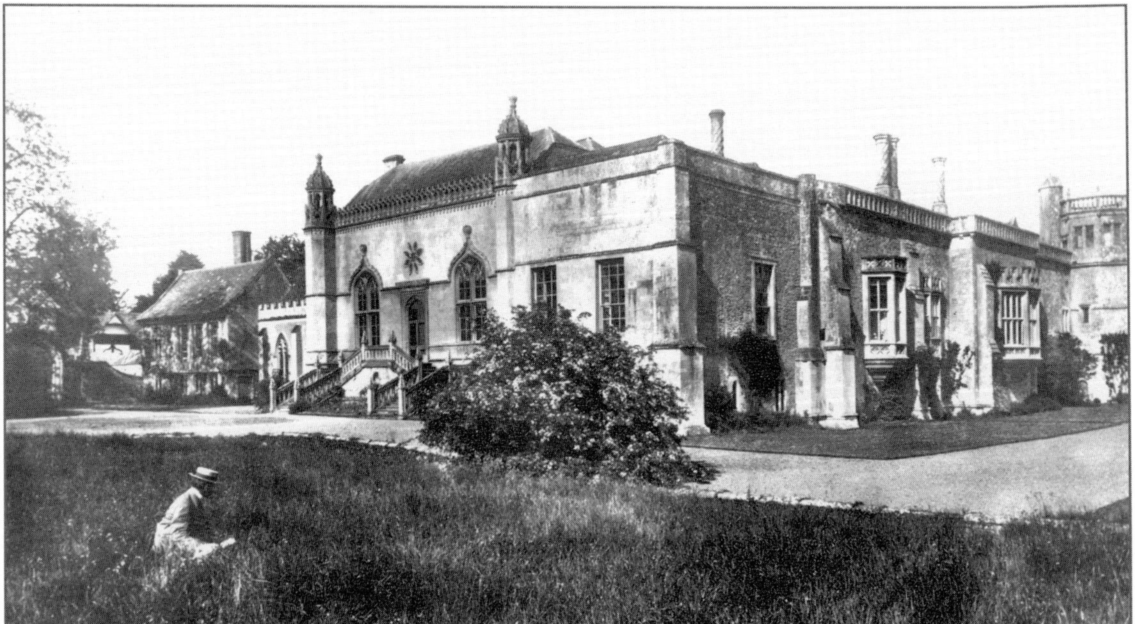

Lacock, The Abbey 1904 51510
Standing on the site of an Augustinian Convent which was founded in 1232, Lacock Abbey is the place where, in 1835, William Henry Fox-Talbot took the world's first photograph - a negative of one of the windows on the south front.

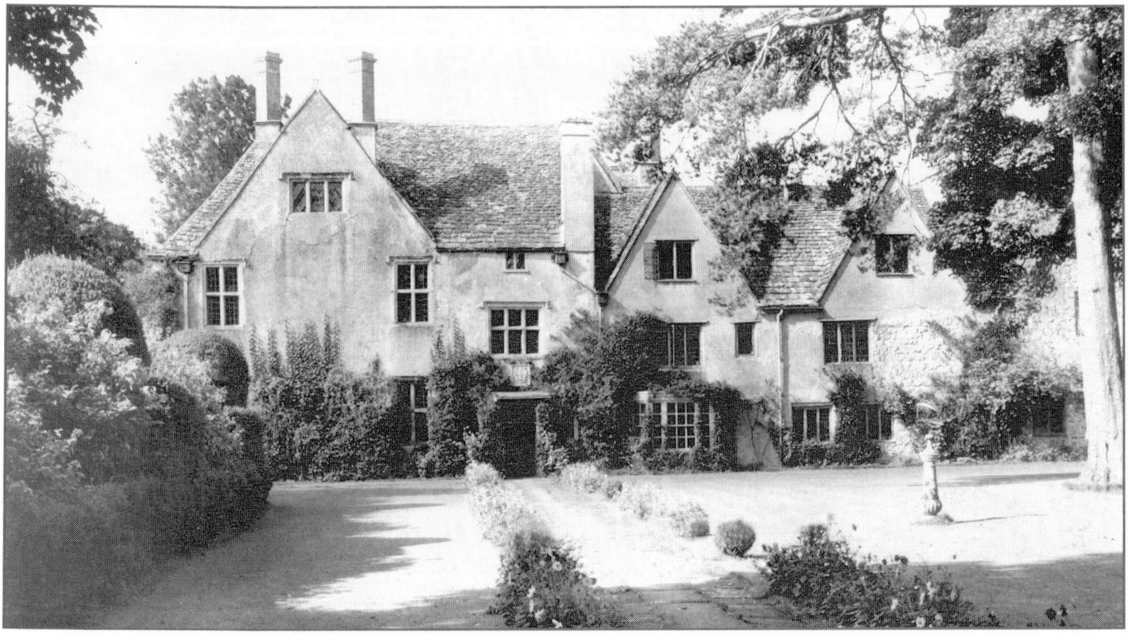

Avebury, The Manor House c1955 A80035

Avebury Manor stands in the great Stone Age circle which dominates the village; the manor was built in 1557 by Sir William Sharington, using profits made while he was in charge of the Bristol Mint. The Great Hall and Chamber were added around 1600.

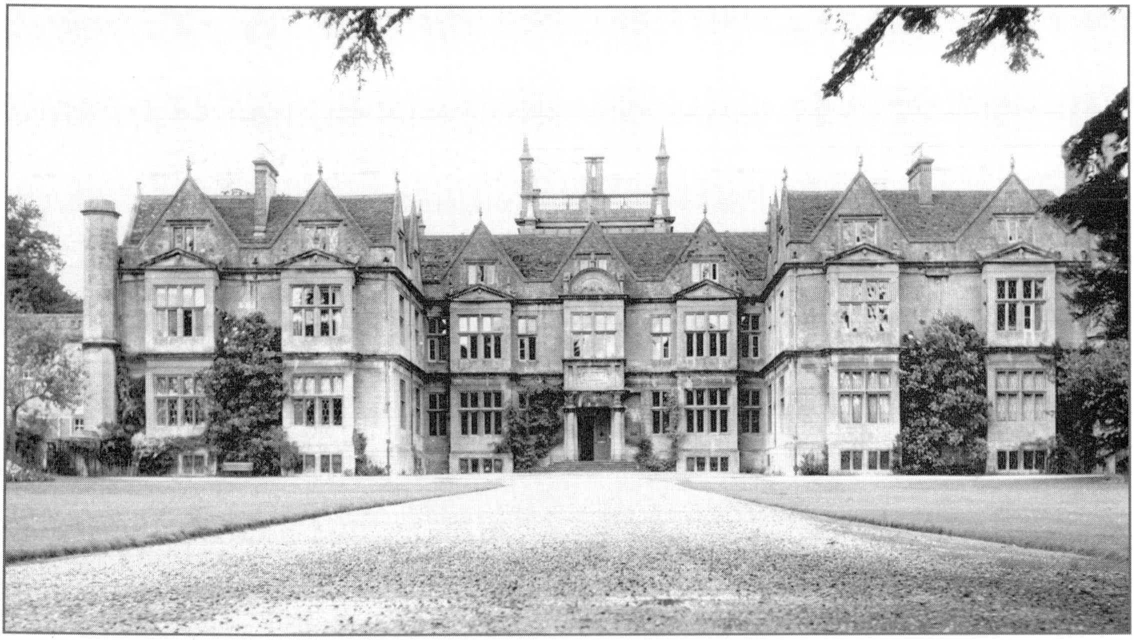

Corsham, Corsham Court c1955 C162026

Built from local stone, Corsham Court was built in 1582 for Thomas Smythe, known as 'Customer' Smythe because of his position as Collector of the Customs of London. The house was remodelled in 1760 by Capability Brown in his less well-known role as architect.

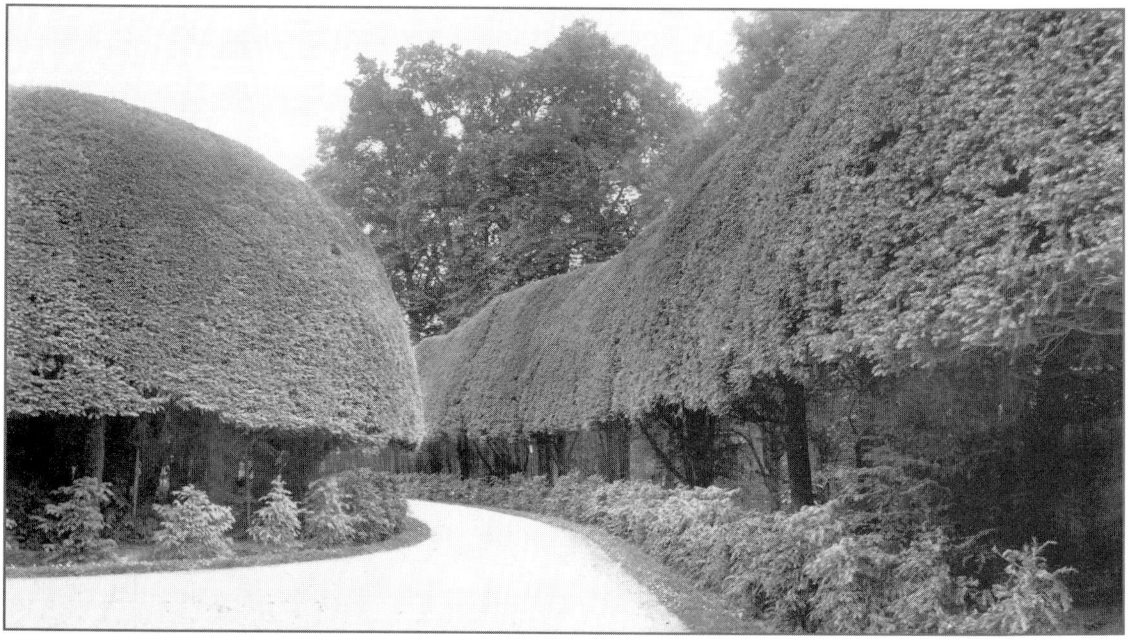

Corsham Court, The Yew Hedge 1907 57810
Topiary was introduced to Britain by the Romans. It reached its height in the 17th century, when imagination ran riot and all manner of beasts could be seen adorning gardens. By the 18th century the style had become rather more restrained and geometric, as seen here.

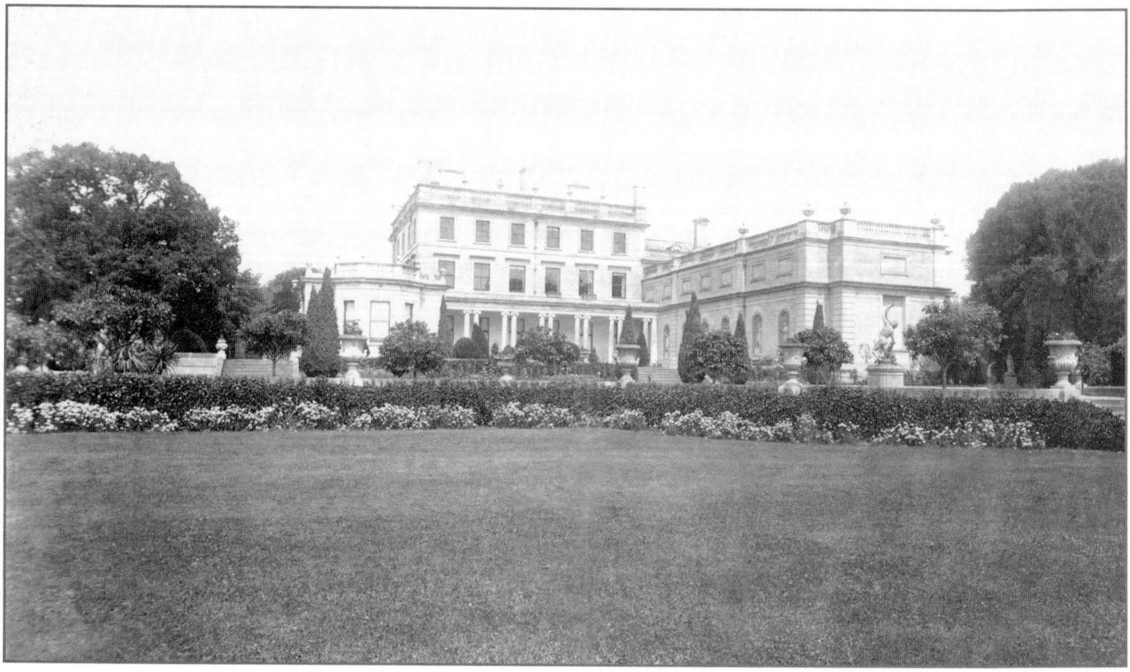

Ringwood, Somerley House 1890 28652
Situated at the edge of the New Forest, Somerley House was designed by Samuel Wyatt in the mid 18th century. In 1825 it passed to the Normanton family, and the sixth Earl still lives there.

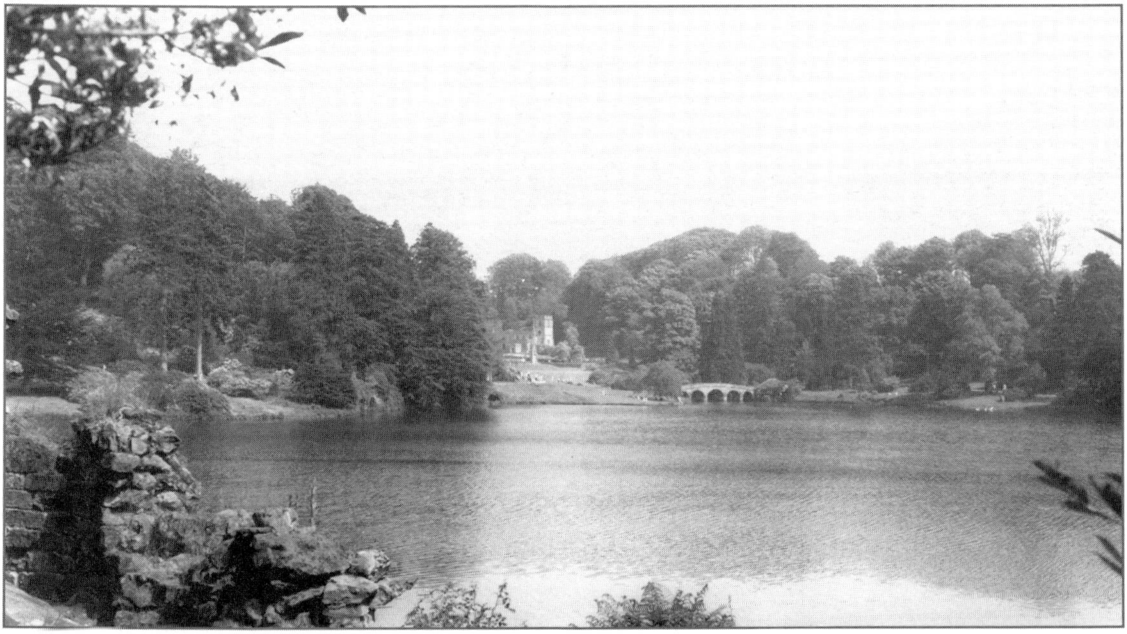

Stourhead, The Pleasure Gardens c1965 S741088

Henry Hoare, a wealthy banker, had Stourhead House built between 1718-24. He had been much impressed by the work of Colen Campbell, an early and leading exponent of the Palladian style, and commissioned Campbell to design the house.

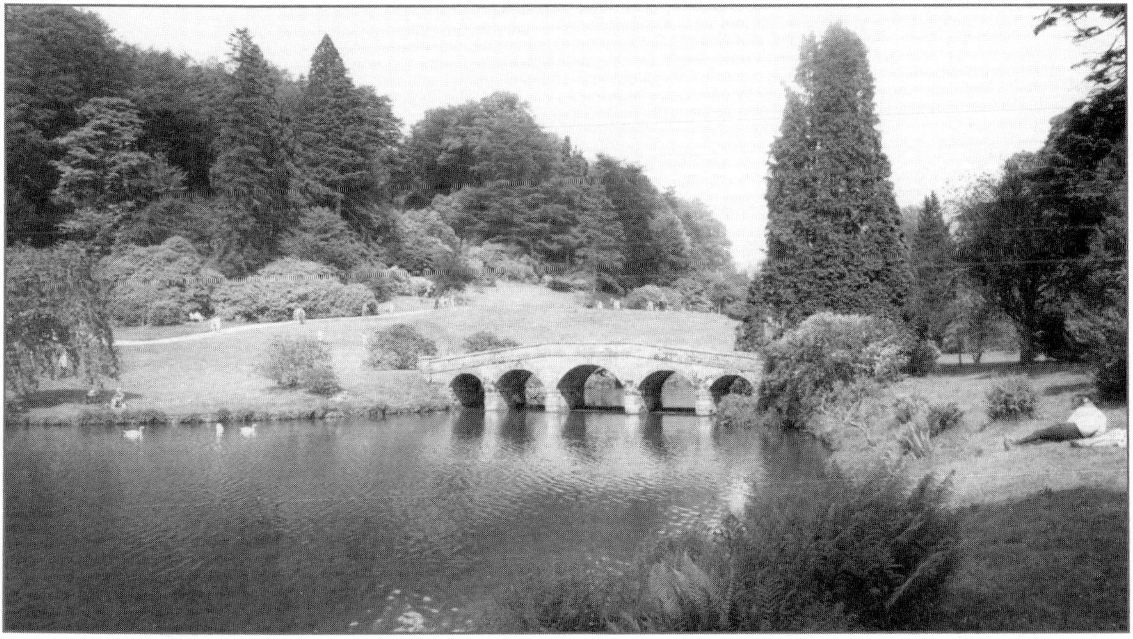

Stourhead, The Pleasure Gardens c1965 S741086

In 1741 Henry Hoare the younger returned from the Grand Tour particularly impressed by what he had seen in Italy. He had become converted to the idea of 'educating' nature, using and modifying the natural contours to produce pleasing compositions. This was to lead him to create one of England's great gardens.

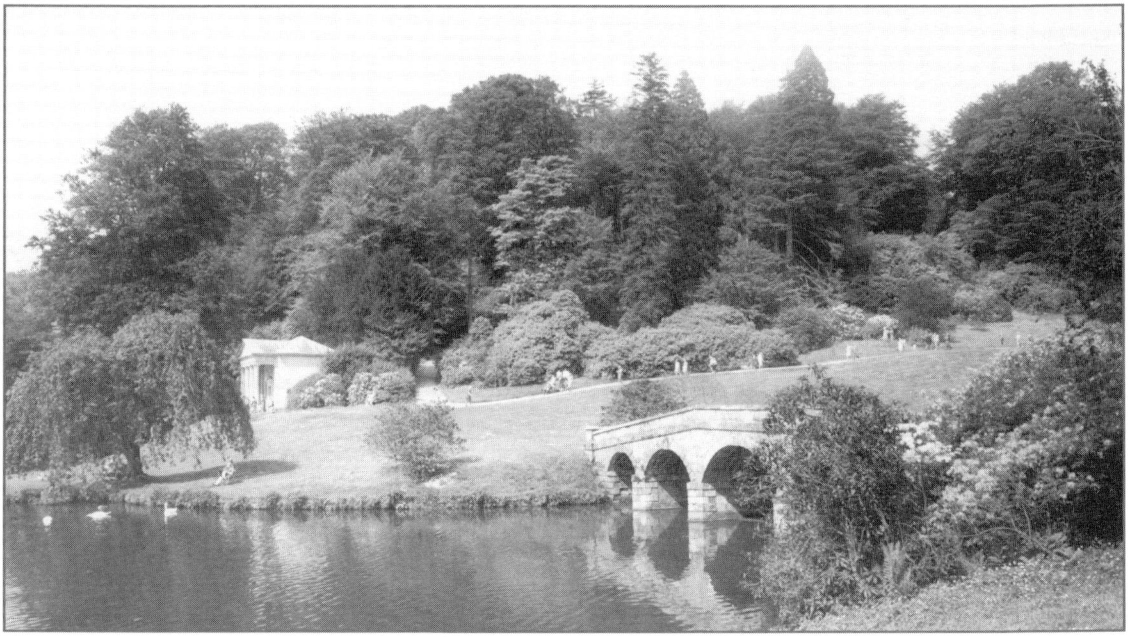

Stourhead, The Pleasure Gardens c1965 S741085
Influenced by artists such as Claude and Poussin, Hoare set about creating their vision of an 'Arcadian' landscape. The lake was created in 1744 with the intention that a walk round its shores would be an allegory of Aeneas's voyage after the fall of Troy.

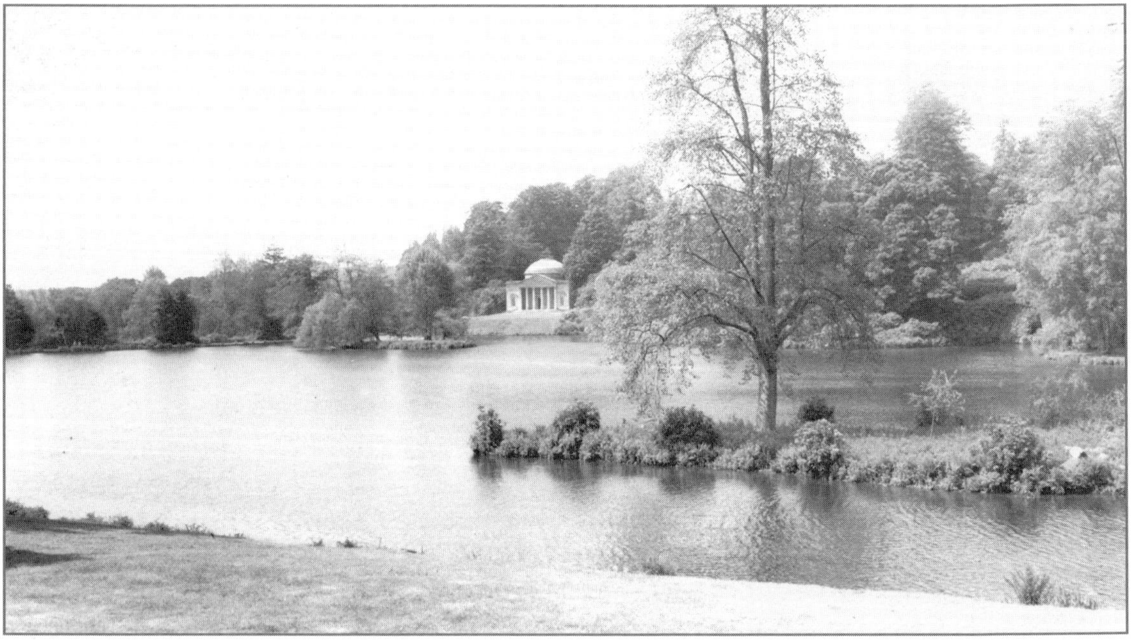

Stourhead, The Pleasure Gardens c1965 S741097
To make his vision a reality, Hoare engaged the services of the architect Flitcroft to create a series of buildings, including the Pantheon (centre), the Temple of Flora and the Temple of Apollo, inspired by the original at Baalbek in the Lebanon.

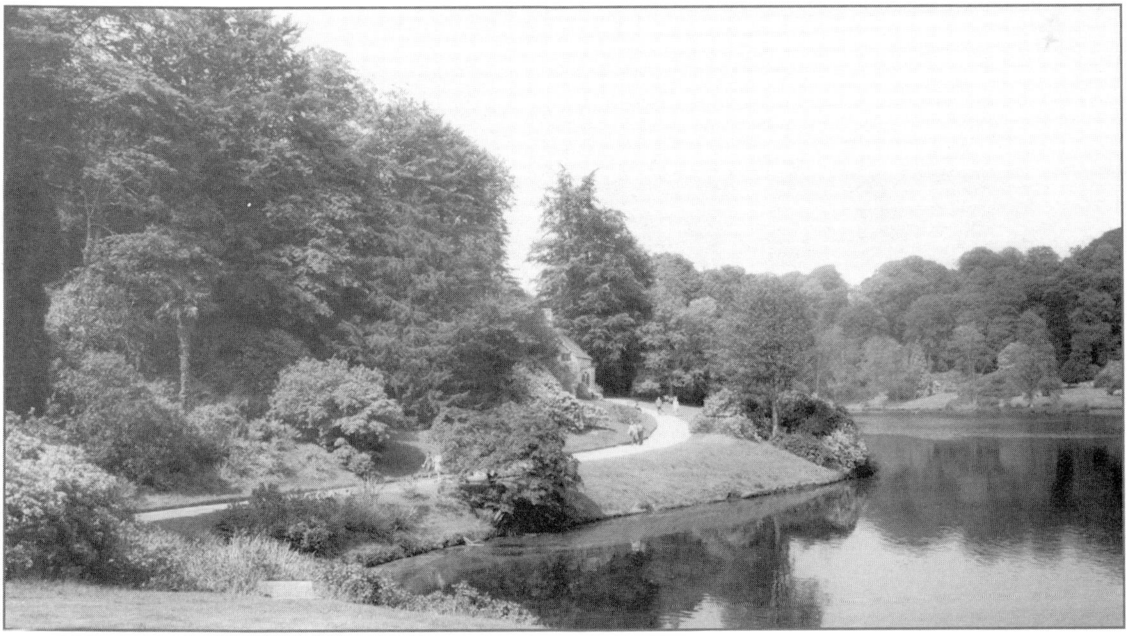

Stourhead, The Pleasure Gardens c1965 S741089
Before the 18th century, garden design had tended to be rigid and geometrical, a symbol of man's imposition of order upon nature. The emergence of men such as Charles Bridgeman, William Kent and Capability Brown was to change all that.

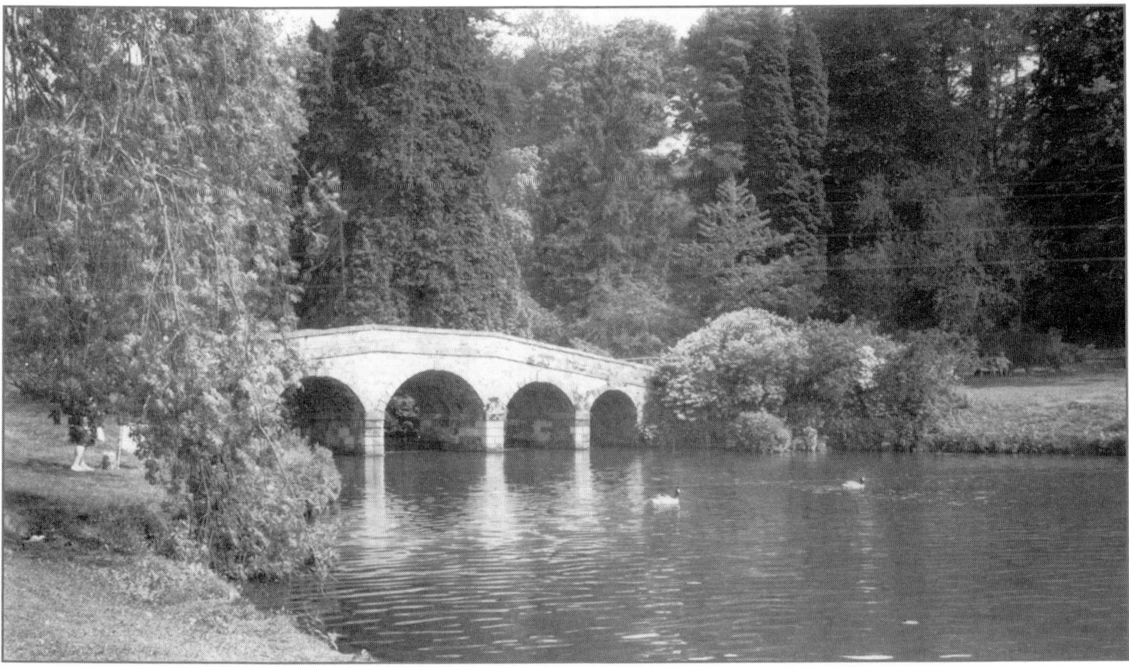

Stourhead, The Pleasure Gardens c1965 S741087
The bridge is based on a five arched bridge at Vicenza in Italy designed by Andrea Palladio, father of the Palladian style.

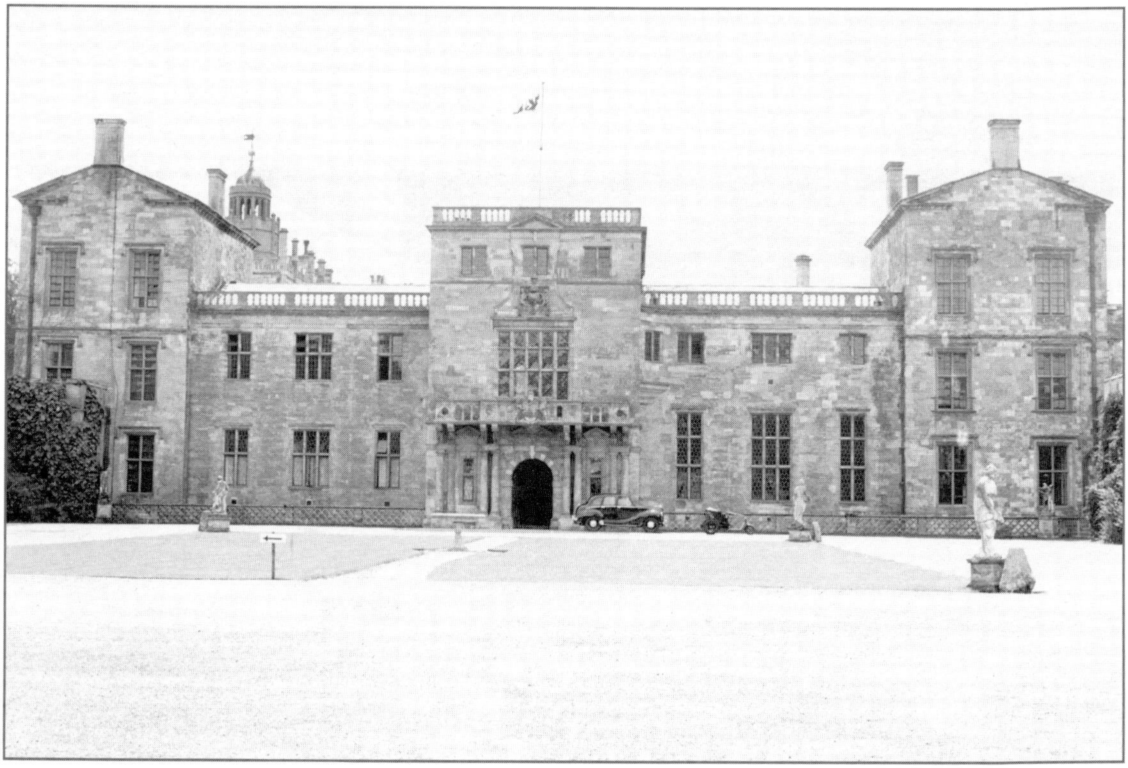

Wilton House c1965 W166059

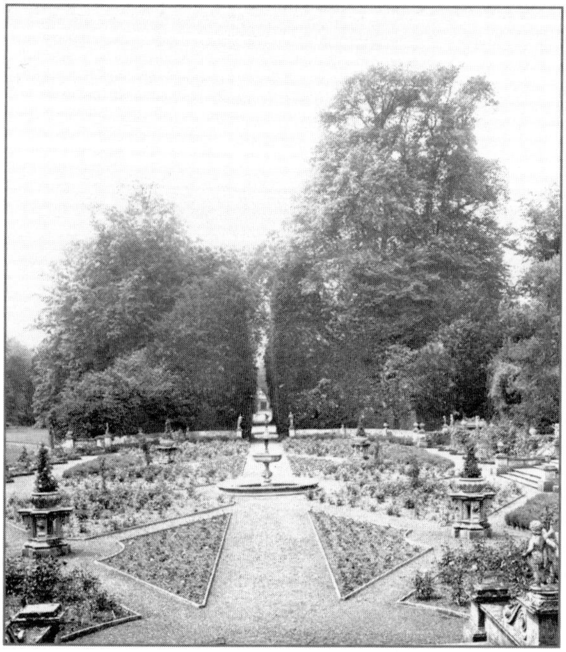

Wilton House, The Park, The Italian Gardens 1919
68934

Wilton House c1965

Reputedly Charles the First's favourite house, Wilton House was built by the French architect Isaac de Caux under instruction from Inigo Jones for Philip Herbert, Earl of Pembroke, in 1630-55. Lord Chamberlain for Charles, the wily Pembroke managed to preserve his power (and possibly his head) when he went over to the Parliamentarian side in the Civil War.

Wilton House
The Park, The Italian Gardens 1919

Wilton once had a magnificent enclosed garden designed by Isaac de Caux before the Civil War, but unfortunately it did not survive. The Italian Garden is a later addition.

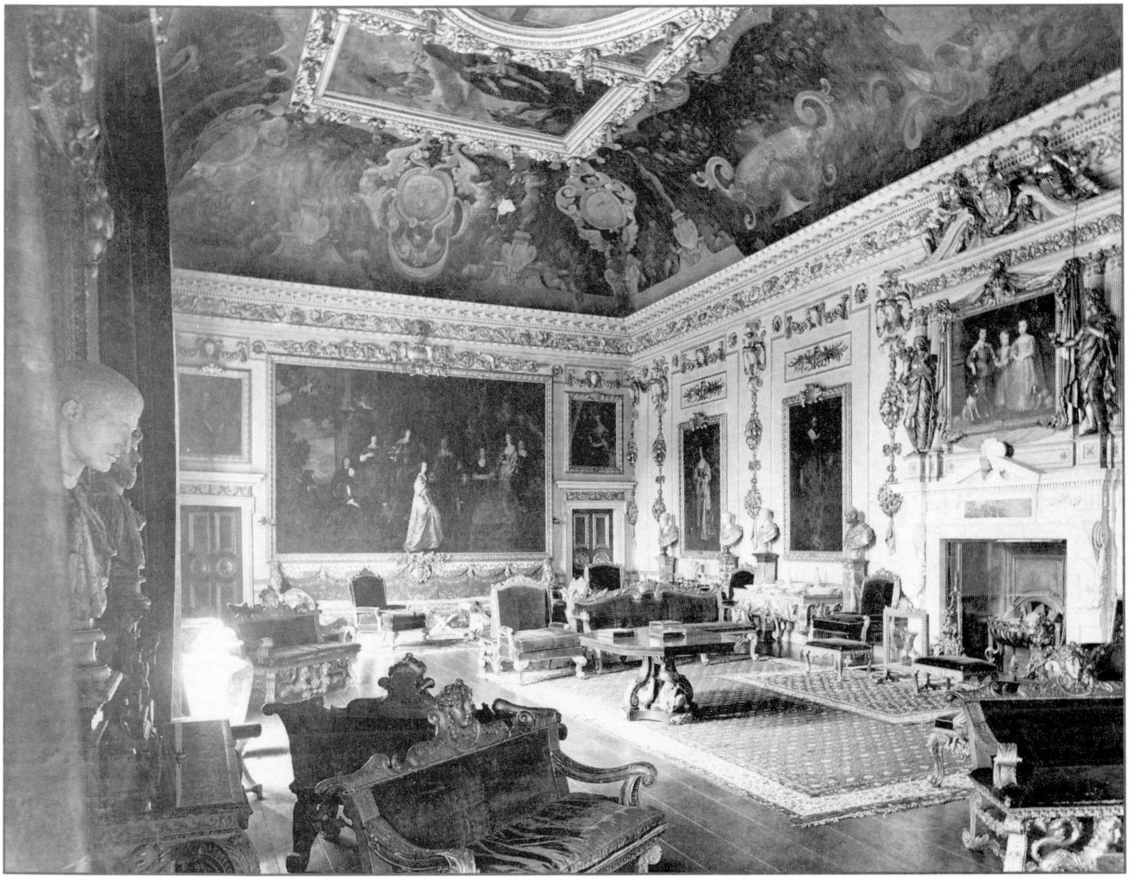

Wilton House

The Double Cube Room 1919 68932

After a fire in 1647, this extraordinary room, sixty feet long, thirty feet wide and thirty high, was redesigned by Inigo Jones to house Sir Anthony van Dyck's portraits of the Herbert family.

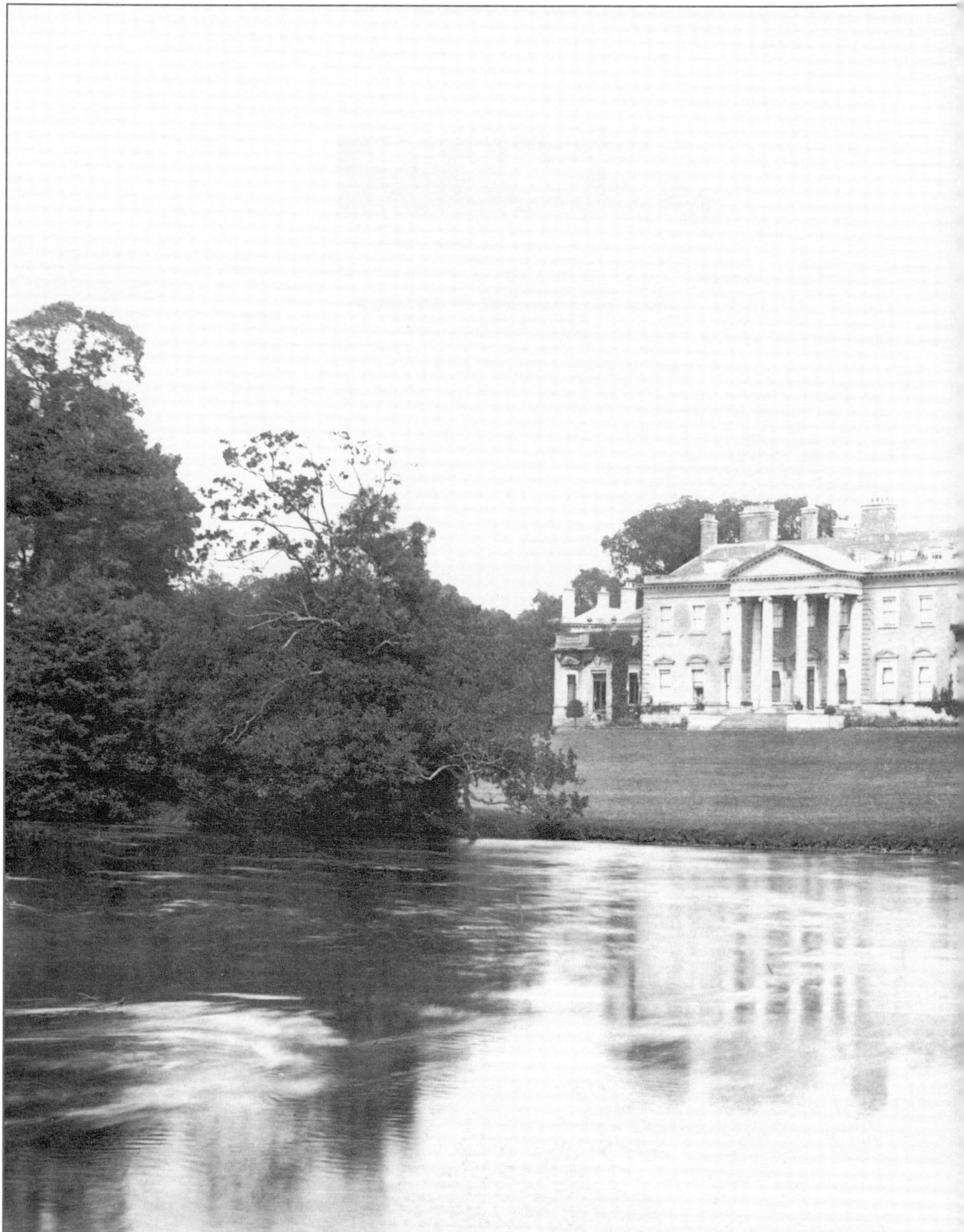

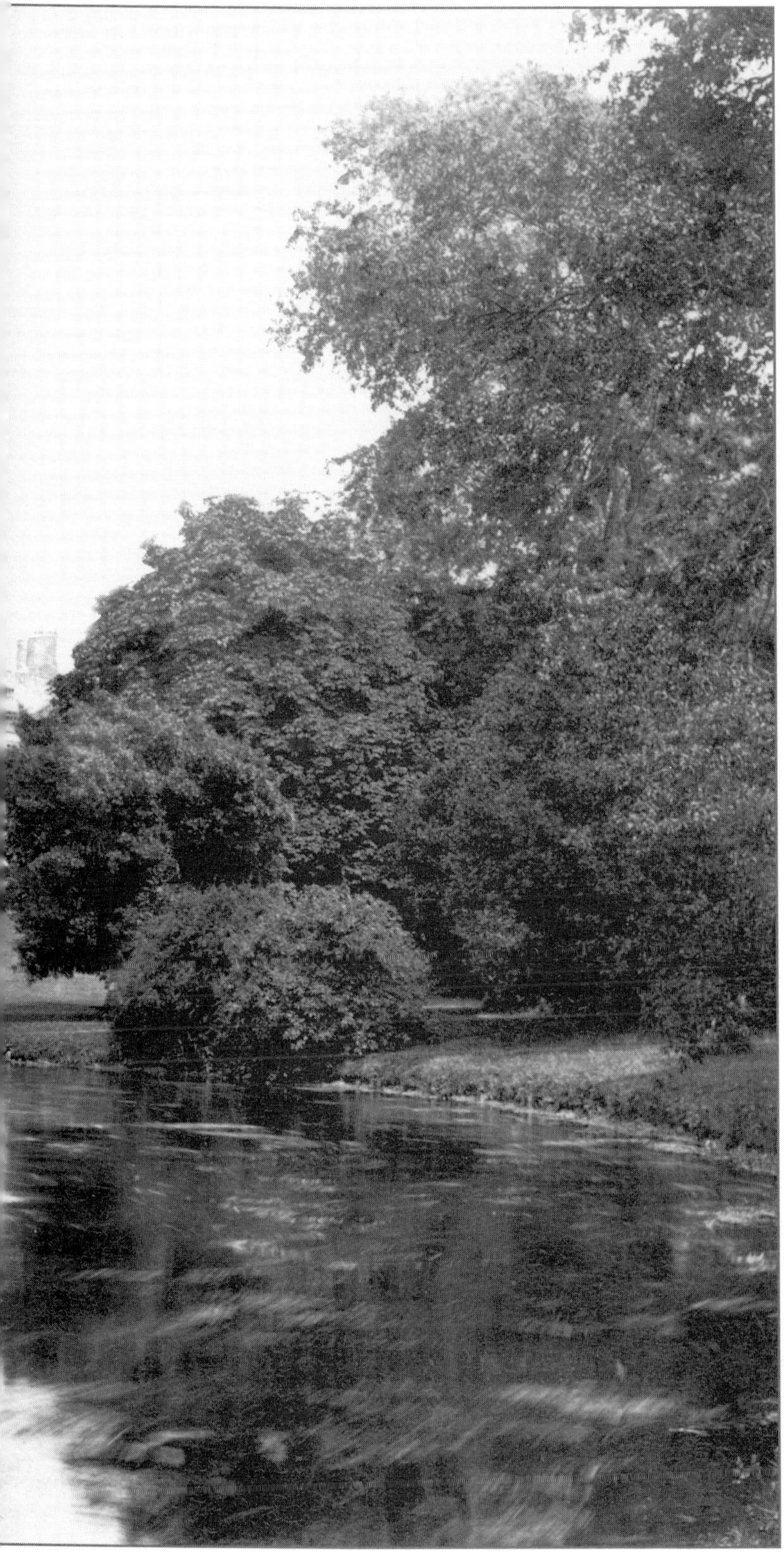

ROMSEY, BROADLANDS 1898 42110
Broadlands was a small Tudor manor until 1736, when the first Viscount Palmerston commissioned William Kent to divert the river. The second Viscount employed Capability Brown to redesign Broadlands as a Palladian mansion.

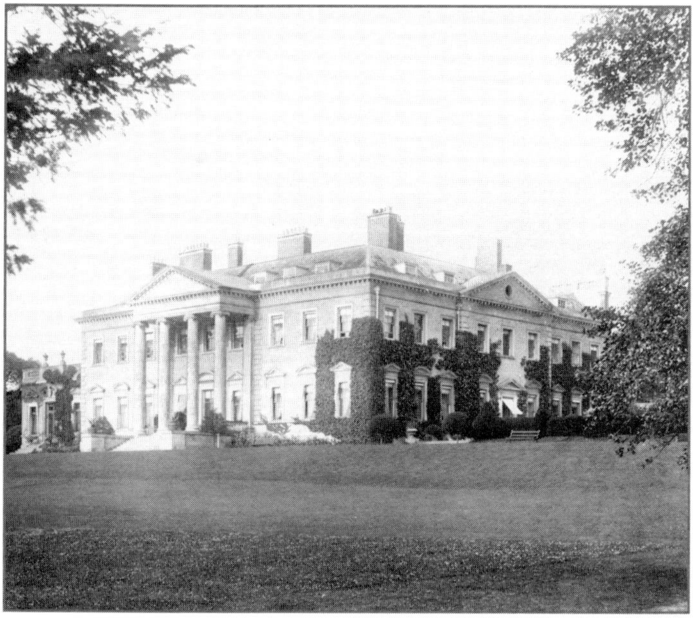

ROMSEY, BROADLANDS 1904 51447

ROMSEY

Broadlands 1904

Capability Brown designed the west front with its beautiful Ionic portico, but other parts of the house were completed by his son-in-law Henry Holland. Houses like this often see subtle changes over the years - in this picture, the chimneys on the left (visible in picture no 42110) have been removed.

ROMSEY

Broadlands 1904

In recent years Broadlands has been most famous as the home of Lord Mountbatten until his death at the hands of the IRA in 1979. Today it contains a museum dedicated to his life.

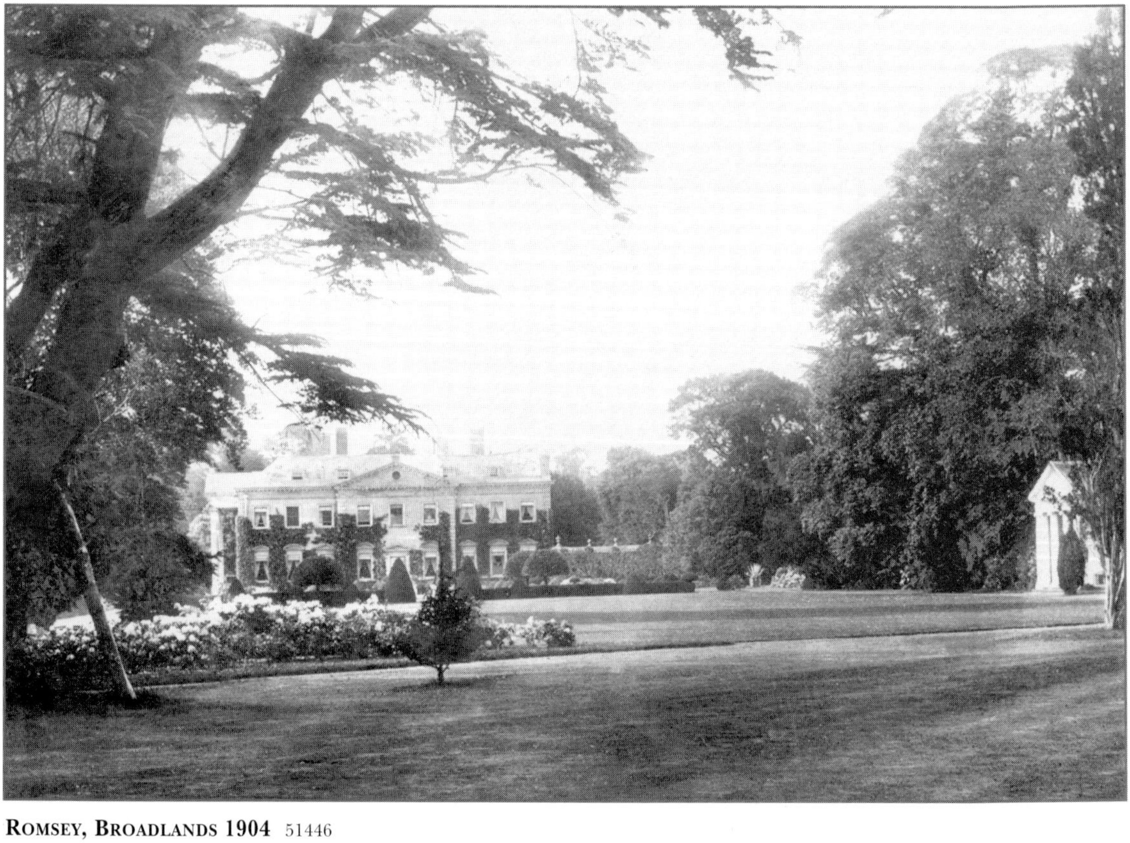

ROMSEY, BROADLANDS 1904 51446

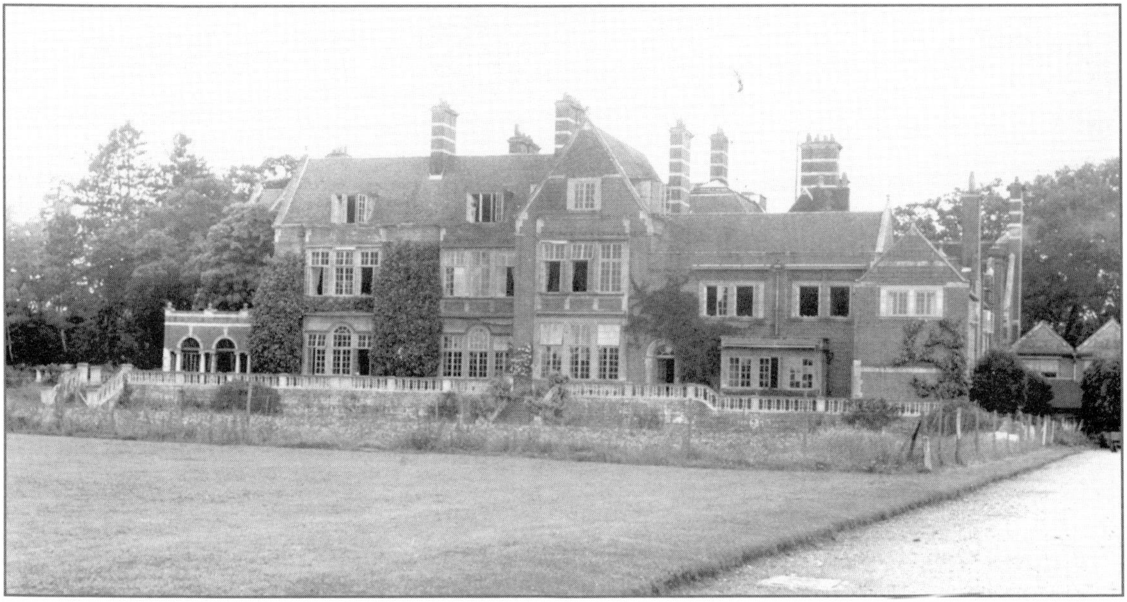

SHERFIELD ON LODDON, NORTH FORELAND LODGE C1955 S631019
Sherfield Manor was built in 1897 by James Benjamin Tailor, a diamond broker and gold prospector who had made his fortune in South Africa. It was subsequently owned by the Earl of Winchelsea. During World War Two it was a nurses' home before becoming a girls' school - it changed its name to North Foreland Lodge after the original school site in Kent.

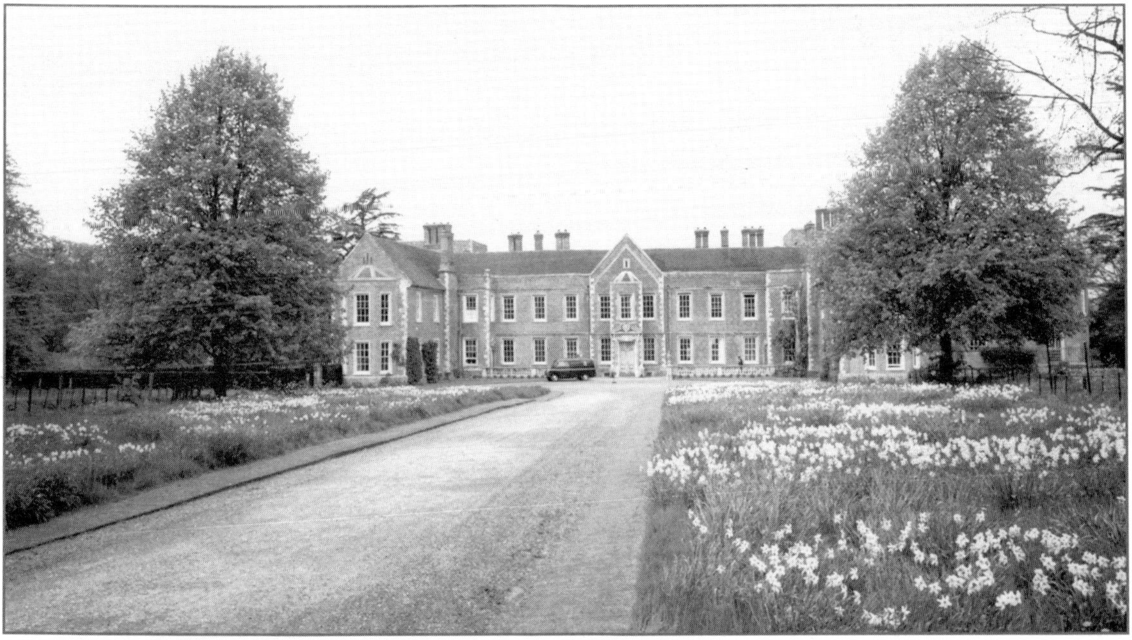

BRAMLEY, THE VYNE C1960 B696032
It is thought that the Vyne takes its name from the Roman Vindomis, or House of Wine, which occupied a site in the area in the 2nd century. The current house was built in the early 16th century for Sir William Sandys, Lord Chamberlain to Henry VIII.

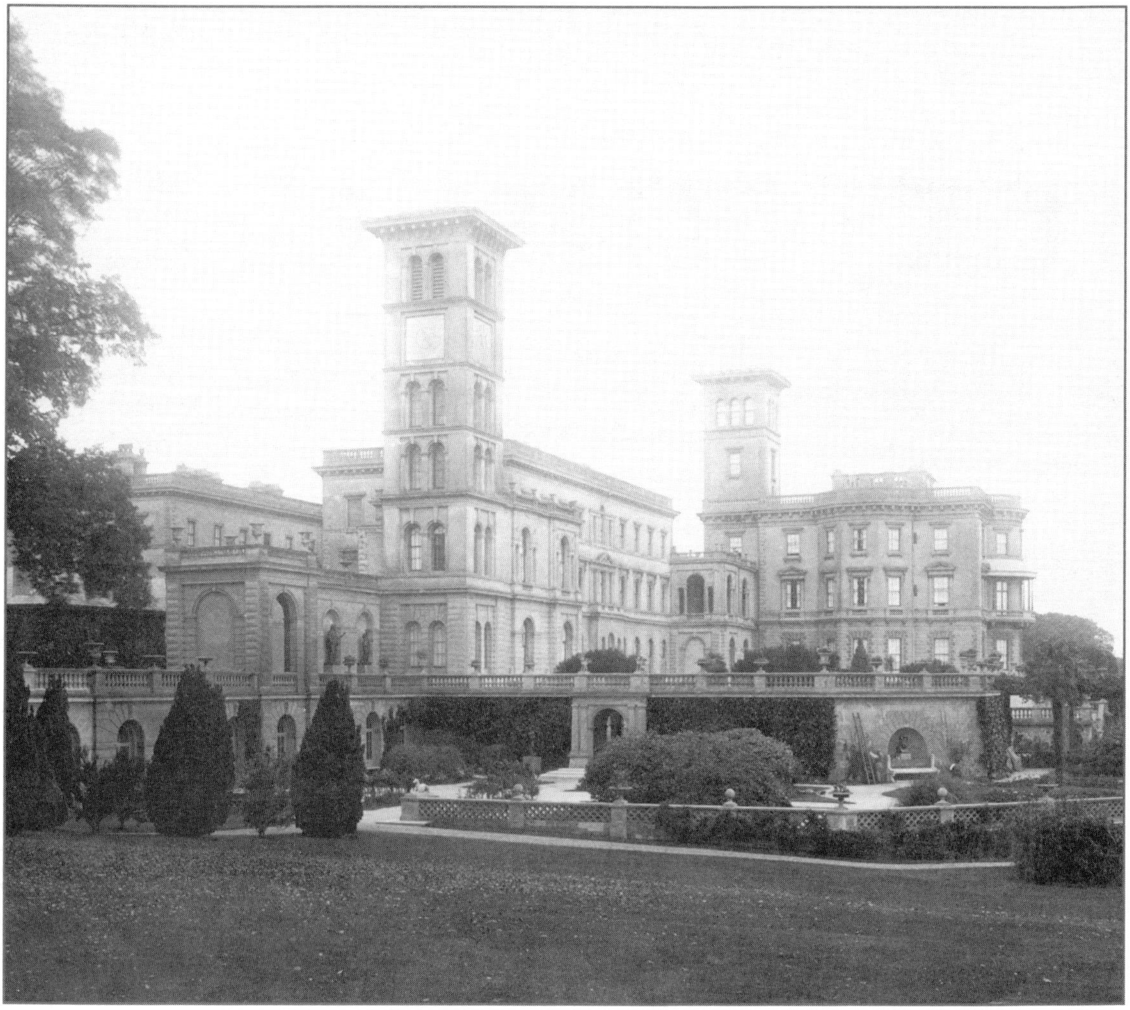

Osborne House 1893 32832
Osborne House was built in 1847-53 for Queen Victoria and Prince Albert, who collaborated on the Italianate design of the house with the architect Thomas Cubitt. When Albert died in 1861, Victoria ordered that Osborne should remain unchanged as a memorial to him.

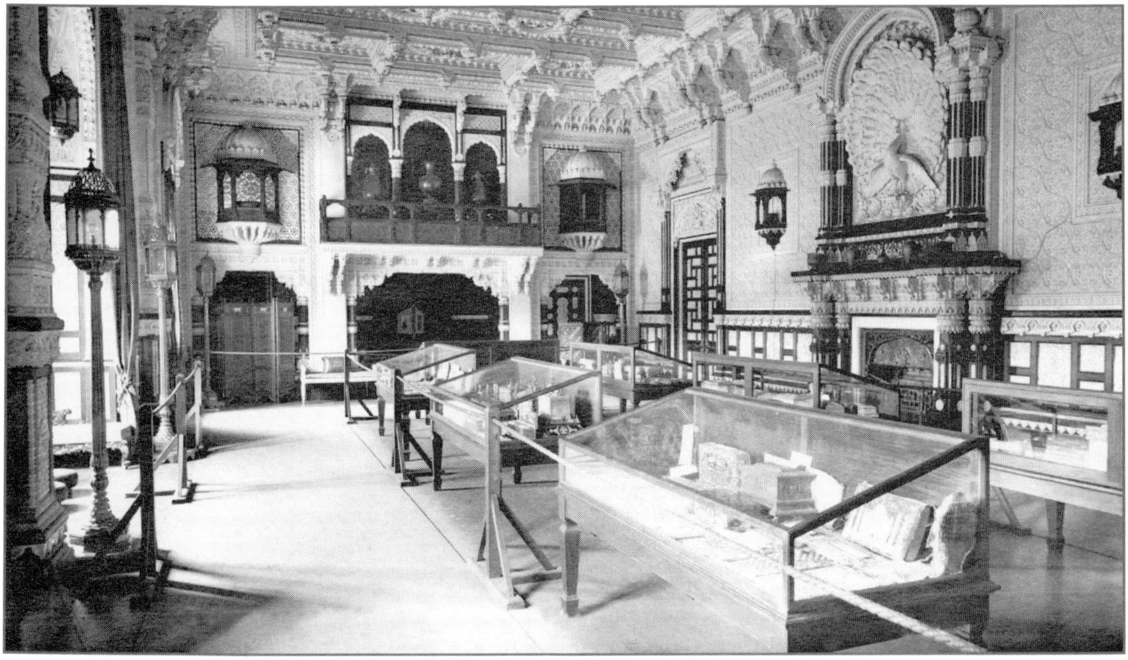

Cowes, Osborne House, The State Apartments, The Indian Durbar Room 1908 60585

The only alteration ever made at Osborne House, the Durbar Room was designed by Bhai Ram Sing and John Lockwood Kipling, whose son would later become the 'Bard of the Empire'.

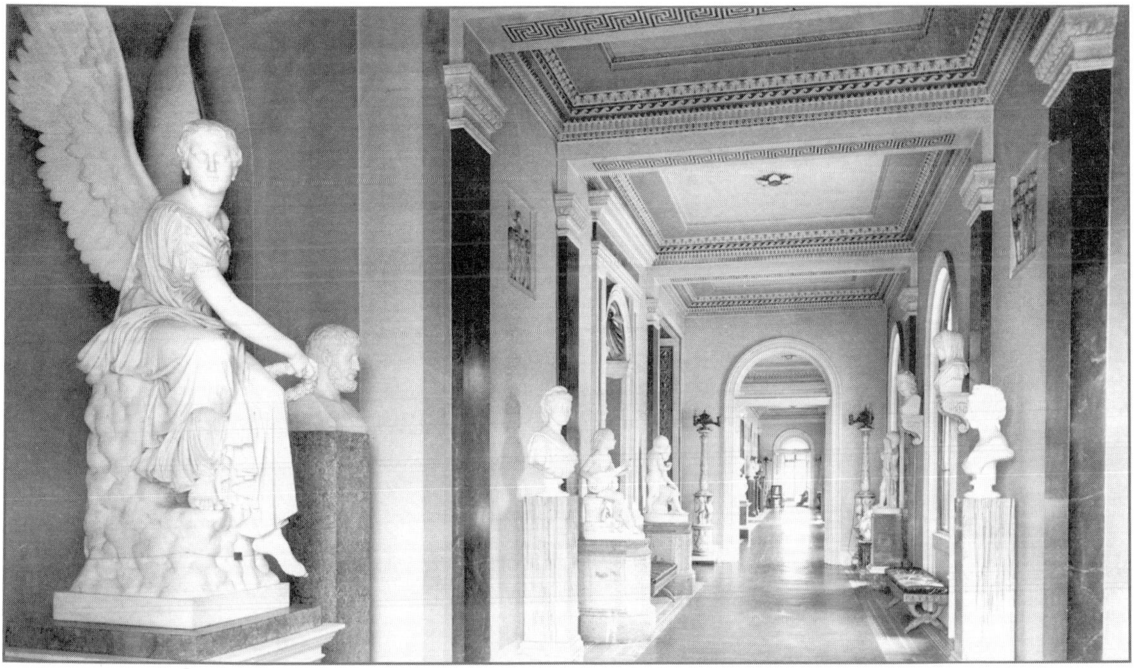

Cowes, Osborne House, The Marble Corridor 1908 60593

This corridor, an early example of open-plan design, runs along three sides of the entrance courtyard and links the Durbar Room with the Billiards Room and Drawing Room.

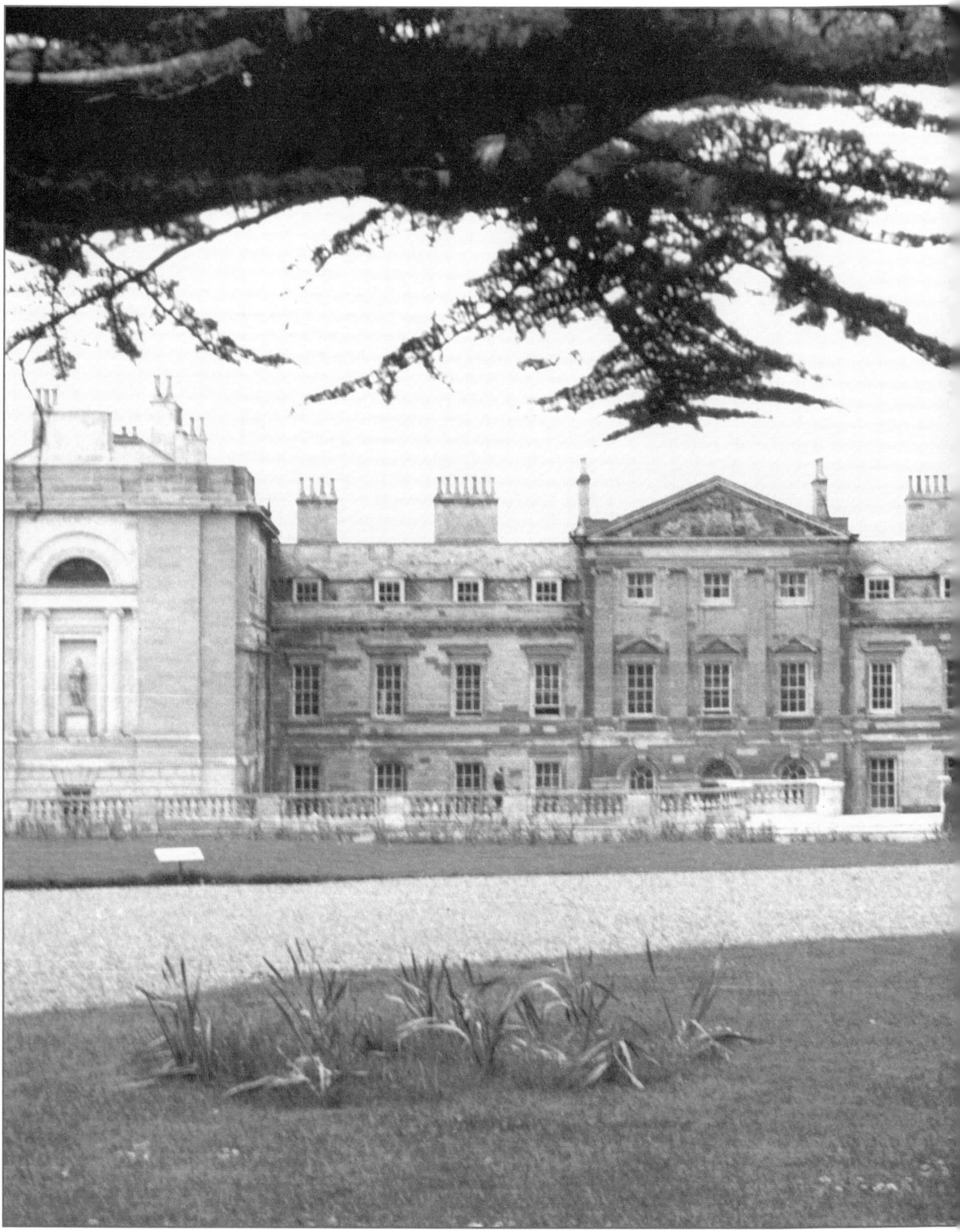

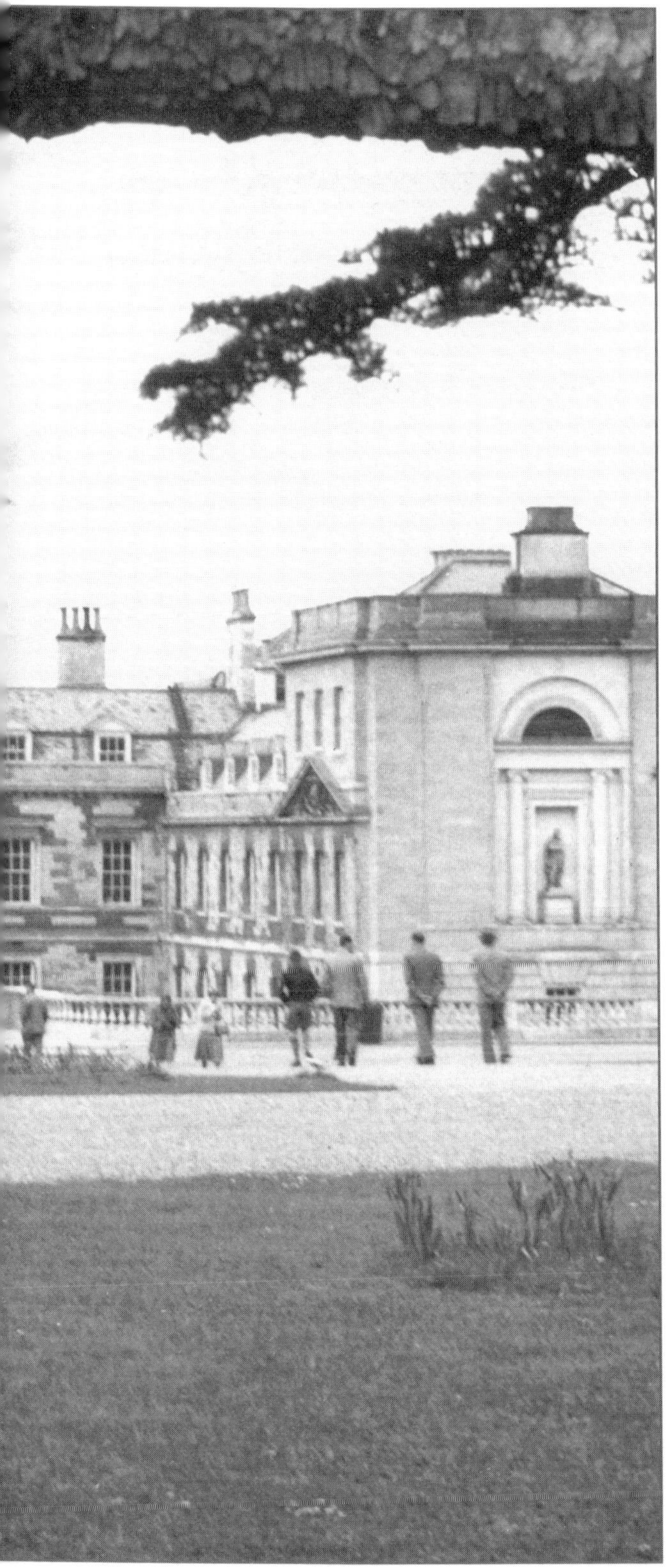

London & The South East

Woburn Abbey, From the Cedars c1955 W301033
The ruined Cistercian house, founded in 1125, was left in his will by Henry VIII to John Russell, first Earl of Bedford. In 1625 the fourth Earl fled the plague in London and commissioned Isaac de Caux to build on the site. The west front was added by the fourth Duke in 1747.

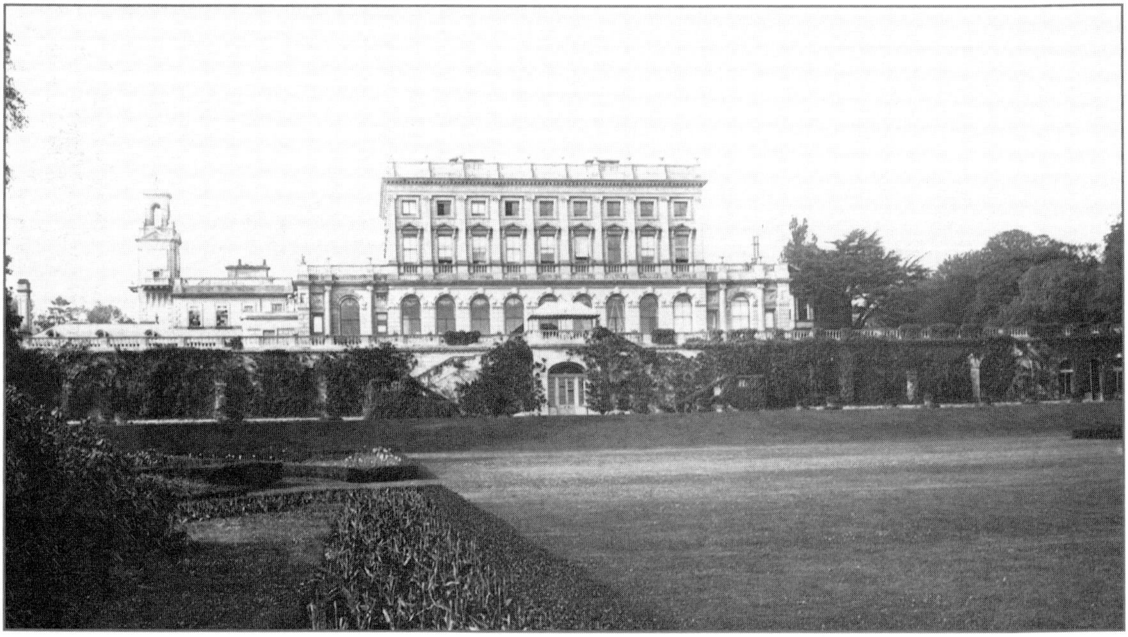

Cliveden House 1893 31758
The magnificent arcaded terrace which looks out on the Thames was built in 1666 by William Winde. The house is the third to occupy the site, and was built in 1851 by Sir Charles Barry. In 1893 it was bought by William Waldorf Astor, the first Viscount Astor. The second Viscount's wife was Nancy Astor, the first woman MP.

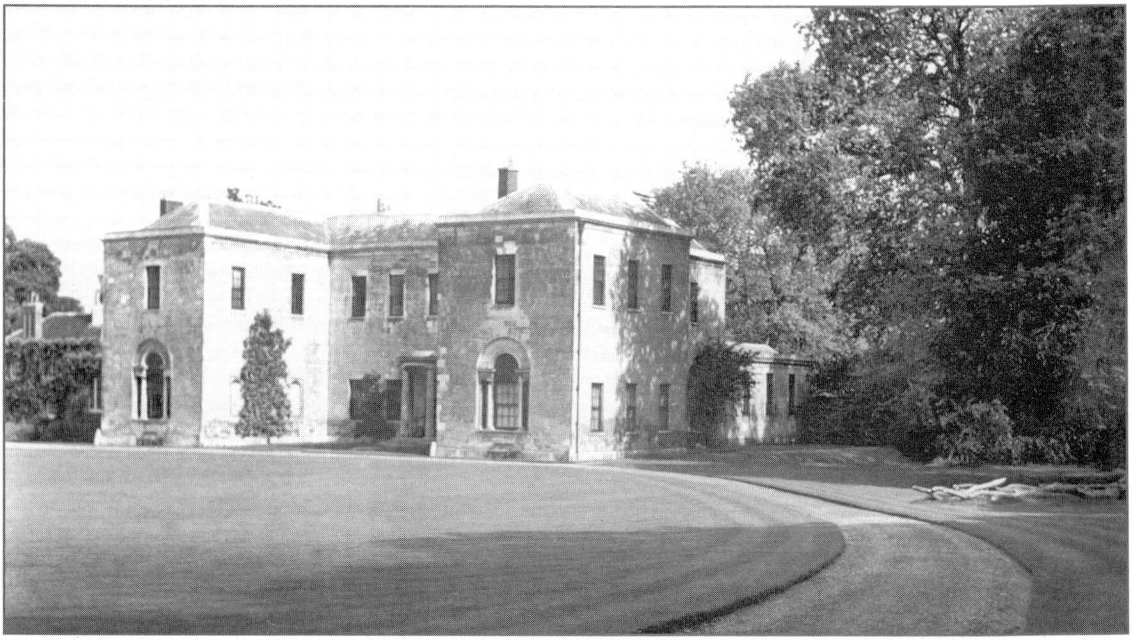

Hitchin, The Priory c1955 H89005
Hitchin Priory was, like so many other religious houses, destroyed in the Dissolution of the Monasteries, and the only original remains are those of the cloisters in the north courtyard. The house that now occupies the site was designed by Robert Adam.

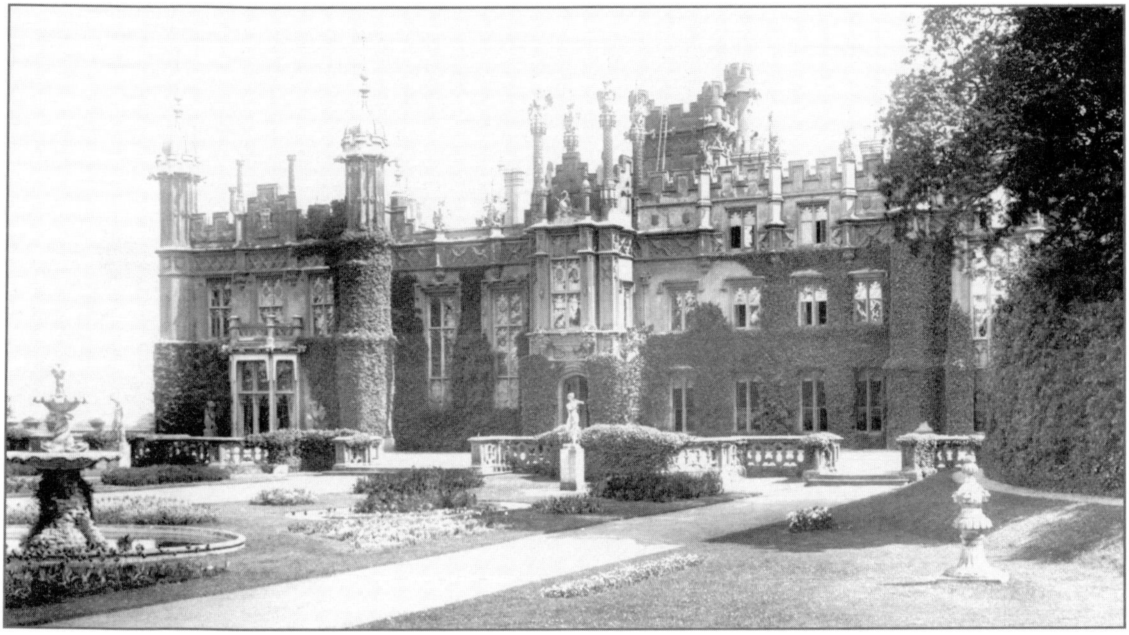

KNEBWORTH HOUSE 1901 46662

Knebworth has undergone several incarnations. Originally a Tudor mansion dating from 1490, this was demolished in 1811 by Mrs Elizabeth Bulwer and rebuilt to a design by Biagio Rebecca. In 1843 it was extensively remodelled by H E Kendall Junior on the instructions of the writer and politician Edward Bulwer-Lytton.

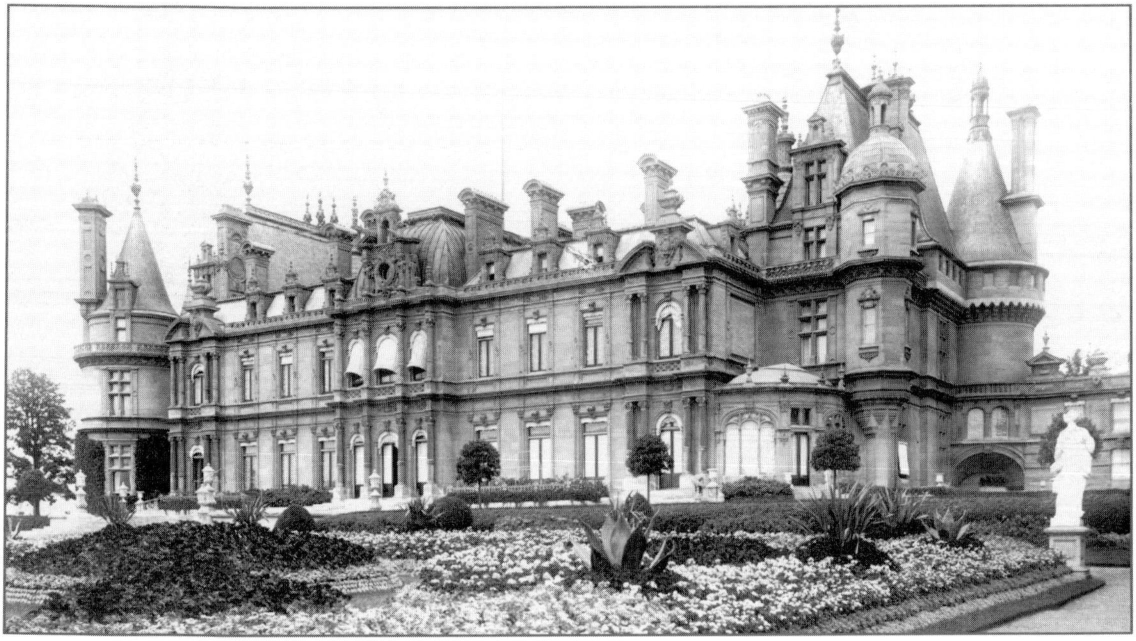

AYLESBURY, WADDESDON MANOR, THE SOUTH FRONT 1897 39653

Modelled on a French chateau by Gabrielle-Hippolyte Destailleur, Waddesdon Manor was built for Baron Ferdinand de Rothschild and was completed in 1889. Among numerous works of art is a fine collection of 18th- and 19th-century buttons, and the wine cellars (as one would expect) are a sight to behold.

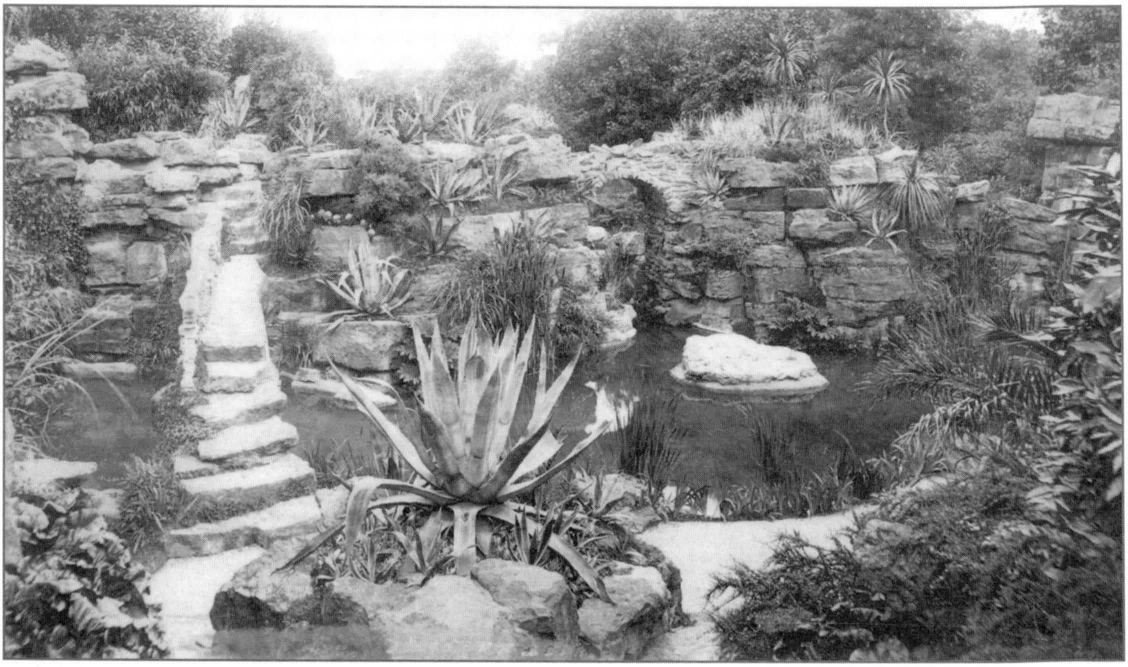

Waddesdon Manor, The Rockery 1897 39660
Waddesdon's gardens were designed by Lain, and are considered to be among the finest Victorian gardens in the country. There is also a Rococo aviary housing exotic birds.

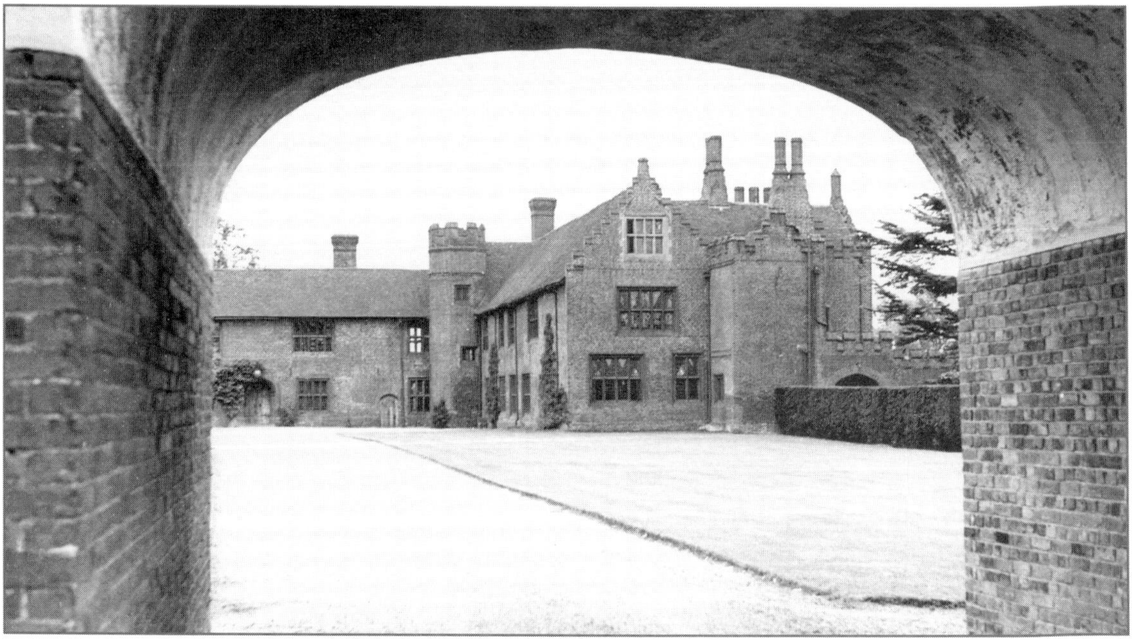

Ingatestone Hall, The Gateway and Courtyard c1955 I10013
This Tudor brick manor was built by Sir William Petre, Secretary of State to Edward VI and Bloody Mary and Privy Counsellor to Henry VIII and Elizabeth I. The Petre family still live here, and the Long Gallery, with a fine collection of family portraits, is open to the public.

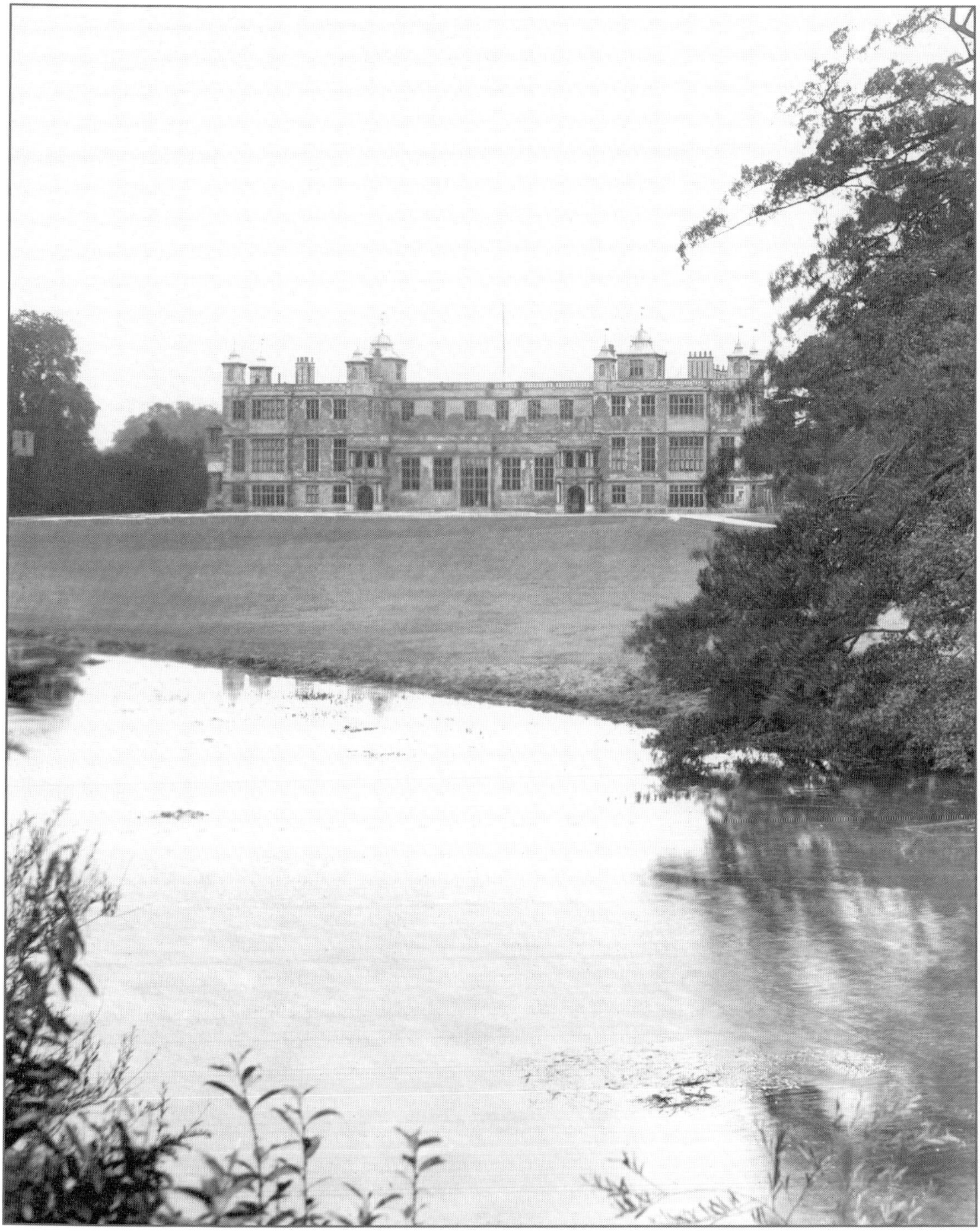

Saffron Walden, Audley End House 1920 69141

Audley End was built in the early 17th century by Thomas Howard, first Earl of Suffolk and Lord Treasurer of England, and designed by Bernard Johnson. Much altered over the years, it has a stair by Sir John Vanbrugh, a great drawing room by Robert Adam, and gardens by Adam and Capability Brown.

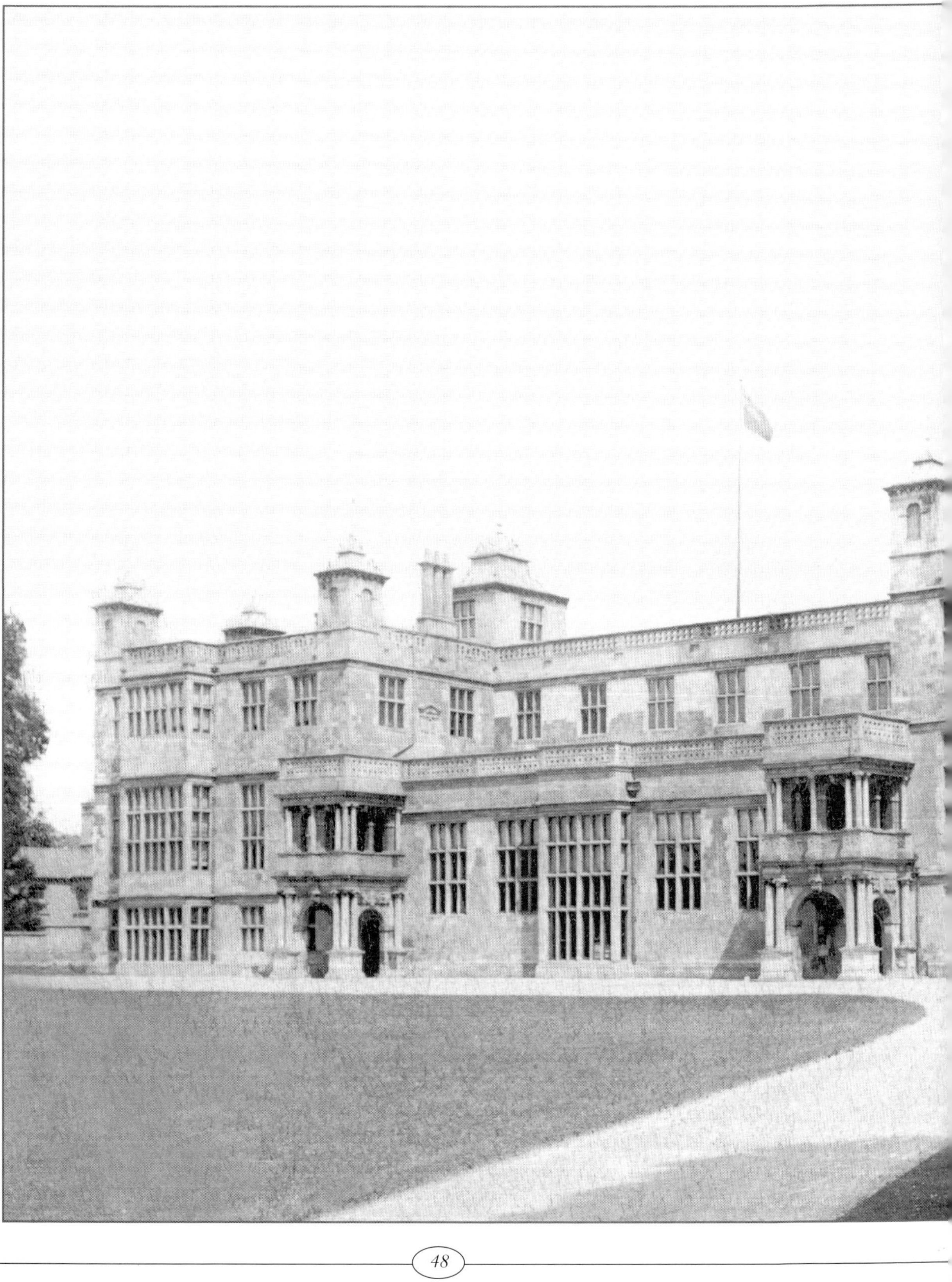

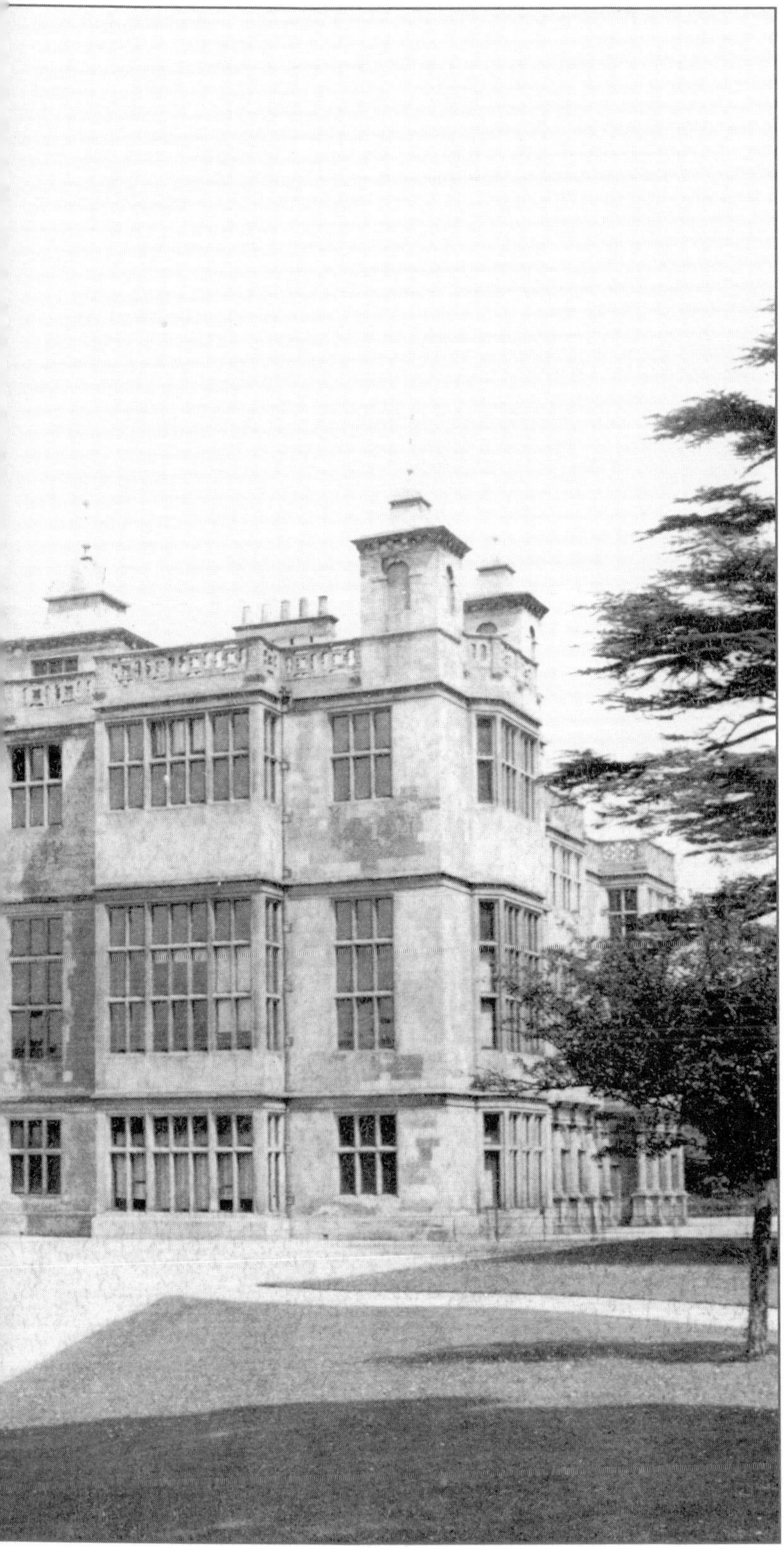

Saffron Walden
Audley End House c1910 A109044
When it was first built, Audley End was twice the size it is now; on seeing it, James I is reputed to have dryly remarked: 'Too large for a king, but might do well for a Lord Treasurer'. In 1614 the Lord Treasurer was tried for embezzlement and fined £30,000.

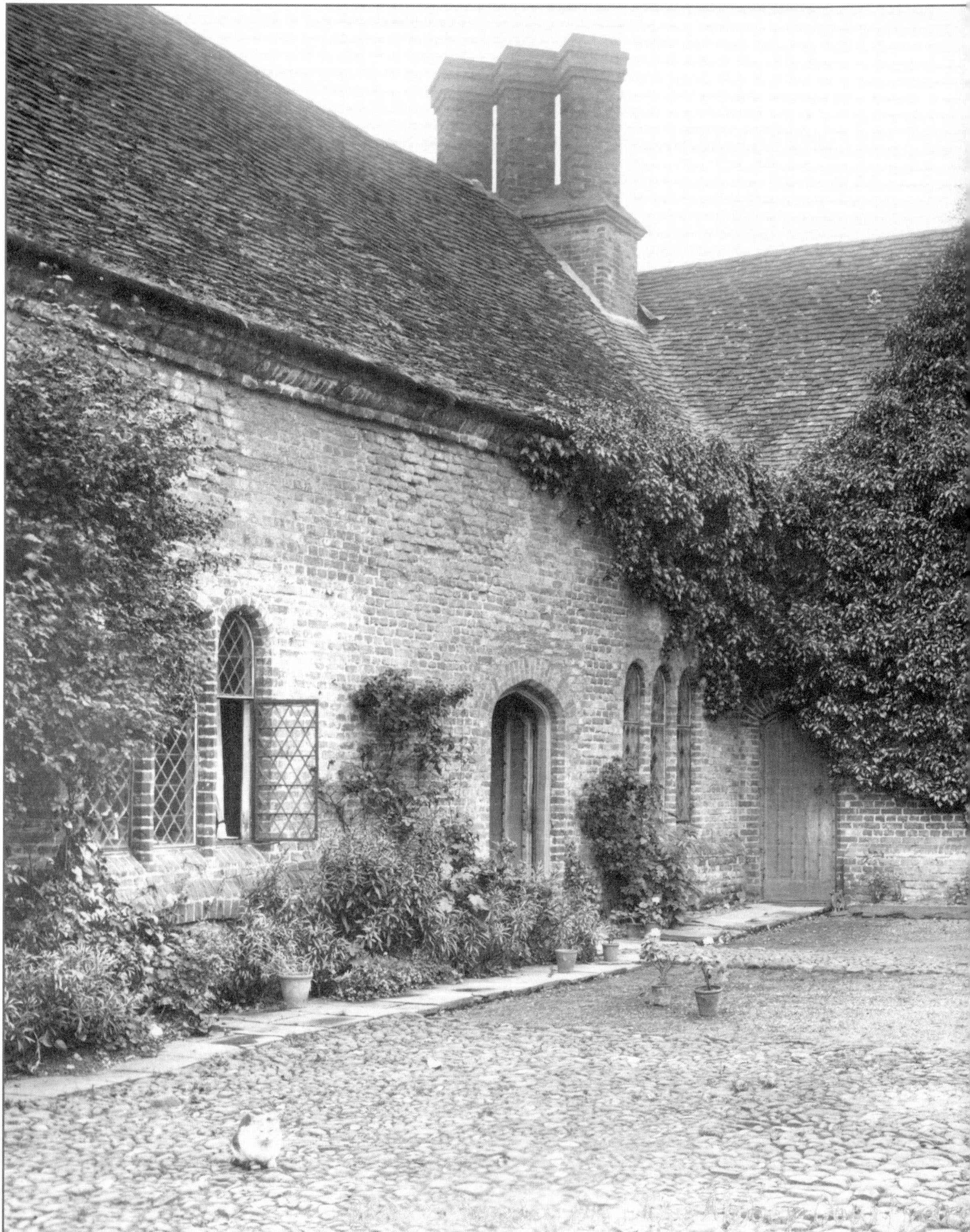

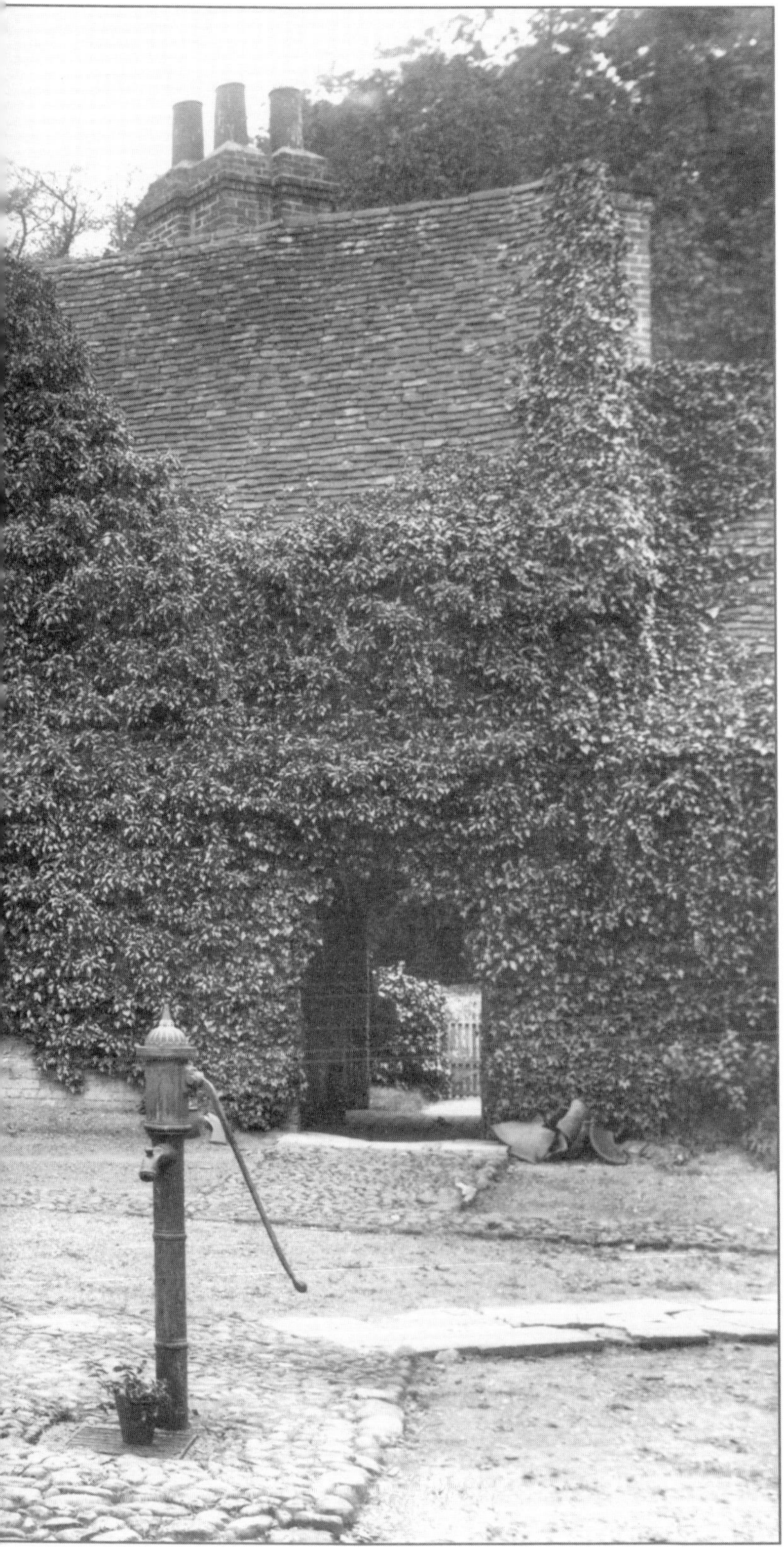

SAFFRON WALDEN, THE ABBEY COURTYARD, AUDLEY END 1907 58832
This is the courtyard of the old Benedictine Abbey, a scene that must have remained the same for centuries: leaded windows, cobbled yard, and handpump. Only the cat looks somehow out of place.

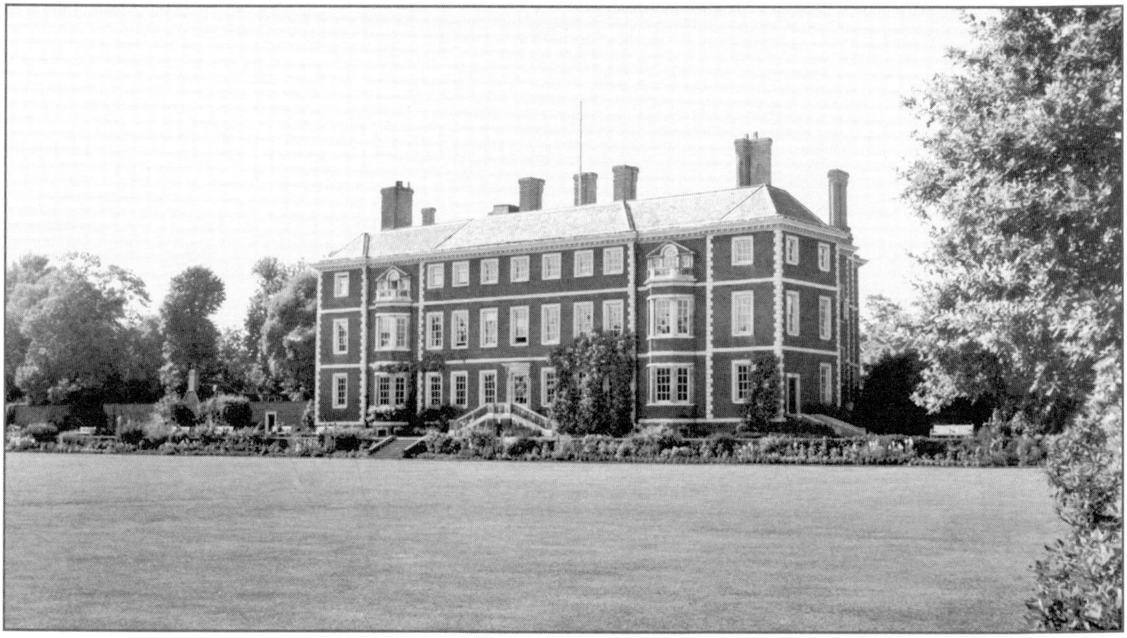

Richmond, Ham House c1955 H352012

This outstanding red brick Stuart house was built in 1610 and was much admired. John Evelyn wrote in his diary in 1678: 'After dinner, I walked to Ham, to see the house and garden of the Duke of Lauderdale, which is indeede inferior to few of the best villas in Italy itself; the house furnished like a great Prince's'. Need one say more?

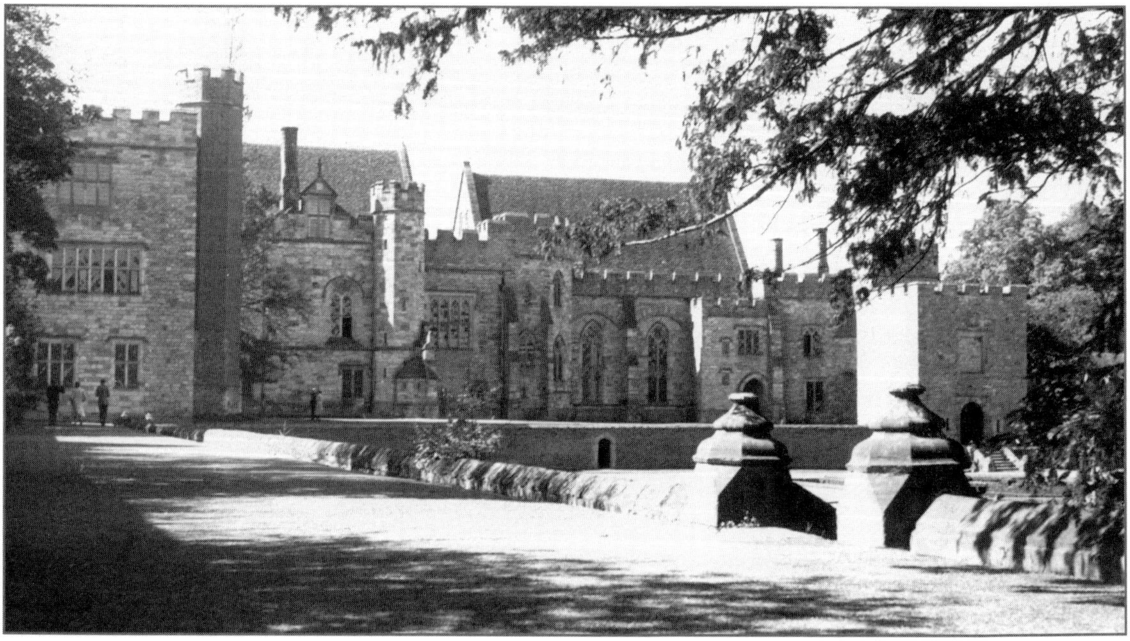

Penshurst Place c1960 P36023

The 14th-century Great Hall at Penshurst has survived almost unaltered, while all around it the house has grown. There are 15th-century additions by the Dukes of Bedford, and 16th- and 18th-century ones by the Sidney family, who still own the house.

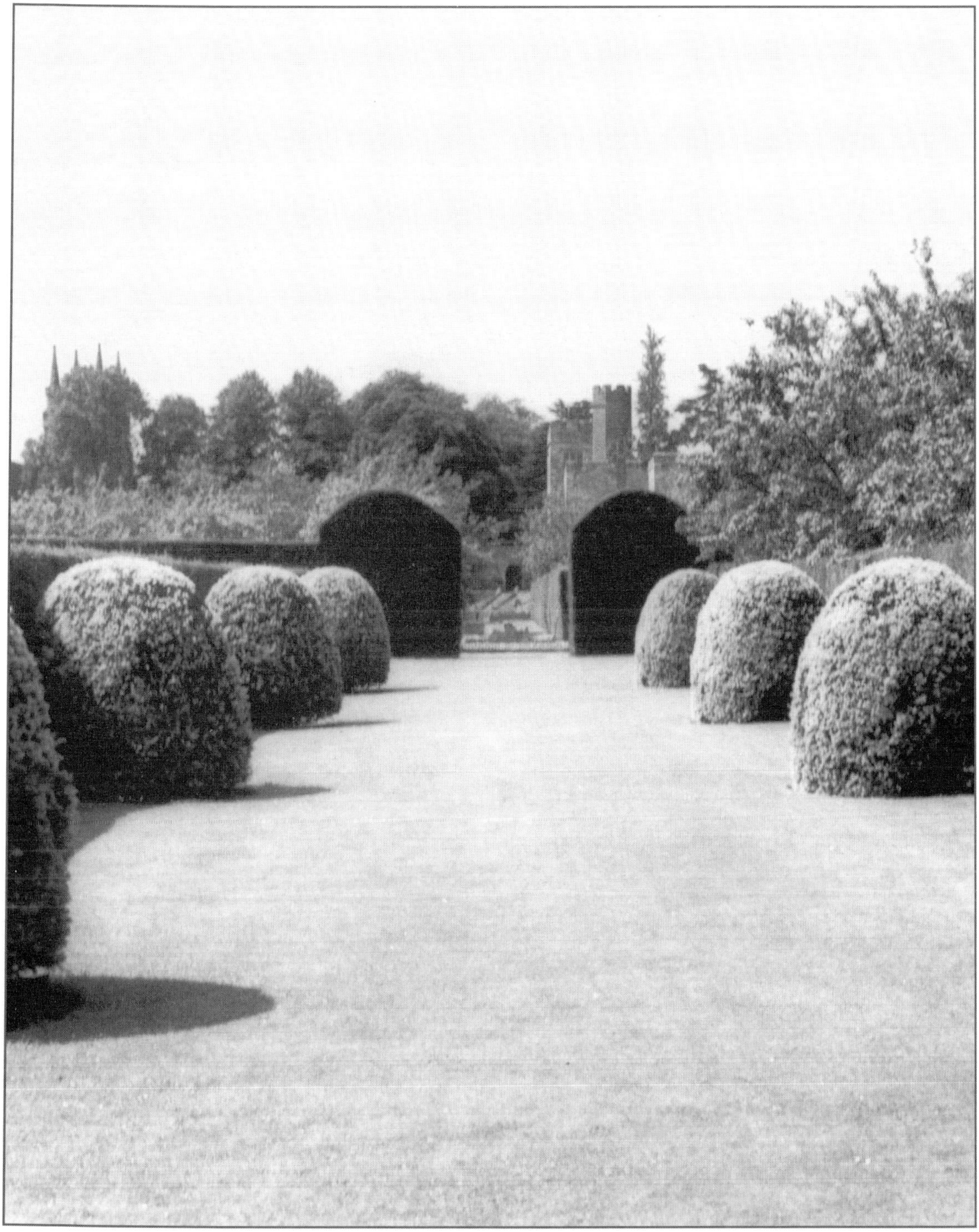

Penshurst Place c1960 P36062

The most famous scion of the Sidney family was the soldier-poet Sir Philip Sidney. He achieved immortality when, fatally wounded in 1586 on a battlefield in Holland, he passed his flask to a common soldier, saying 'Thy necessity is greater than mine'.

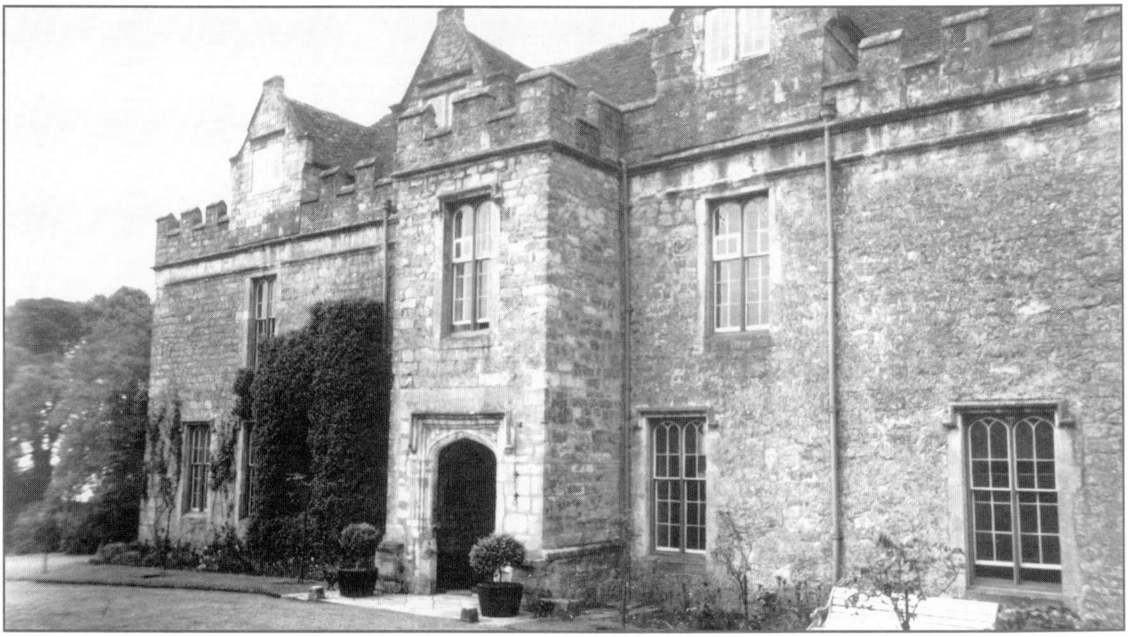

Boughton Monchelsea Place c1960 B576002

Set on top of a hill, in a deer park and with magnificent views of the Weald, Boughton Monchelsea was built on the site of an old fortified manor by Robert Rudston in the 1560s. Although altered in Regency times, it still has a Tudor kitchen and tithe barn.

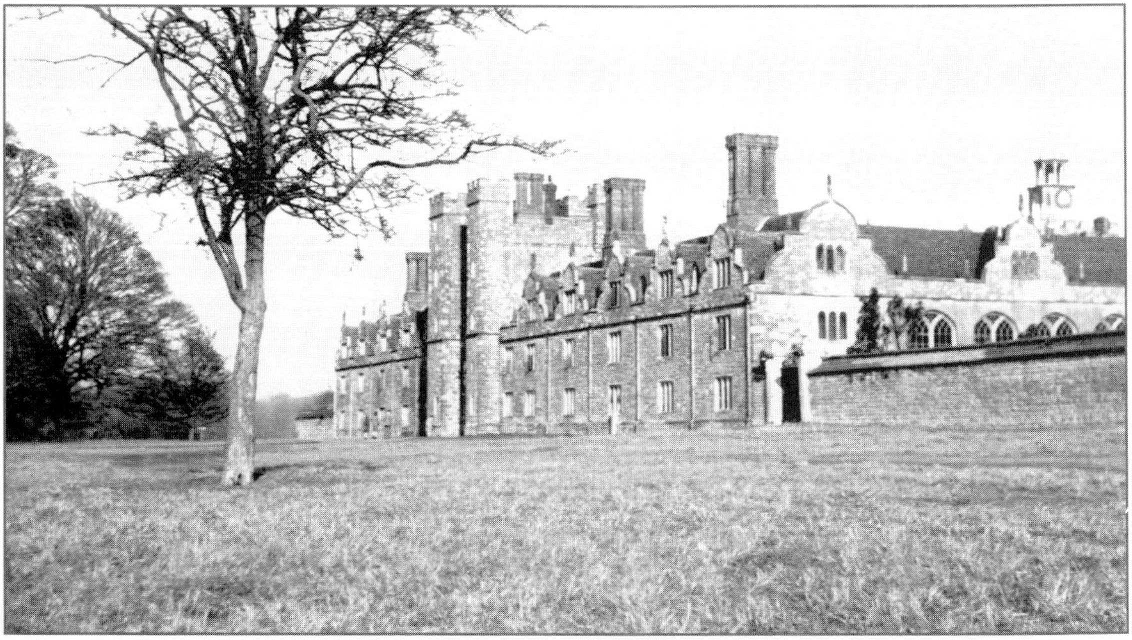

Sevenoaks, Knole c1960 K45003

Knole was owned by the Archbishops of Canterbury until Henry VIII confiscated it after falling out with Thomas Cranmer. Elizabeth I gave the house to Thomas Sackville, Earl of Dorset in 1566, and it has remained in the Sackville family ever since.

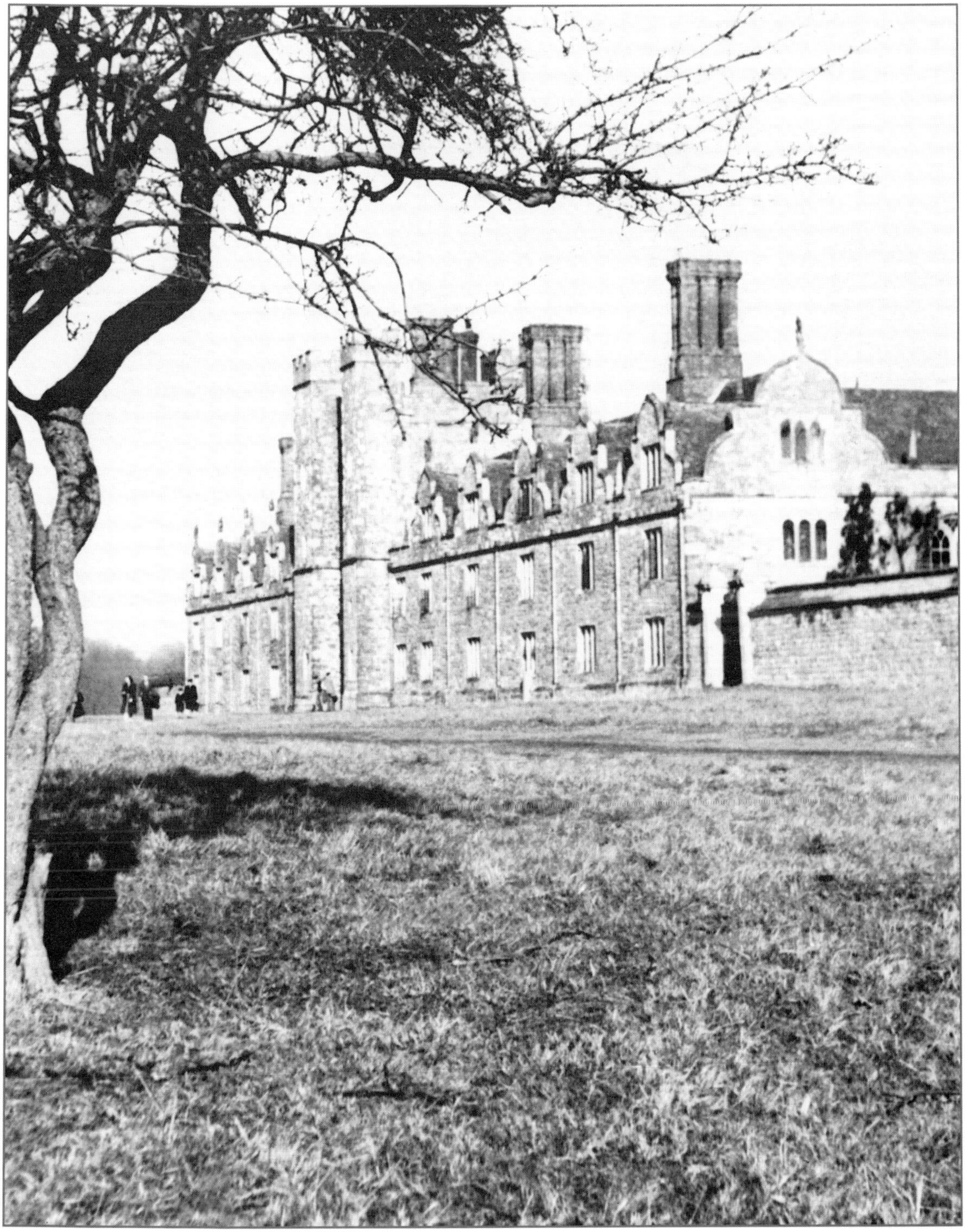

Sevenoaks, Knole c1955 S98002

Built around a series of grassed and paved quadrangles, Knole reputedly has one room for every day of the year, although counting them is apparently a little tricky! Vita Sackville-West's novel 'The Edwardians' was set at Knole.

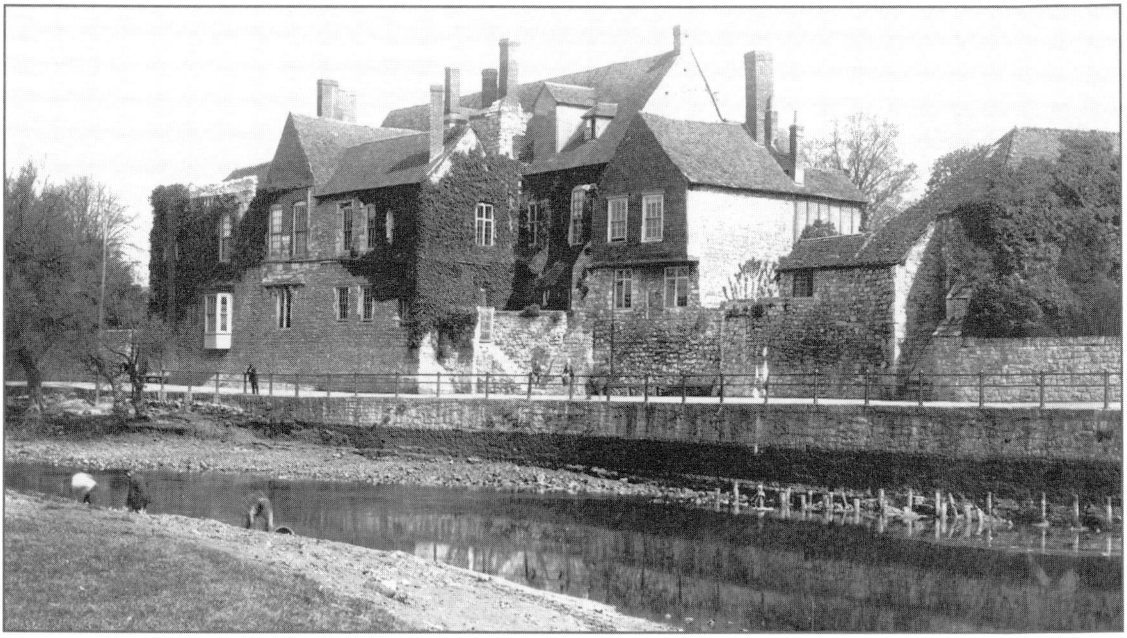

MAIDSTONE, THE ARCHBISHOP'S PALACE 1892 31489
Built overlooking the River Medway in 1348, this fine old building was the property of the Archbishops of Canterbury until a slight misunderstanding with Henry VIII. It stands next to the Perpendicular church of All Saints, built in 1395 by Archbishop Courtenay.

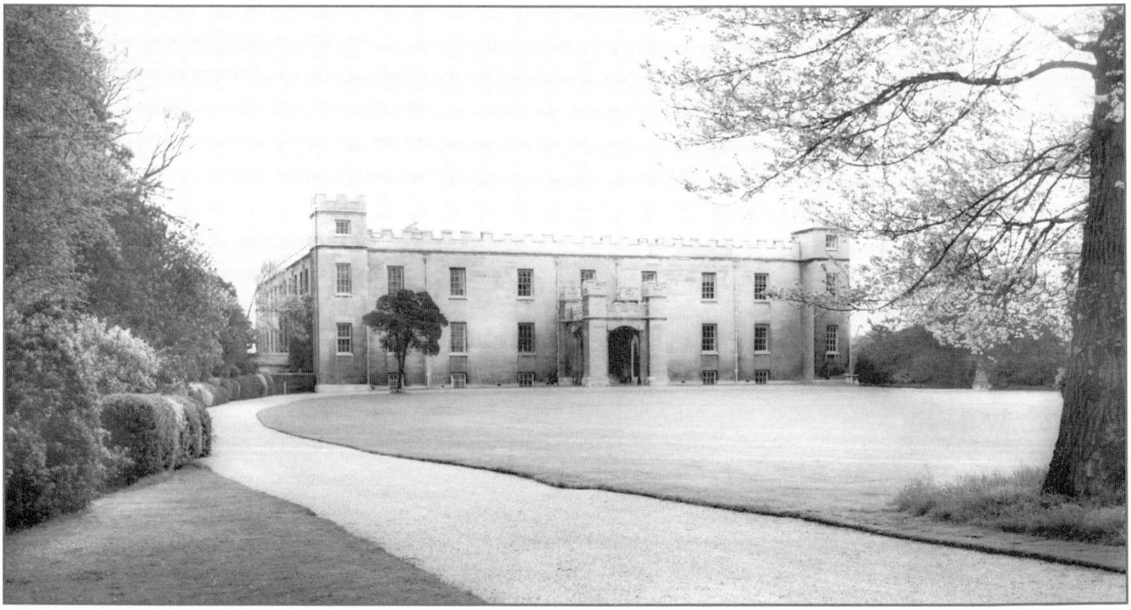

BRENTFORD, SYON HOUSE c1960 B400042
Originally a monastery, Syon House, like so many others, was seized by Henry VIII in 1539. It has an unlucky history. Katherine Howard was incarcerated here prior to her execution; Lady Jane Grey was offered the crown here, accepted it and was shortly executed; and the Earl of Northumberland, given Syon by Elizabeth I, was imprisoned in the Tower for fifteen years after the gunpowder plot.

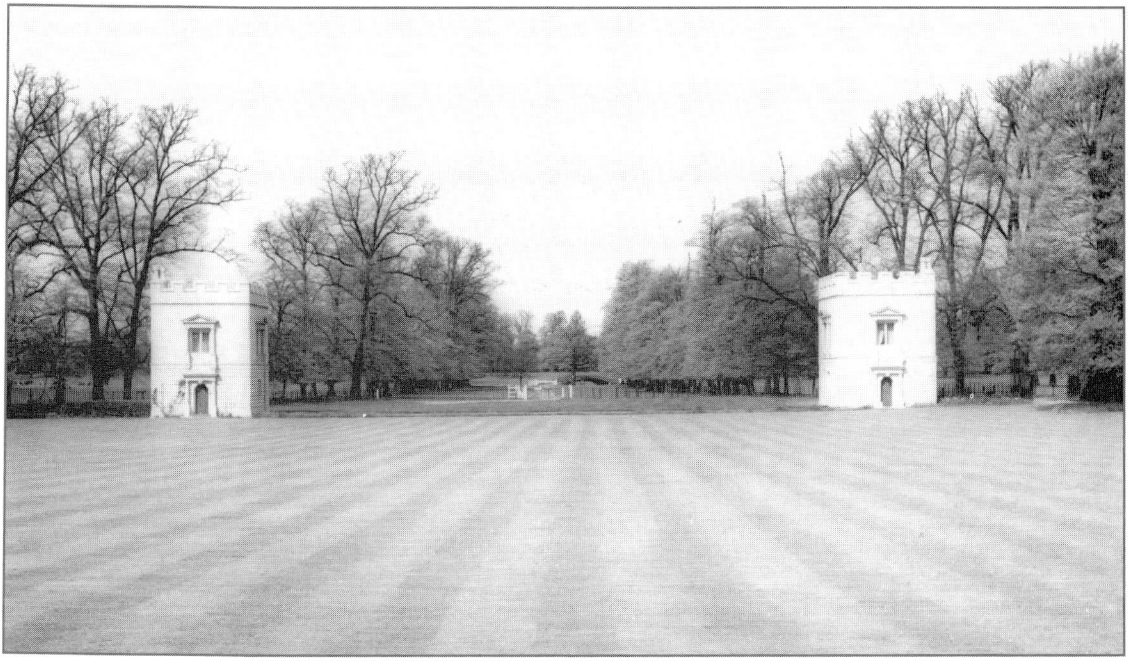

BRENTFORD, SYON HOUSE c1960 B400046
Converted from the original nunnery to a castellated mansion by Edward Seymour, Duke of Somerset, Syon was repaired in the 17th century by Inigo Jones. The gardens were designed by Capability Brown.

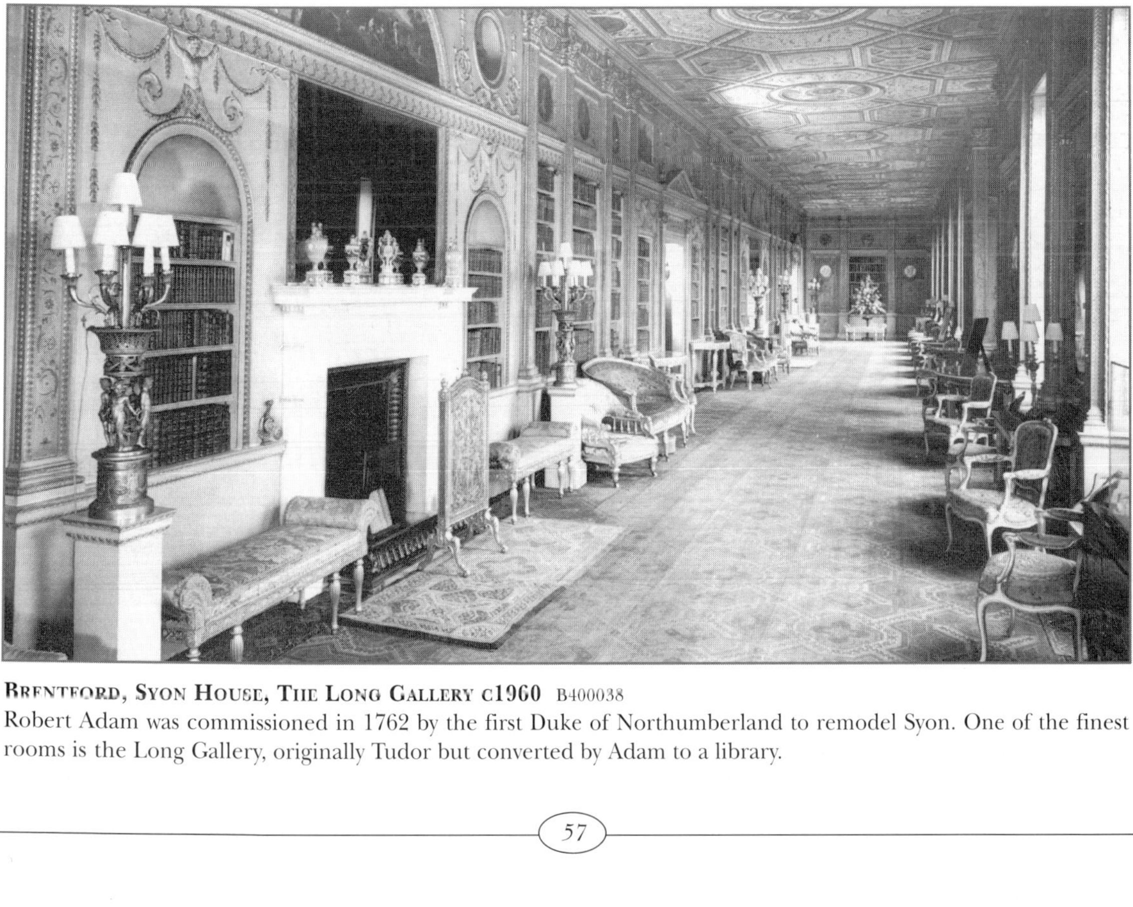

BRENTFORD, SYON HOUSE, THE LONG GALLERY c1960 B400038
Robert Adam was commissioned in 1762 by the first Duke of Northumberland to remodel Syon. One of the finest rooms is the Long Gallery, originally Tudor but converted by Adam to a library.

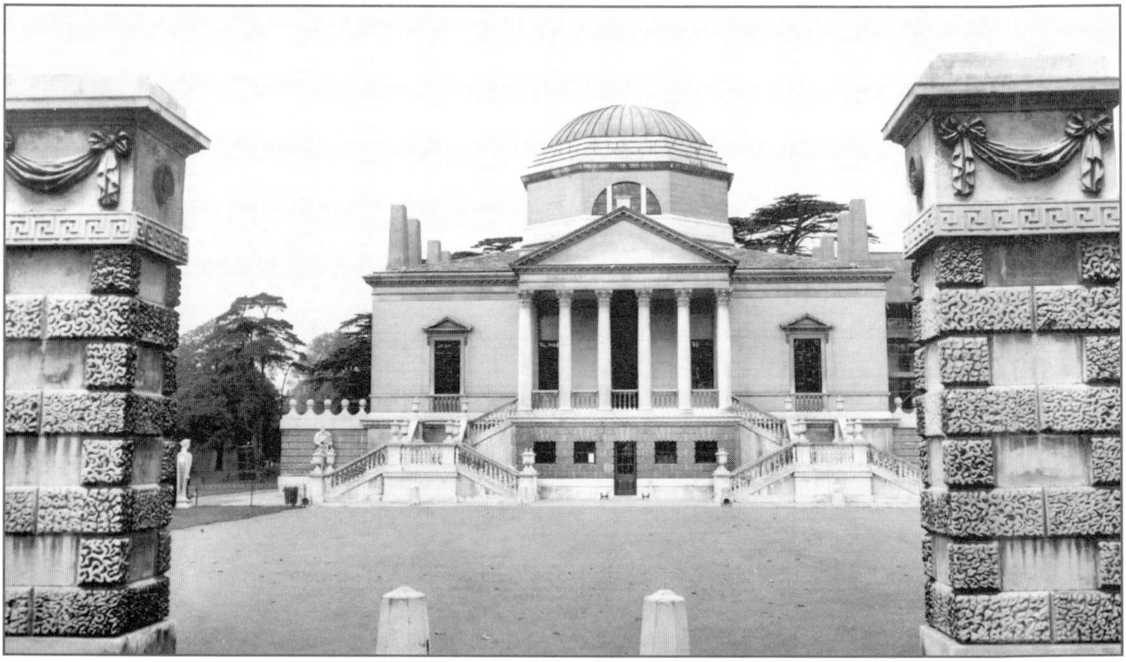

CHISWICK HOUSE c1960 C318025
The publication in 1715 of Colen Campbell's 'Vitruvius Britannicus' was a major influence for Richard Boyle, third Earl of Burlington, and following Campbell's vision he began building Chiswick House in 1725 to his own design.

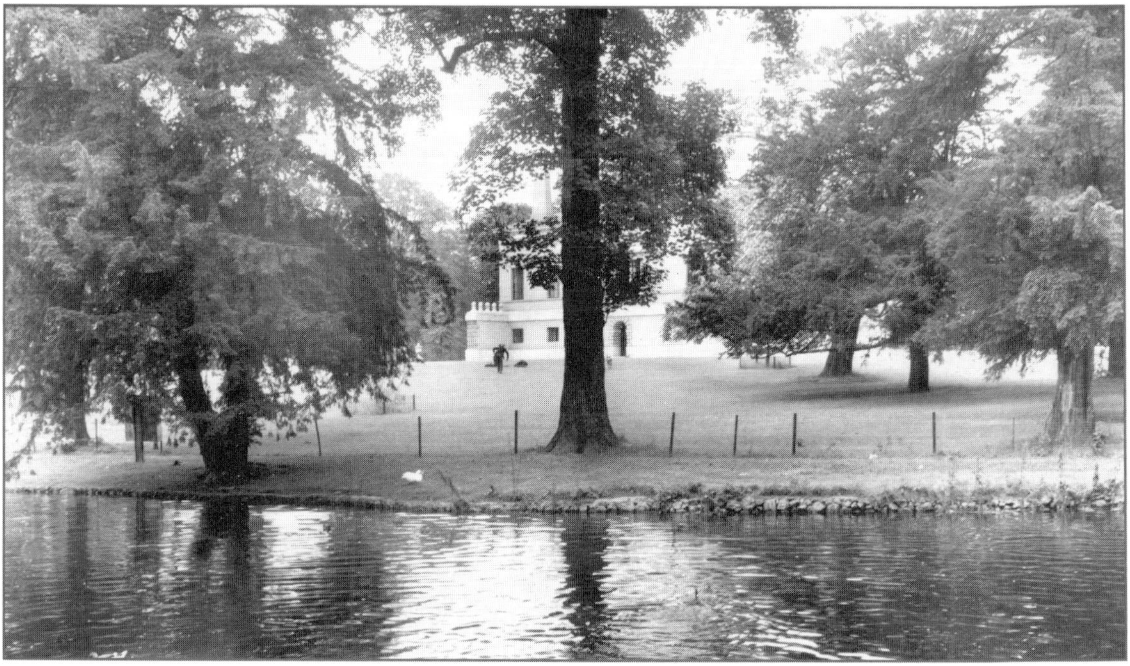

CHISWICK HOUSE c1960 C318020
Campbell was a disciple of the 16th-century Italian Andrea Palladio, and the design of Chiswick House is very Italian-influenced. The interior and gardens are by William Kent.

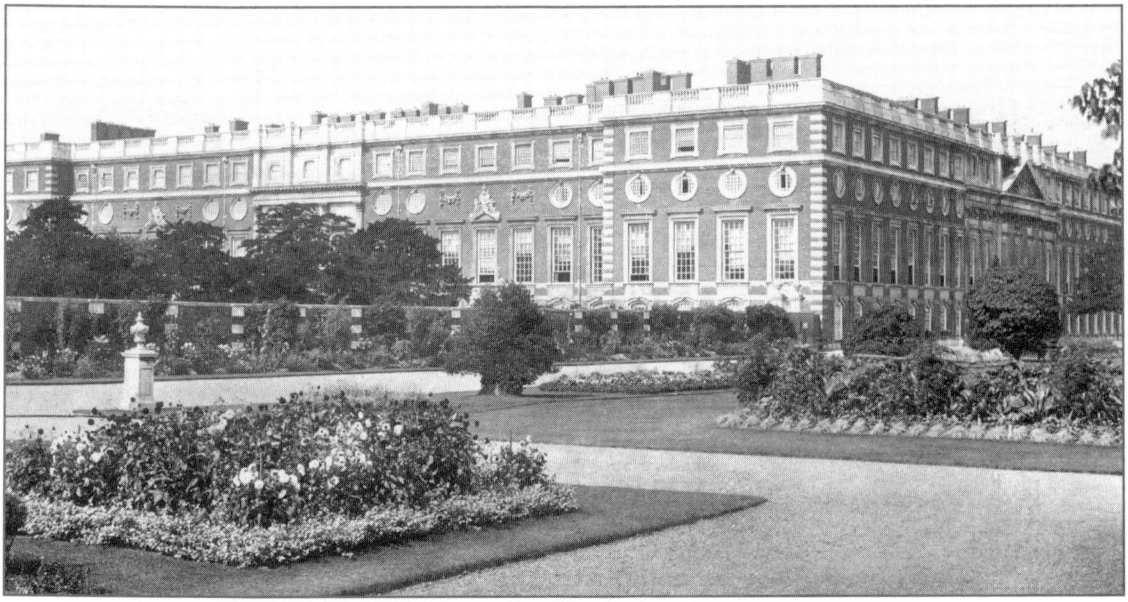

Hampton Court Palace 1899 43045

Hampton Court has 1,000 rooms, three miles of lead plumbing and was five years in the building by a workforce of 2,500 men: an impressive monument for a butcher's boy from Ipswich. Ultimately, Cardinal Wolsey gave Hampton Court Palace to Henry VIII in order to placate him over the Cardinal's refusal to grant the king a divorce from Catherine of Aragon, but to no avail - his star was waning, and he died awaiting trial for treason.

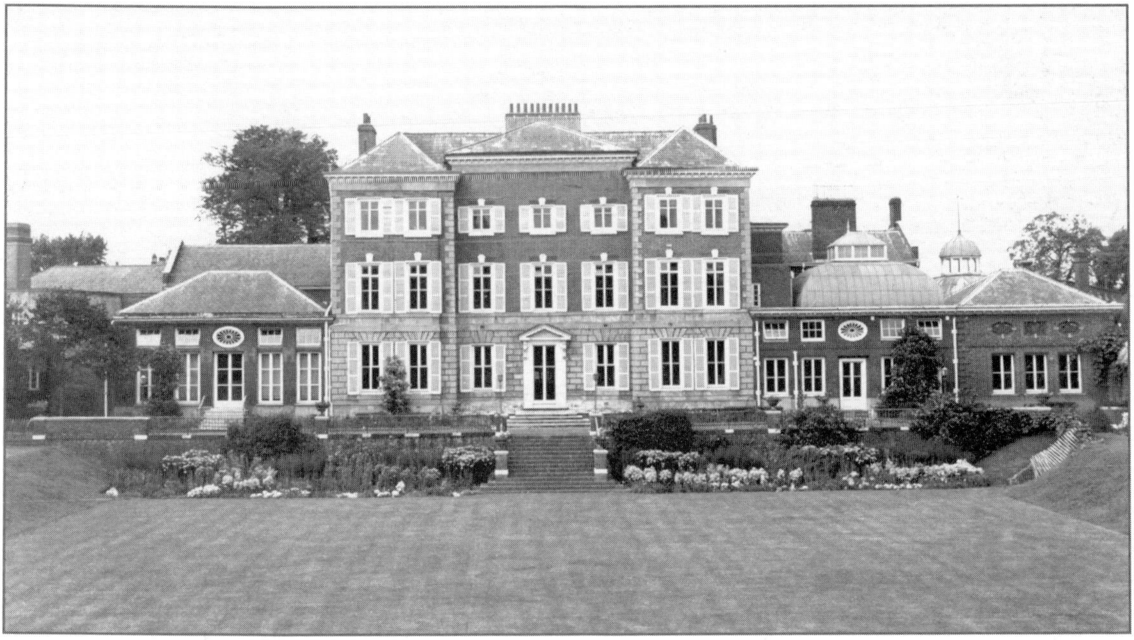

Twickenham, York House from the Bridge c1955 T91016

York House was built in 1626-7 for the Duke of Buckingham by the brilliant Dutch polymath Sir Balthazar Gerbier; in between being a diplomat, courtier and promoter, Gerbier did a little architecture on the side. The Dutch influence shows in the shutters - unusual in an English house.

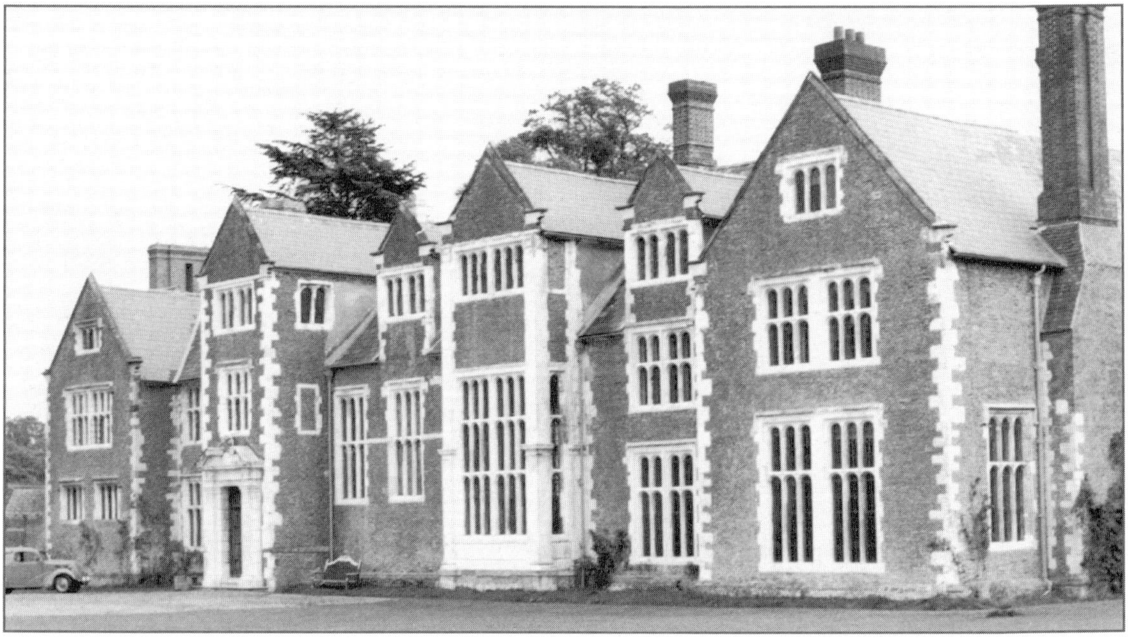

COMPTON, LOSELEY HOUSE c1955 C146019
Sir William More, adviser to Elizabeth and related to Sir Thomas More, built this Elizabethan mansion in 1568 for the princely sum (then) of £1,640 19s 6d. Some of the stone came from Waverley Abbey, another victim of the Dissolution of the Monasteries.

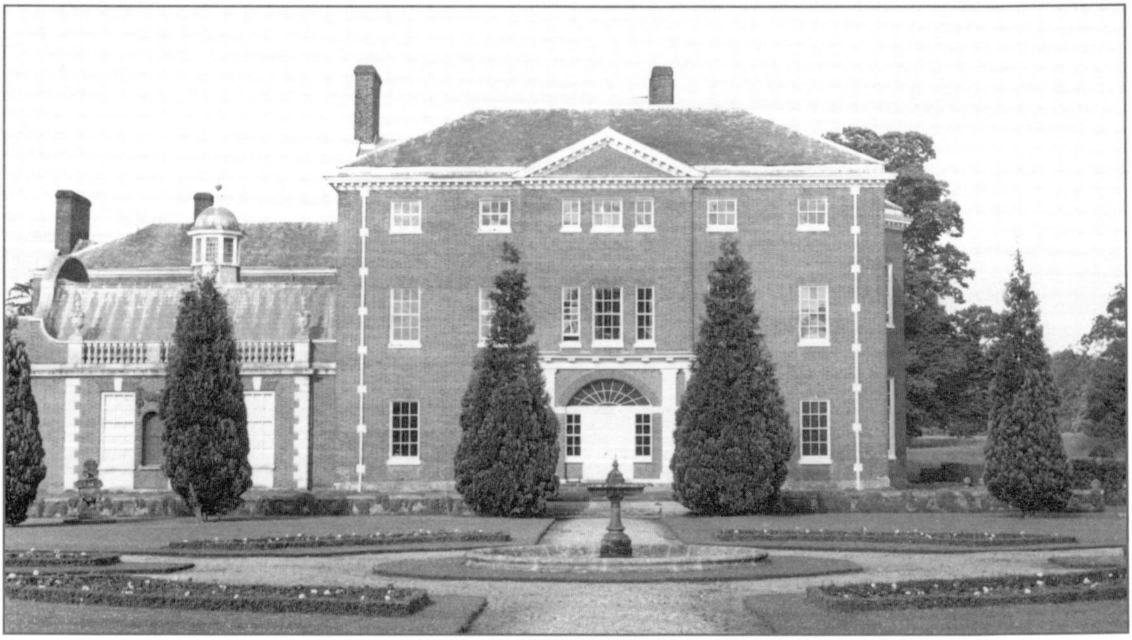

EAST CLANDON, HATCHLANDS c1955 E175002
Admiral Edward Boscawen, a relative of the Boscawen family of Tregothnan in Cornwall, built and possibly designed Hatchlands in a slightly odd Palladian style in 1757. Two years later he gave the job of designing the interior to an up-and-coming young man by the name of Robert Adam.

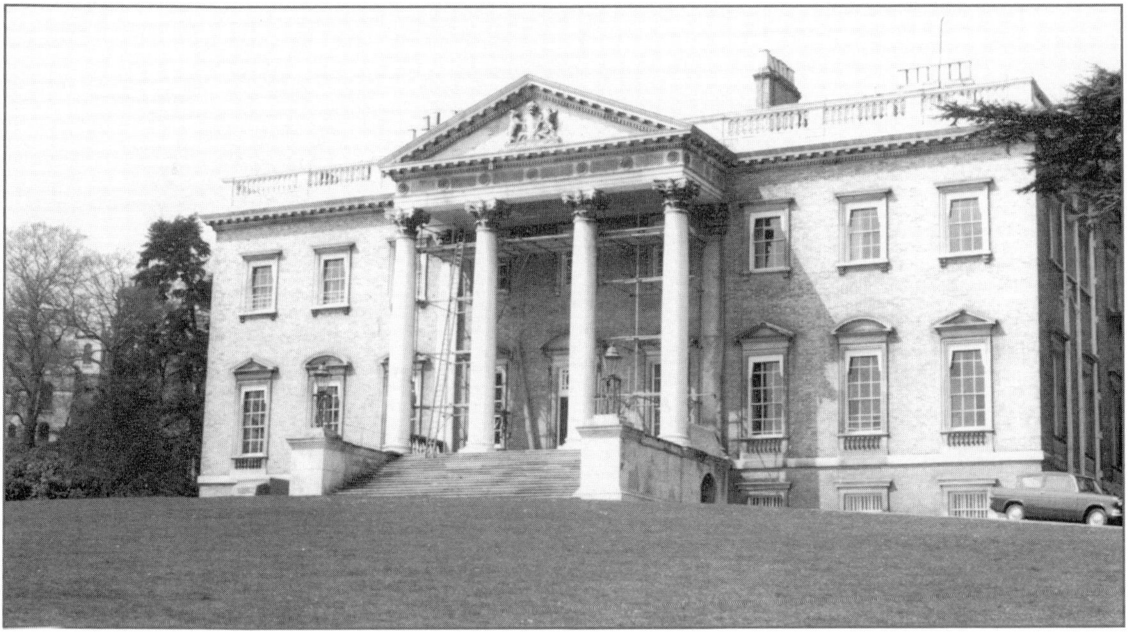

Esher, Claremont School c1965 E64045

Capability Brown and Henry Holland began work on this house for Lord Clive of India in 1771. It was completed in 1774, not long before Clive committed suicide. Apparently, Clive used to stop the windows rattling during gales by wedging them with guineas; the servants retrieved these when the wind dropped and hoped for more gales.

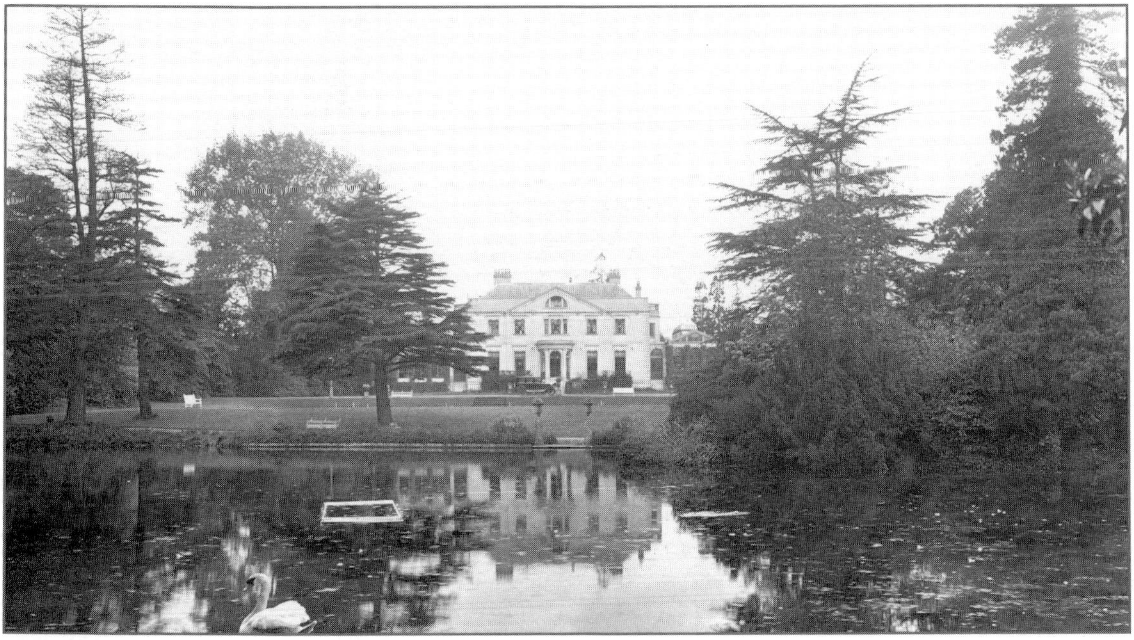

Ewell, Bourne Hall 1924 75380

Occupying the site of a 15th-century mansion, Bourne Hall was built in 1770 for Philip Rowden and passed through the hands of several owners before Margaret Henrietta Glyn left it to Epsom Rural District Council in 1945. In 1962 it was demolished, and the site is now a museum, library and exhibition gallery.

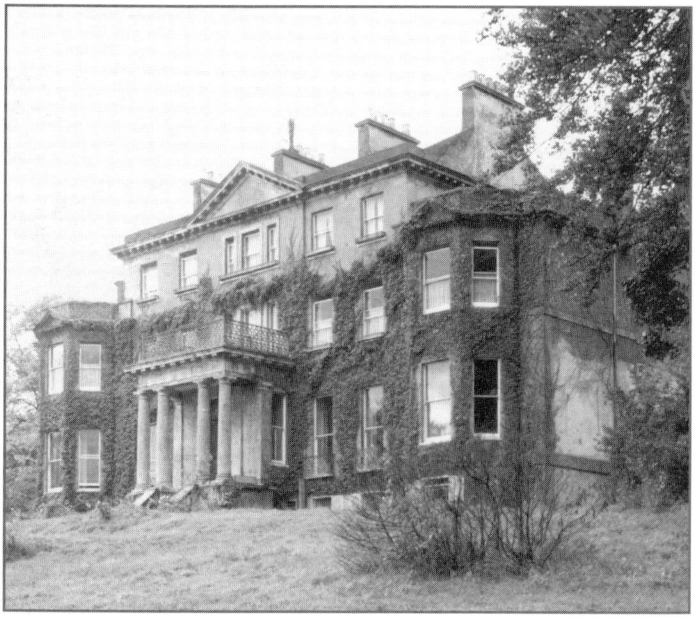

GOMSHALL, NETLEY HOUSE c1955 G29011

GOMSHALL
Netley House c1955
The original red brick house was built in 1790 by Edmund Shallett Lomax. It burned down in the mid 19th century; the present house, which includes as its central section part of the original building, was built in 1860.

VIRGINIA WATER
Holloway Sanatorium c1955
Designed by W H Crossland and opened in 1884, Holloway Sanatorium is described by Pevsner as 'the summit of High Victorian design ... a sort of Franco-Flemish brick-and-stone Gothic carried through with a verve that is entirely its own'.

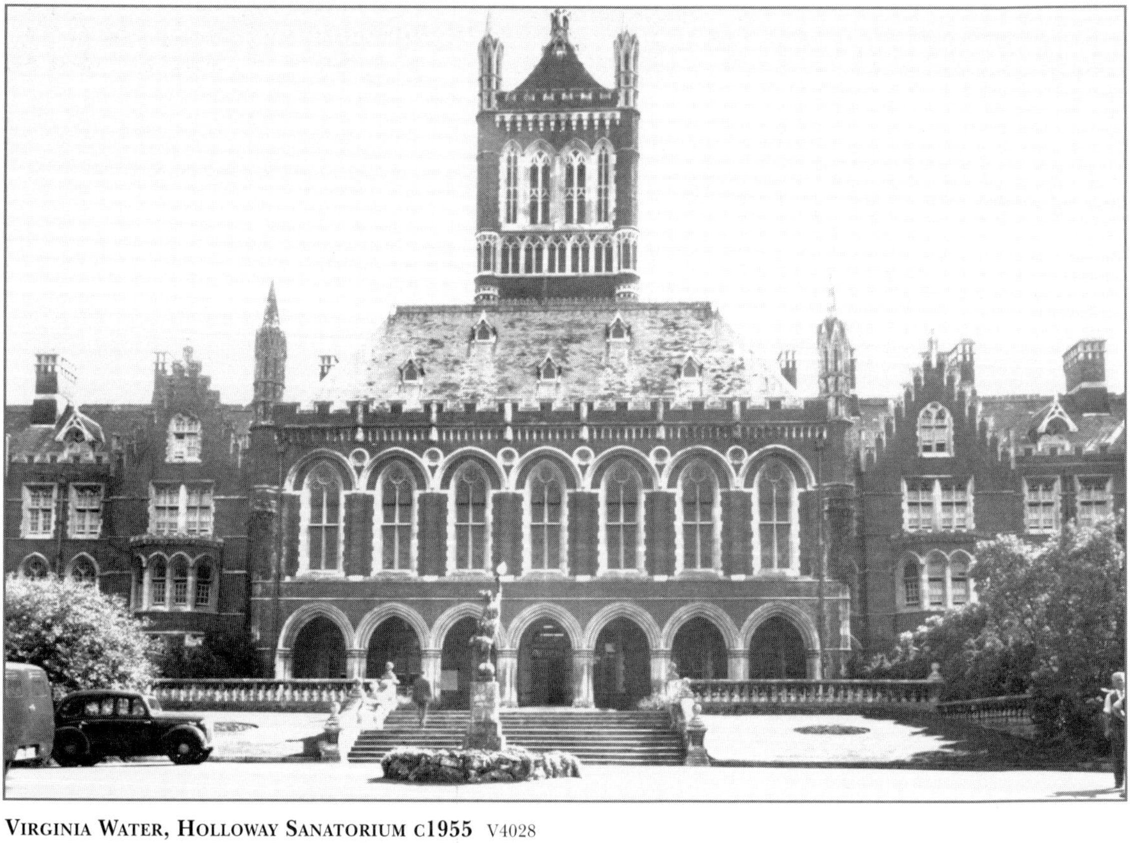

VIRGINIA WATER, HOLLOWAY SANATORIUM c1955 V4028

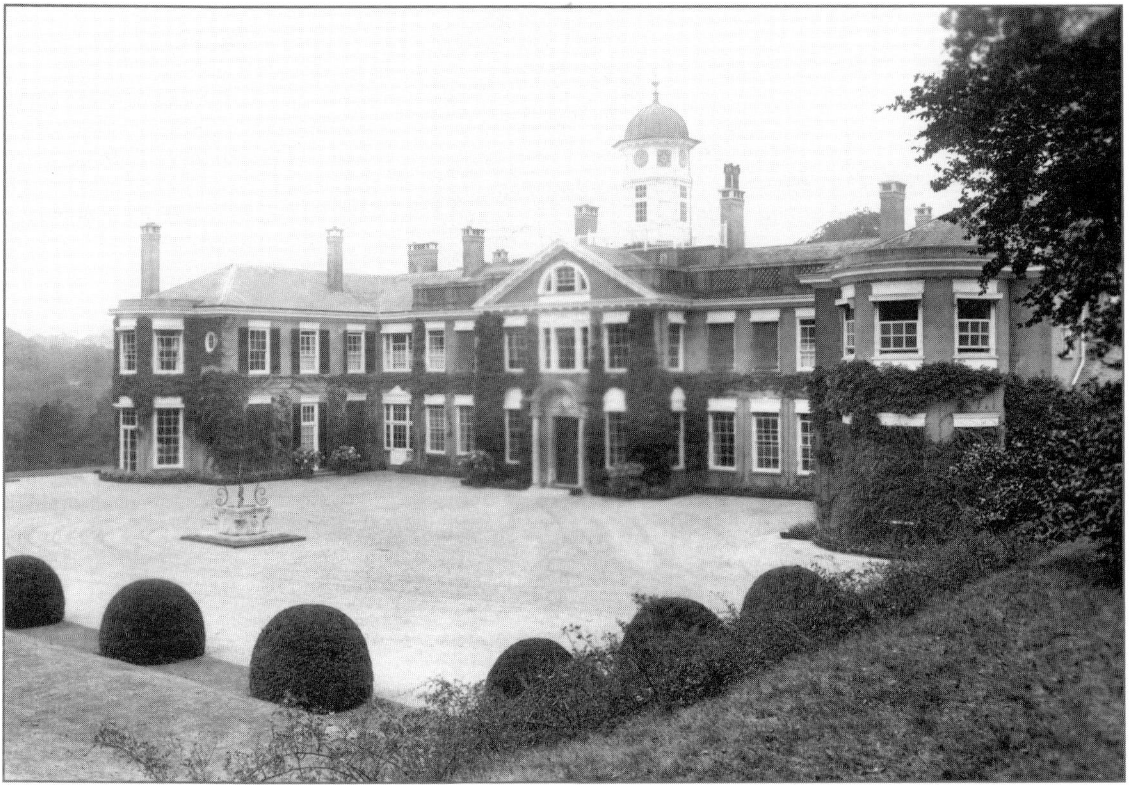

Great Bookham

Polesden Lacey 1929 82423

The dramatist Richard Brinsley Sheridan once owned a house on this site. It was demolished in 1824 by Thomas Cubitt to build the present house, which was extended in 1906 by Ambrose Poynter. George VI and Queen Elizabeth spent part of their honeymoon here in 1924.

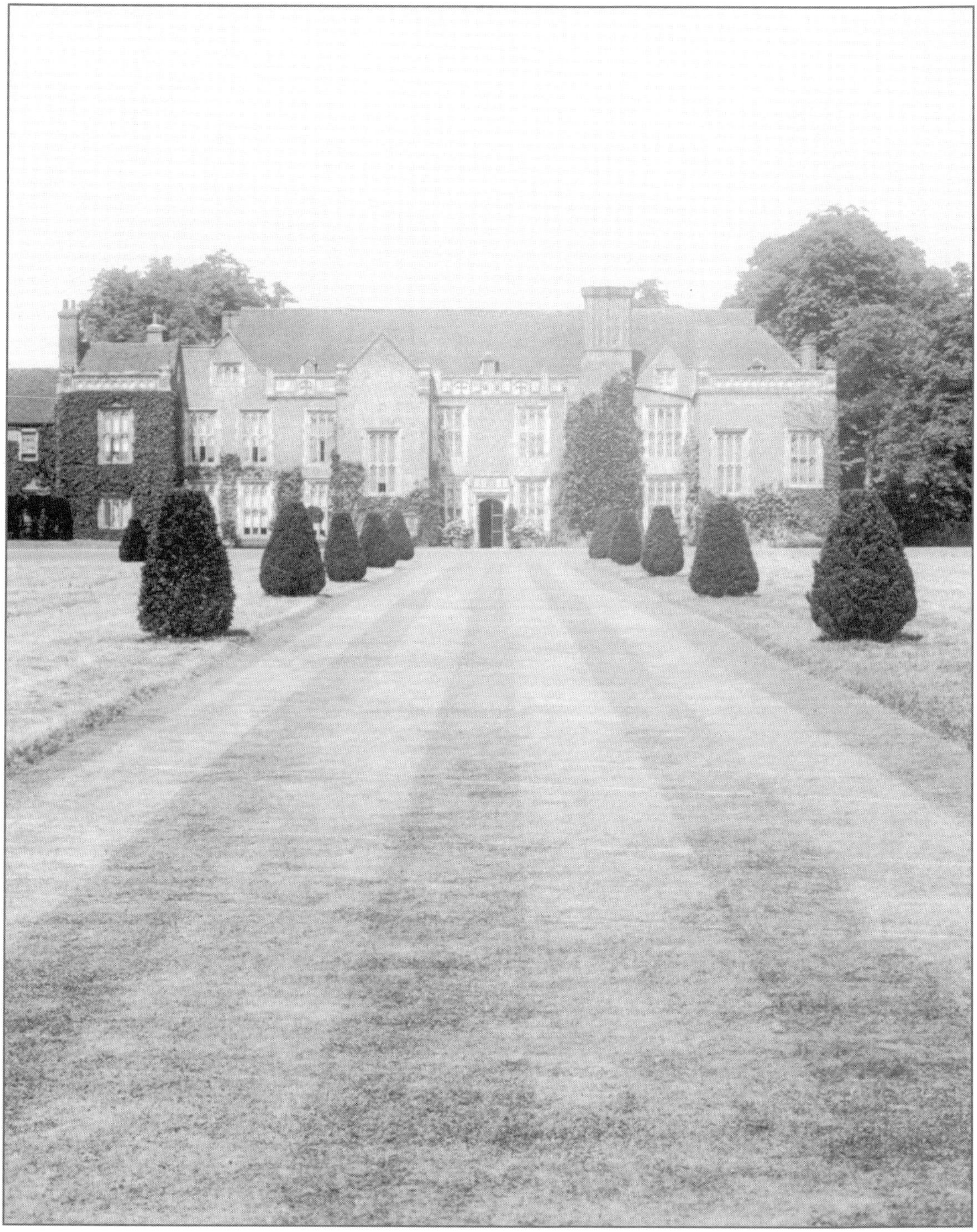

Guildford, Sutton Place, South Front 1914 67044

One of the first non-fortified mansions in Britain, Sutton Place was built in 1521-30 for Sir Richard Weston, a courtier to Henry VIII. Sutton Place has an important place in English history, for it was here, reputedly, that Henry first met Anne Boleyn.

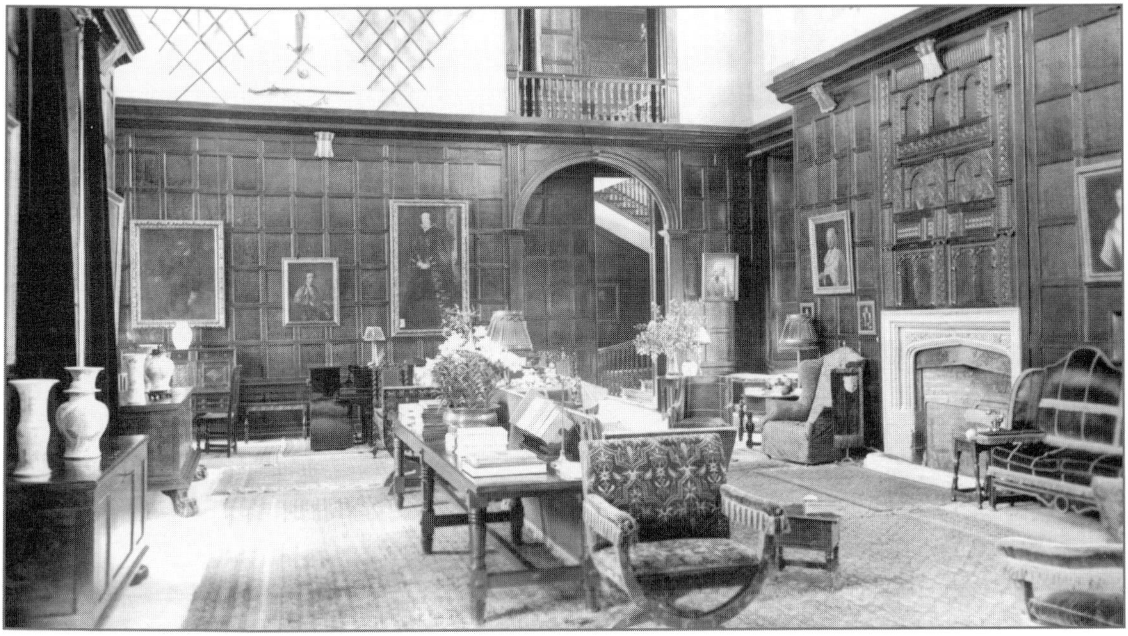

Guildford, Sutton Place, The Hall 1914 67045

The airy look of Sutton Place's hall is due to the very large rectangular windows - a feature that is not seen elsewhere until late Elizabethan times. In 1536 Francis Weston, son of Sir Richard, was accused of being one of Anne Boleyn's lovers and beheaded.

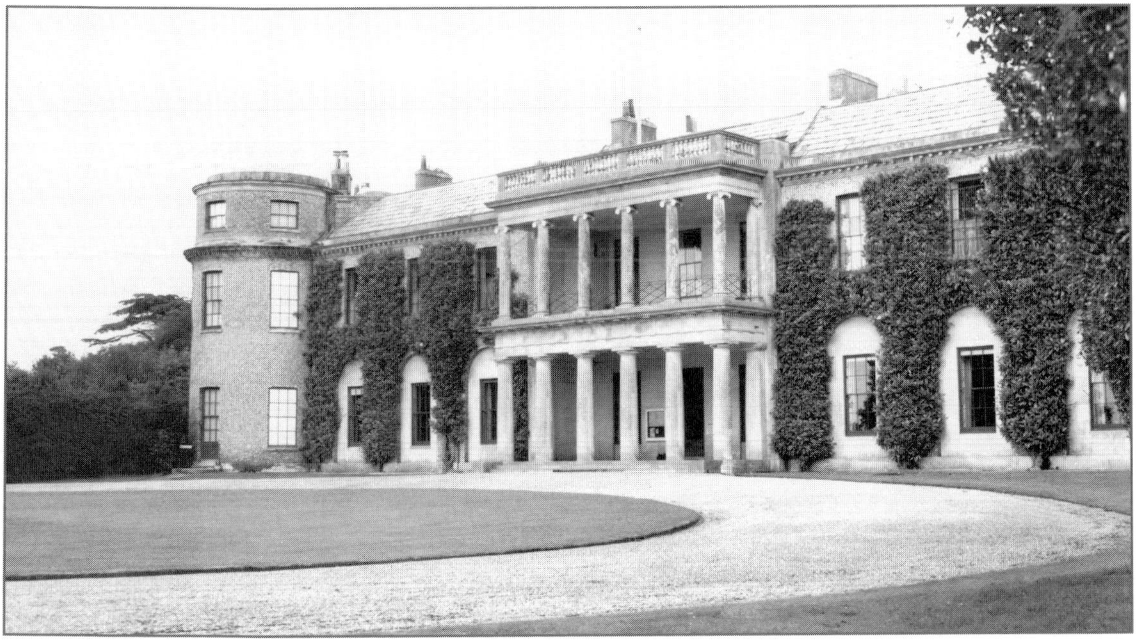

Chichester, Goodwood House c1965 C84107

Built in flint in 1790 1800 for Charles Lennox, third Duke of Richmond and Gordon, Goodwood House was designed by James Wyatt and includes in its structure parts of a previous house built in 1720. It has spectacular views of the South Downs and Chichester Cathedral, and contains paintings by Canaletto, Van Dyck and Stubbs.

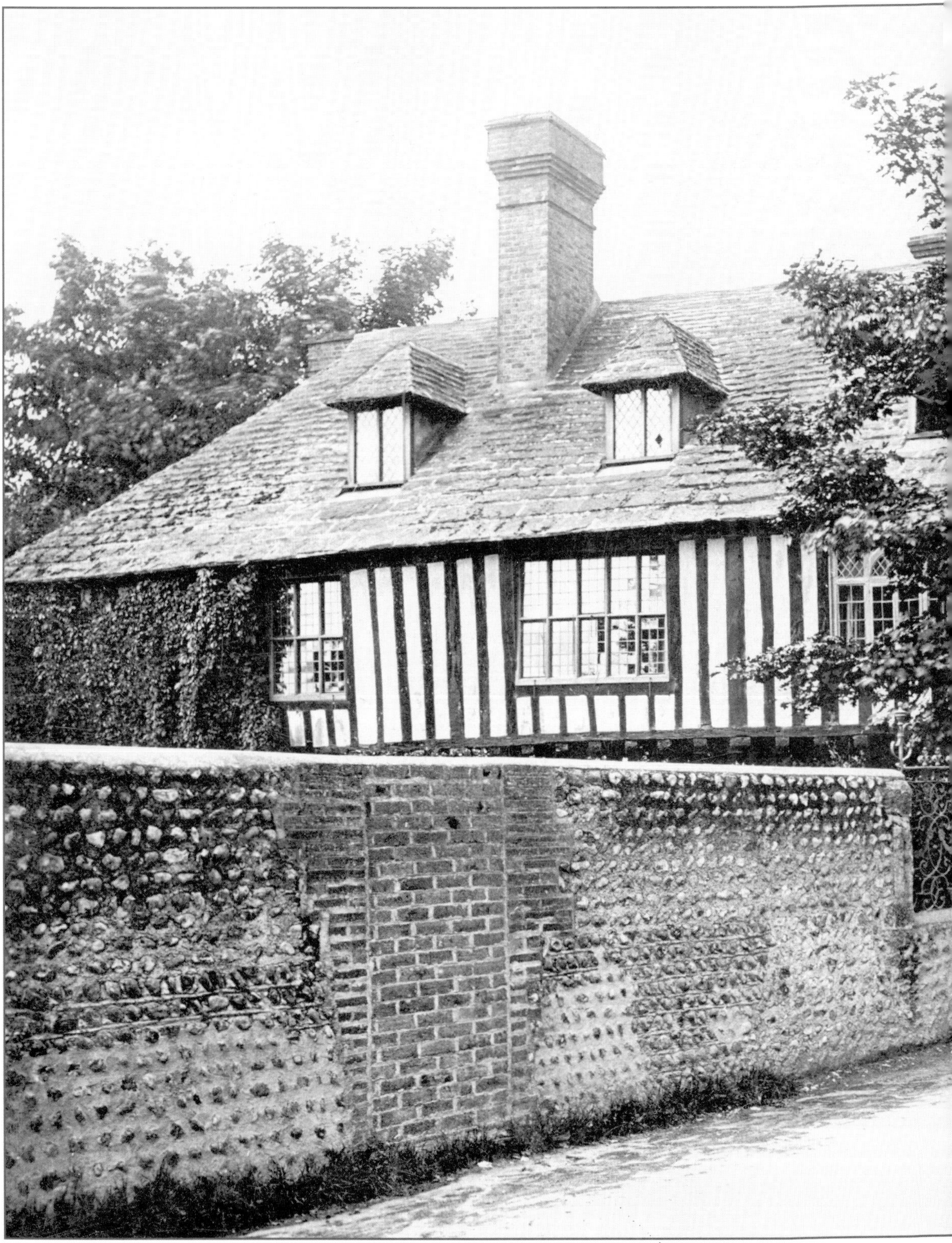

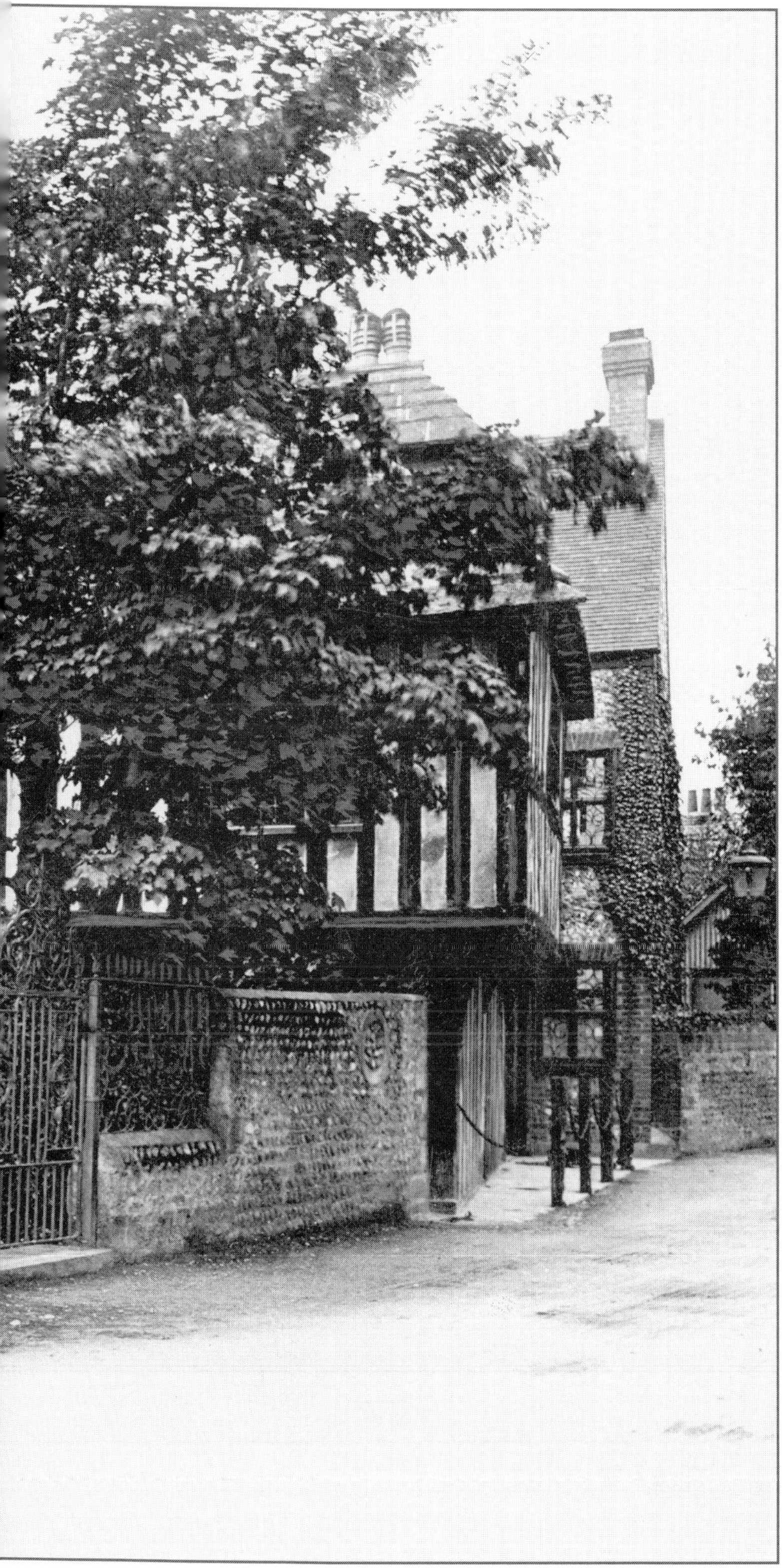

BRAMBER
ST MARY'S HOUSE C1930 B179501
This 15th-century timber-framed house was once the residence of the monks of nearby Sele Priory, who were wardens of Bramber Bridge over the River Adur. It has some particularly rare 17th-century painted panelling.

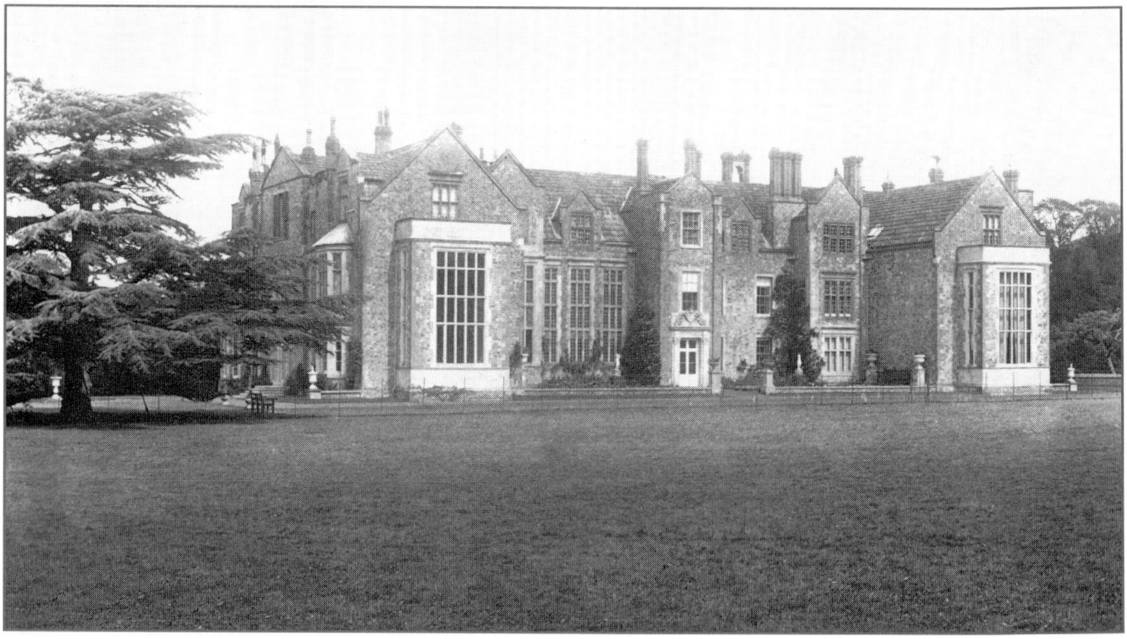

Parham 1894 34403
Almost unaltered and built from local stone, Parham was built on the classic Elizabethan E-plan in 1577 by Thomas Palmer, who was later to sail with Drake to Cadiz to 'singe the King of Spain's beard'. The foundation stone was laid by his grandson Thomas (only two-and-a-half at the time) in accordance with Elizabethan custom.

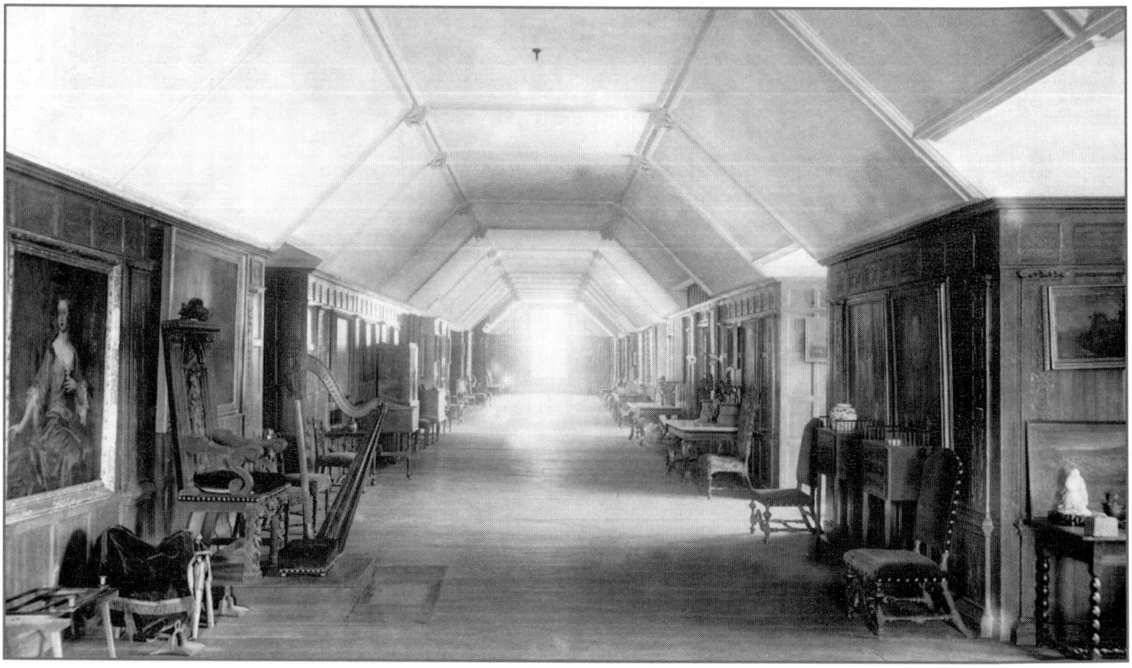

Parham, The Portrait Gallery 1896 38196
At 160 feet, this gallery is one of the longest in Britain and beautifully lit by mullioned windows. The ceiling looks different now: in the 1930s it was painted with a pattern of intertwined tendrils by Oliver Messel.

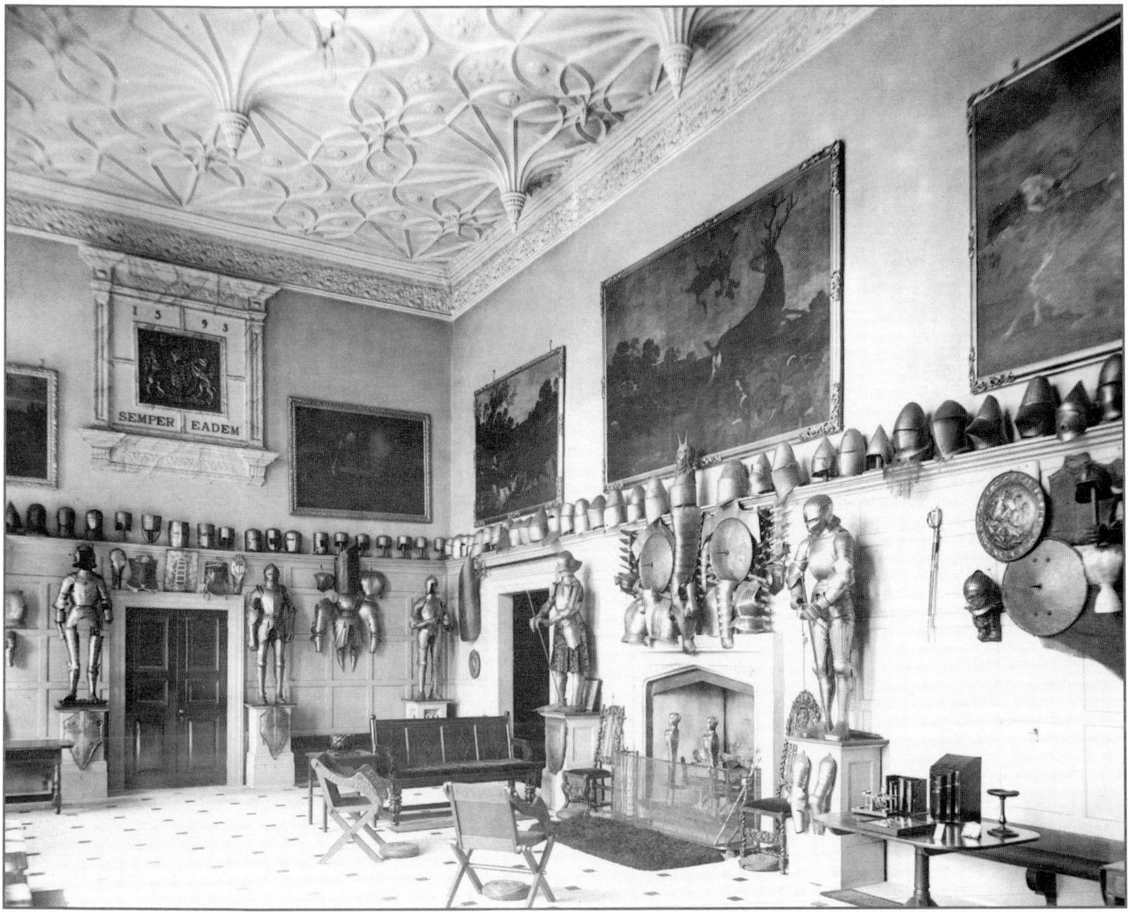

Parham

The Hall 1896 38195

Parham's Hall, with its high mullioned windows and magnificent plaster ceiling, is unusual in that instead of having a minstrel's gallery it has two windows through which the steward could keep an eye on the behaviour of the house servants. The motto on the clock translates as 'always the same'.

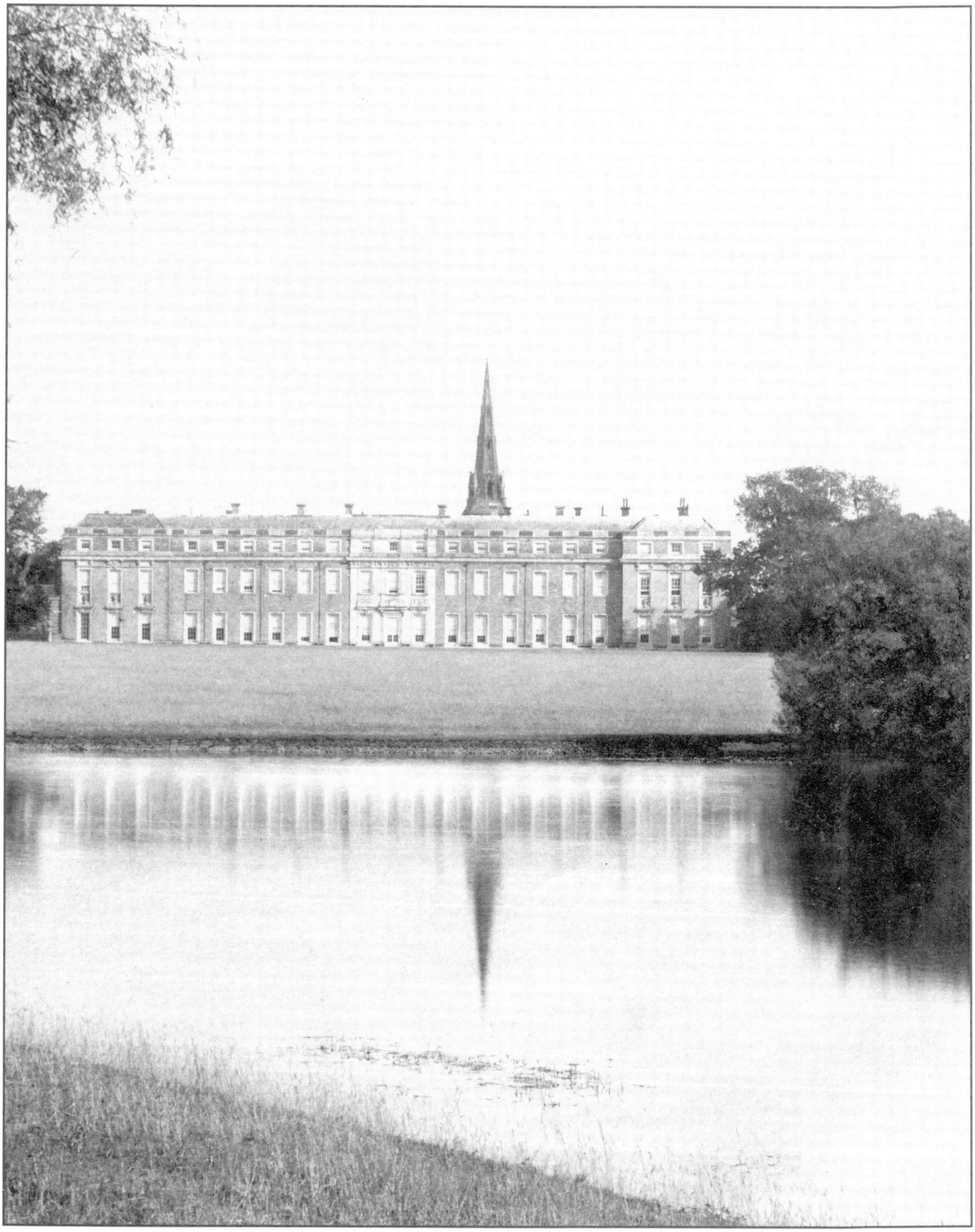

PETWORTH HOUSE 1898 42839
Originally owned by the Percy family, Earls of Northumberland, the estate passed by marriage to the sixth Duke of Somerset, who built the present house, designed by the French architect Daniel Marot, in 1688-93. The gardens were laid out by Capability Brown in the 18th century. The spire is that of St Mary's church.

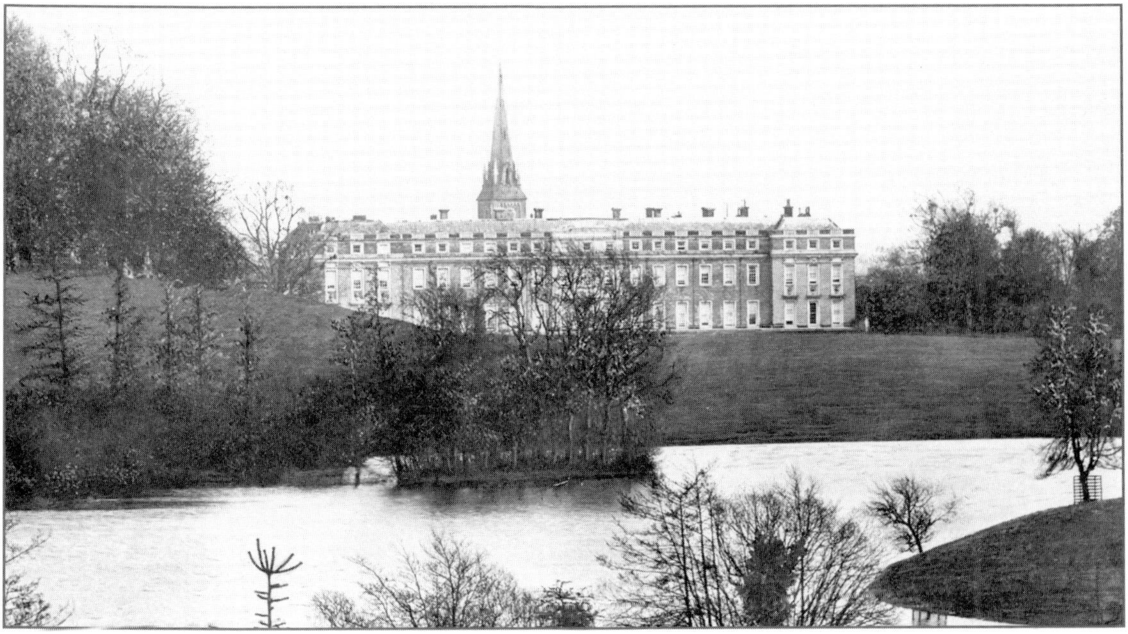

Petworth House 1898 42840A

A frequent visitor to Petworth in the 1830s was the painter J M W Turner; he drew inspiration from the house and grounds, and began to develop the brilliant interweaving of light and colour that characterised the last phase of his work. He had a studio in the Old Library above the Chapel, and thirteen of his pictures still hang there.

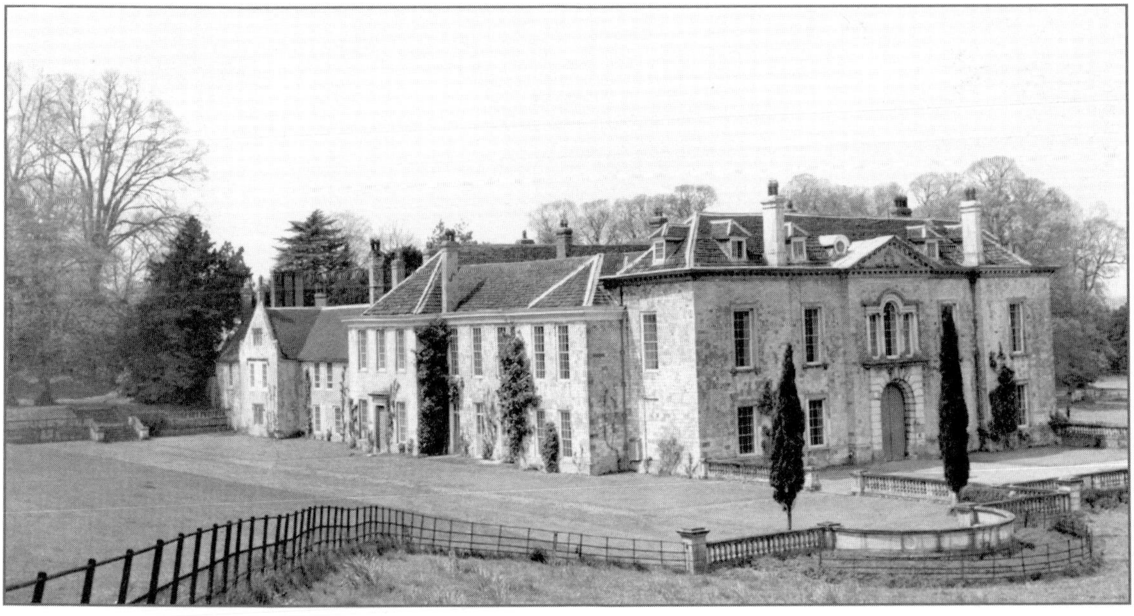

West Firle, Firle Place c1960 F171010

The pointed gable on the far left is part of the original Tudor manor built by Sir John Gage in the 16th century. The rest of the house was rebuilt in 1745 by the local architect John Morris of Lewes. By this time, the Gage family (who live at Firle Place to this day) had converted to become Protestants after many years of fines because of their Catholicism.

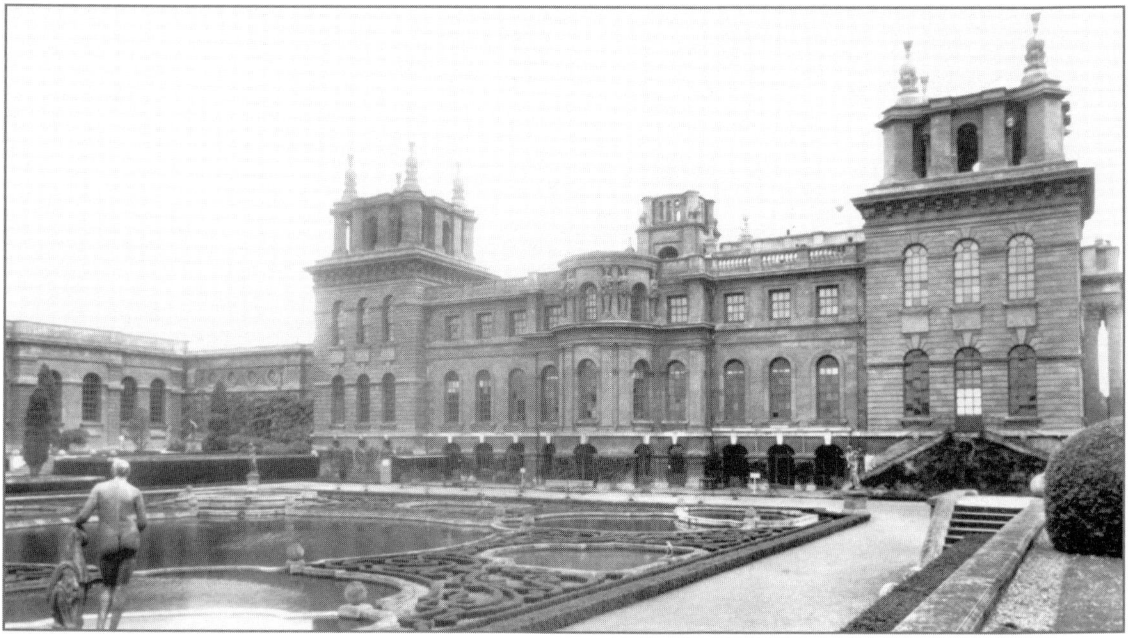

WOODSTOCK, BLENHEIM PALACE, THE WATER TERRACE c1960 W258044
The 'English Versailles' was built as a gift to the Duke of Marlborough after his victory over the French at Blenheim in 1704. Designed by Sir John Vanbrugh, its building was bedevilled with problems, including the Duke's fall from grace and a series of disputes between Vanbrugh and the Duchess which eventually caused Vanbrugh to resign.

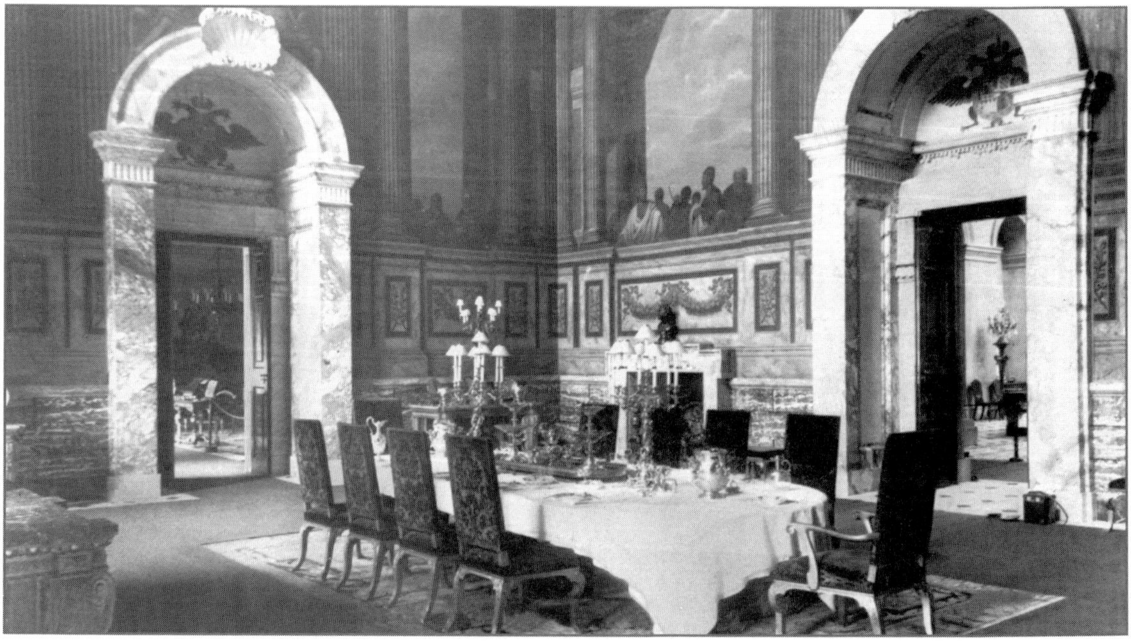

WOODSTOCK, BLENHEIM PALACE, THE SALOON c1960 W258033
On Vanbrugh's resignation, Nicholas Hawksmoor took over the building; among other features, he designed the doorways of the Saloon in white marble. The walls were painted by Louis Laguerre after it was decided that Sir James Thornhill's price of 25s per yard was too expensive.

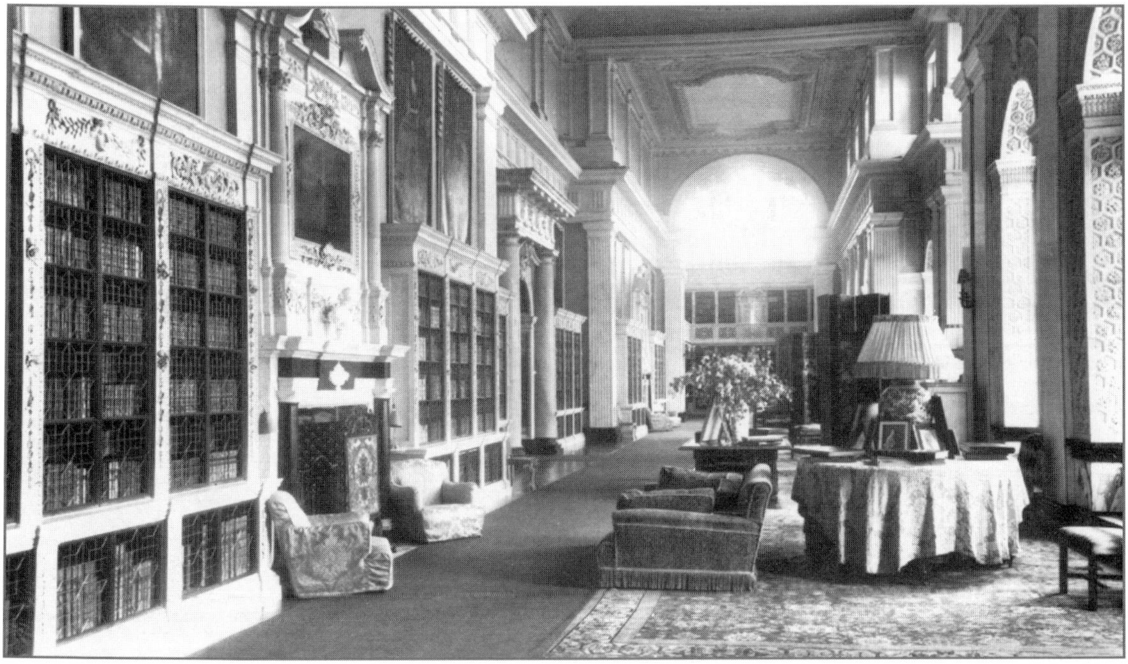

Woodstock, Blenheim Palace, The Long Library c1960 W258041
The Long Library, which runs the entire length of the West Front, was still undecorated at the time of the Duke of Marlborough's death in 1722. Hawksmoor hired Isaac Mansfield to do the plasterwork.

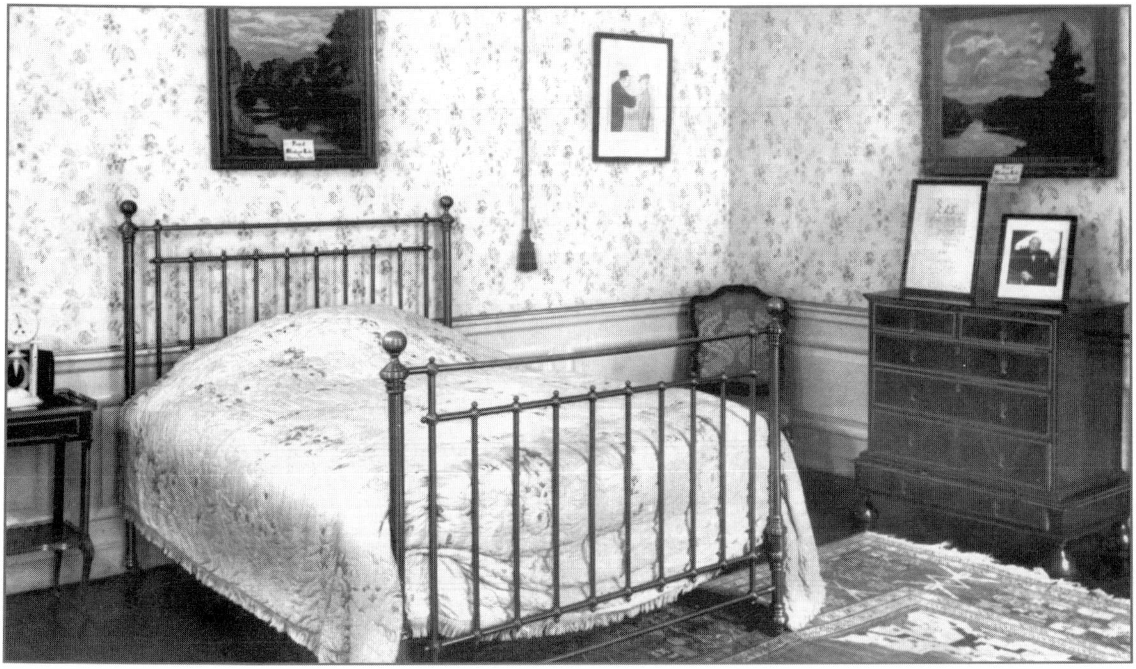

Woodstock, Blenheim Palace, Sir Winston Churchill's Bedroom c1960 W258029
'At Blenheim', wrote Winston Churchill, 'I took two very important decisions: to be born and to marry. I am happily content with the decisions I took on both those occasions'.

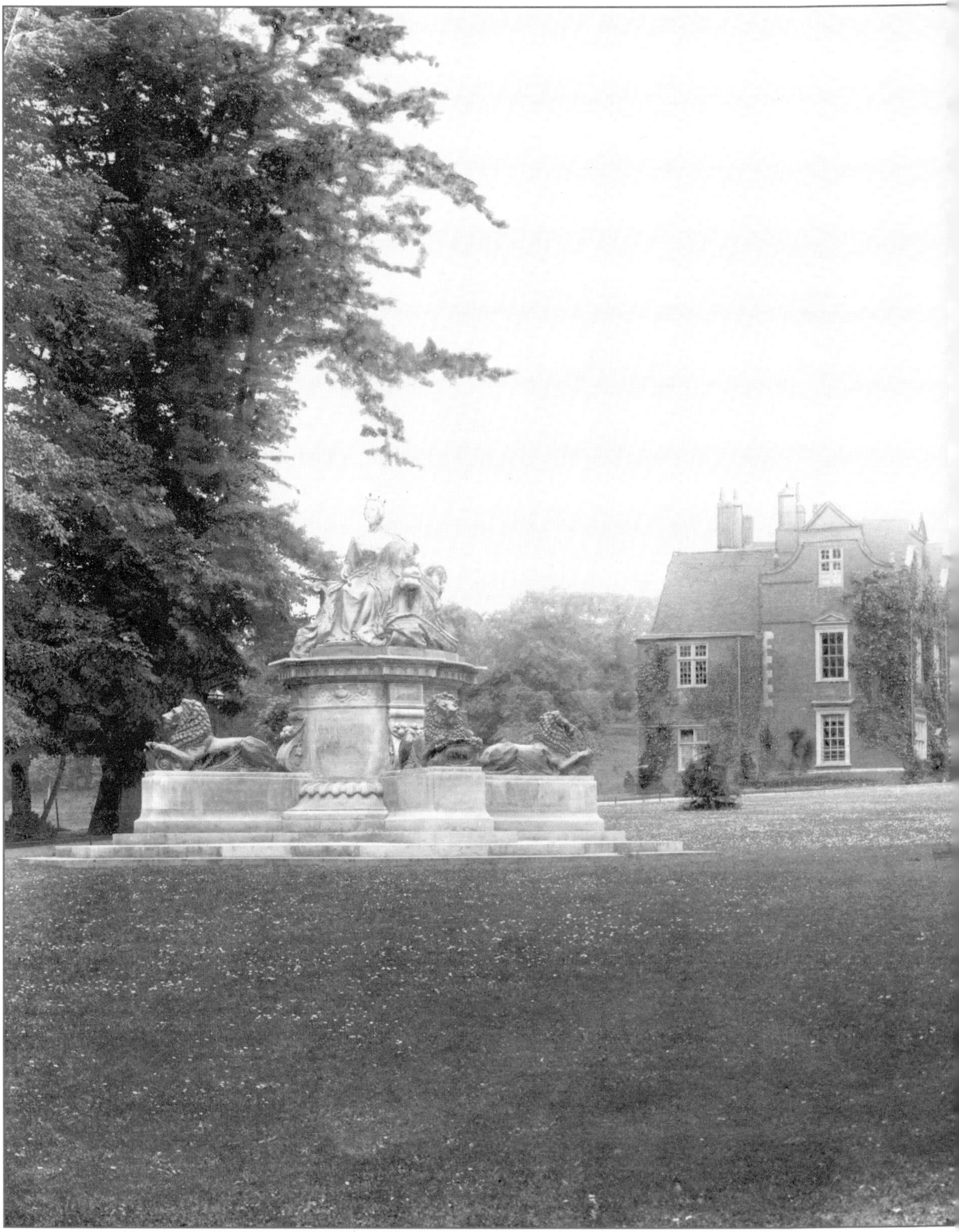

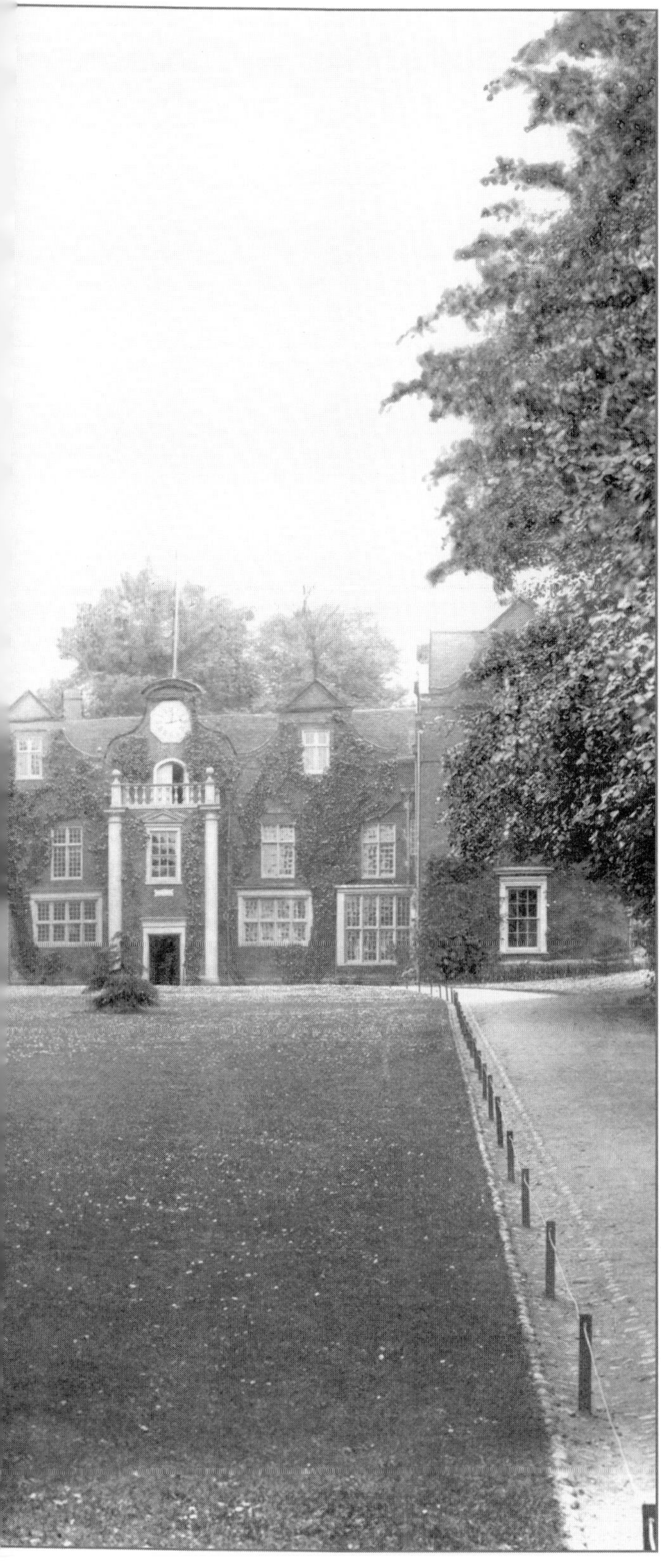

East Anglia

Ipswich, Christchurch Mansion Christchurch Park 1904 51248
Christchurch Mansion occupies the site of the old Priory of the Holy Trinity, and was built in 1548-50. The upper storey was rebuilt after a fire in 1760, and at the end of the 19th century the mansion was endowed as a town museum by F T Cobbold.

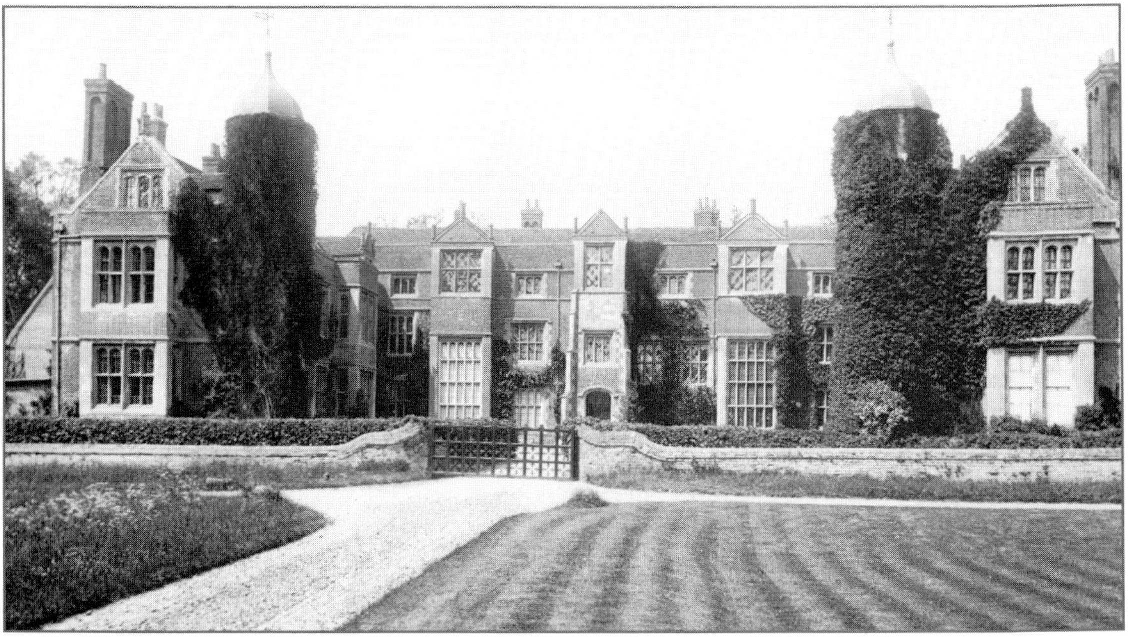

Long Melford, Kentwell Hall 1895 35495
Standing at the end of a mile-long avenue of lime trees, Kentwell Hall was built by William Clopton in 1560. It was badly damaged in a fire in 1822 and remodelled by Thomas Hopper, who managed to preserve its original Tudor appearance.

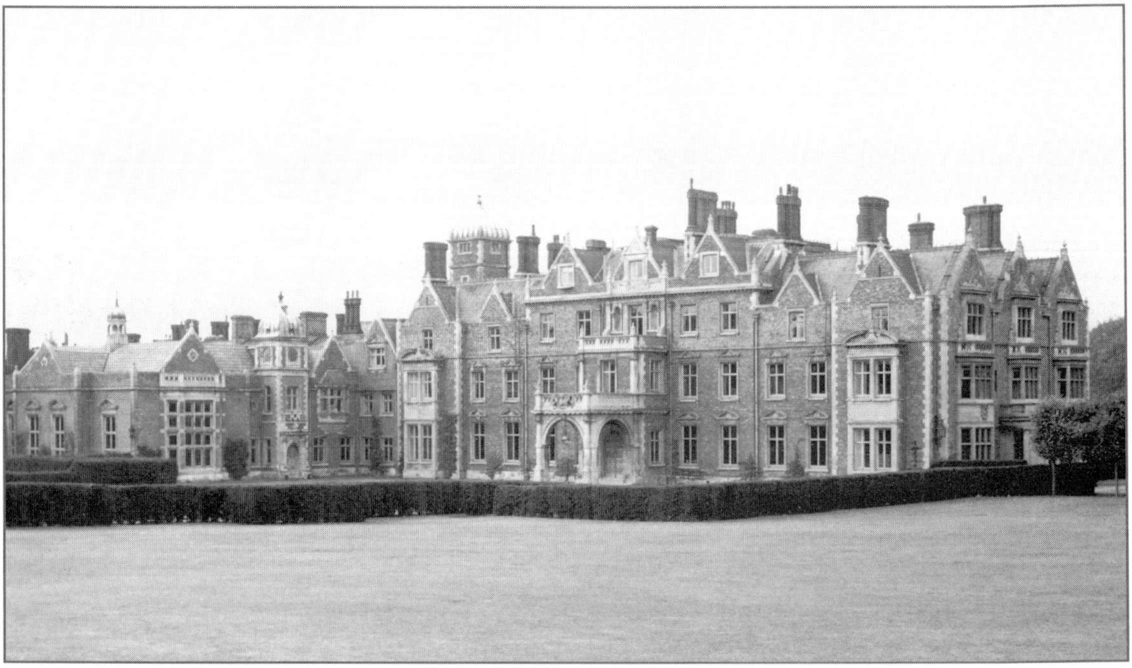

Sandringham House c1965 S58151
Sandringham was bought by Queen Victoria in 1862 as a shooting lodge for her son Albert, the Prince of Wales, who later became Edward VII. Using dues from the Duchy of Cornwall, he had this Jacobean-style house finished by 1870.

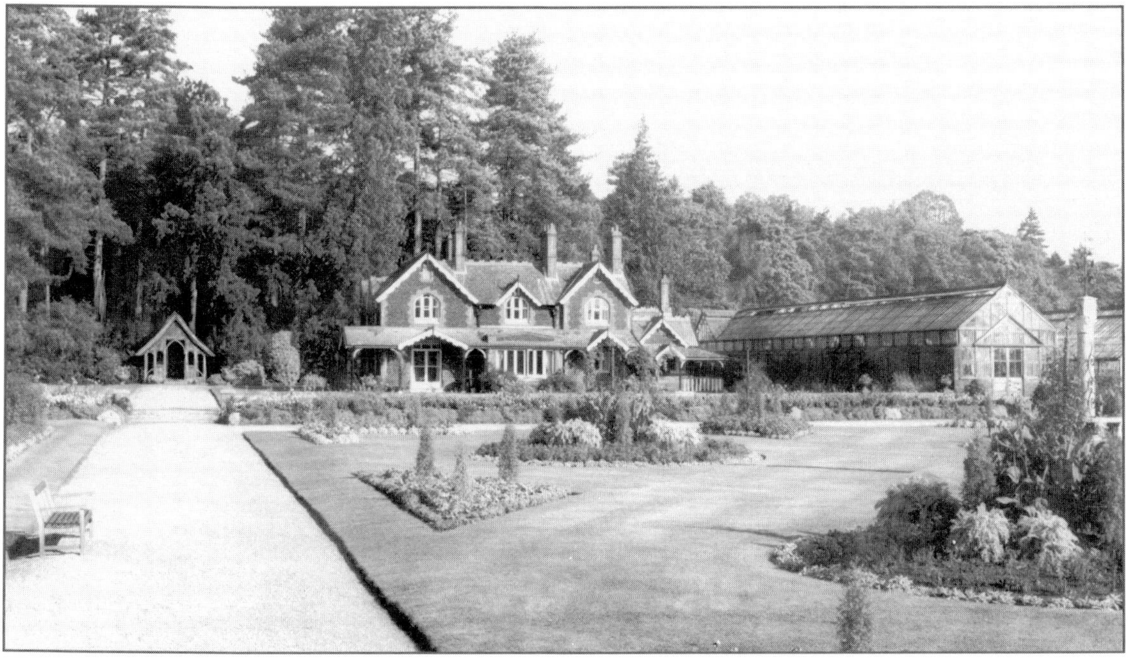

SANDRINGHAM, THE HEAD GARDENER'S HOUSE c1965 S58156
Sandringham became one of the favourite royal residences; the royal family spend New Year there, and both George V and George VI died there. When the family is not in residence, the grounds are open to the public.

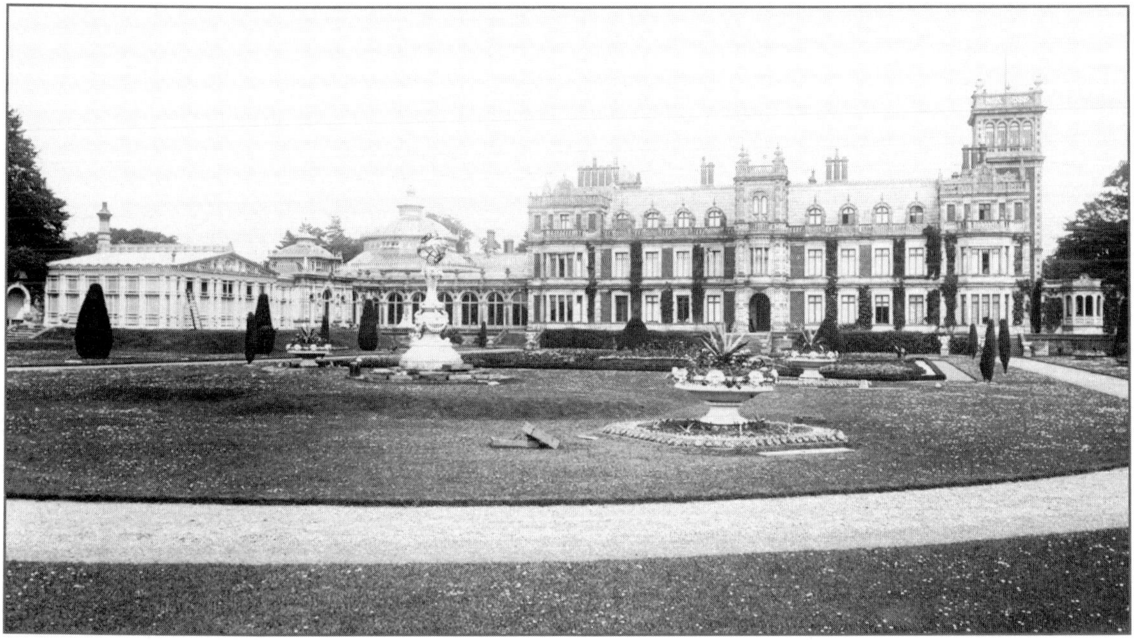

SOMERLEYTON HALL 1891 28725
A couple of rooms from the original Elizabethan manor survive in this flamboyant example of High Victorian architecture, built by railway entrepreneur Sir Morton Peto MP in 1844-54 and designed by John Thomas. It was described by local writer George Borrow as 'pandemonium in red brick'.

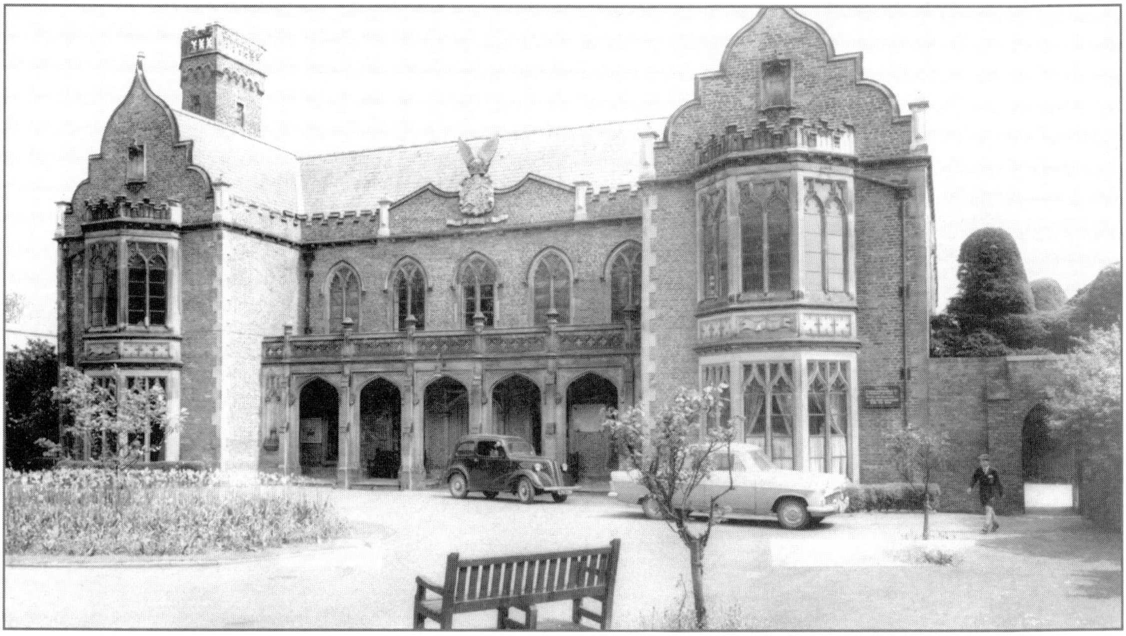

Spalding, Ayscoughfee Hall c1960 S388230

Now a natural history museum, Ayscoughfee Hall was built in the 15th century and restored in the 18th century by Maurice Johnson; he was the founder of the Spalding Gentlemen's Society, which included among its members Alexander Pope and Isaac Newton.

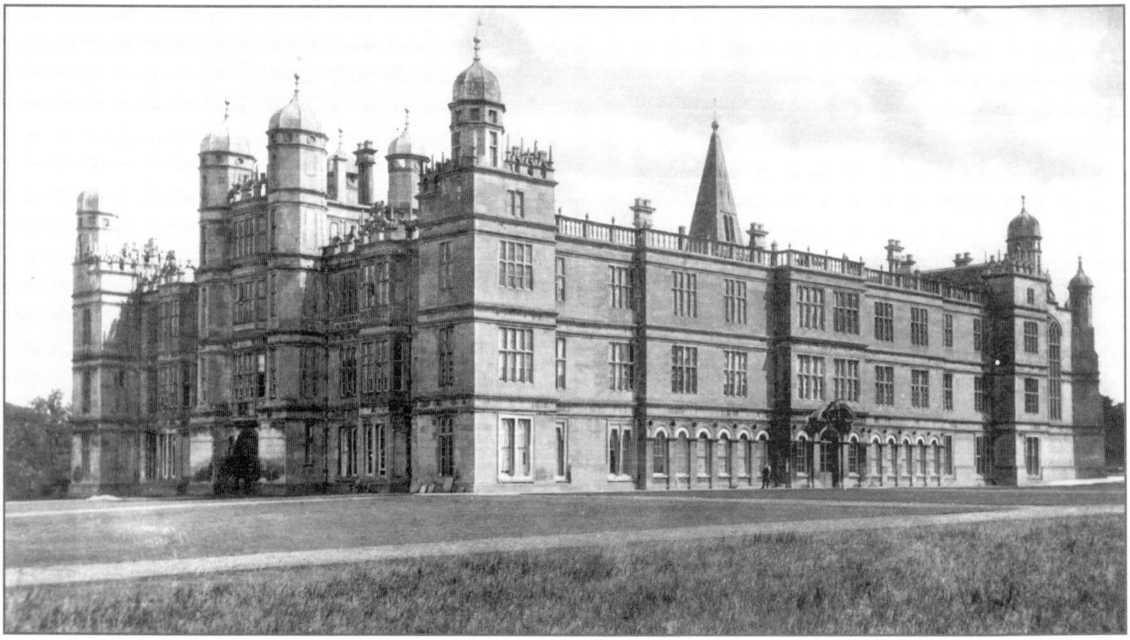

Stamford, Burghley House 1922 72323A

Burghley was built by William Cecil, Secretary of State to Queen Elizabeth, between 1552 and 1587. The interior was redesigned in the late 17th century, and includes carving by Grinling Gibbons, plasterwork by Edward Martin and painting by Verrio. The Deer Park, Gothic Orangery and stables are the work of Capability Brown.

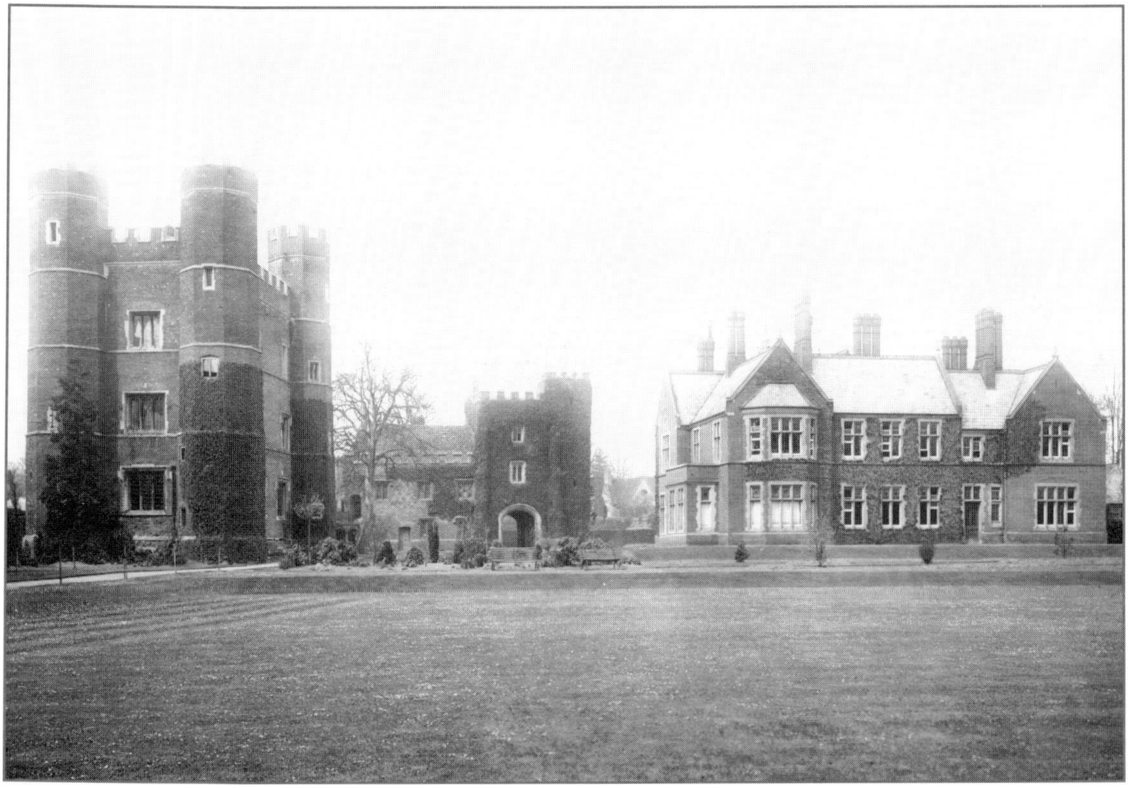

BUCKDEN
The Gatehouse and the Palace 1906 55430
This was built between 1480 and 1494 as the Bishop's Palace by Bishop Russel, whose coat of arms still stands above the inner gateway. Katherine of Aragon was briefly imprisoned in one of the towers before she was moved to Kimbolton Castle.

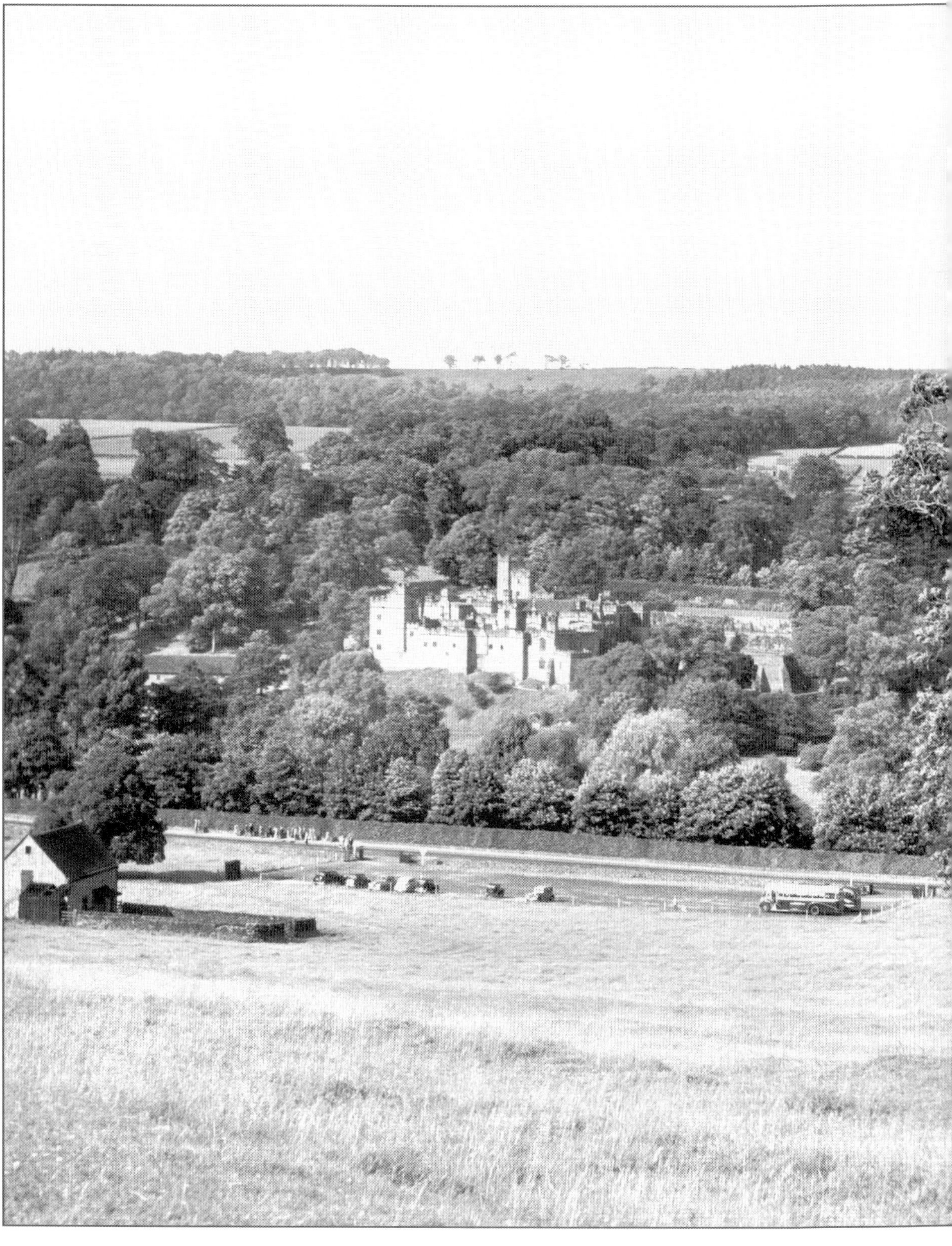

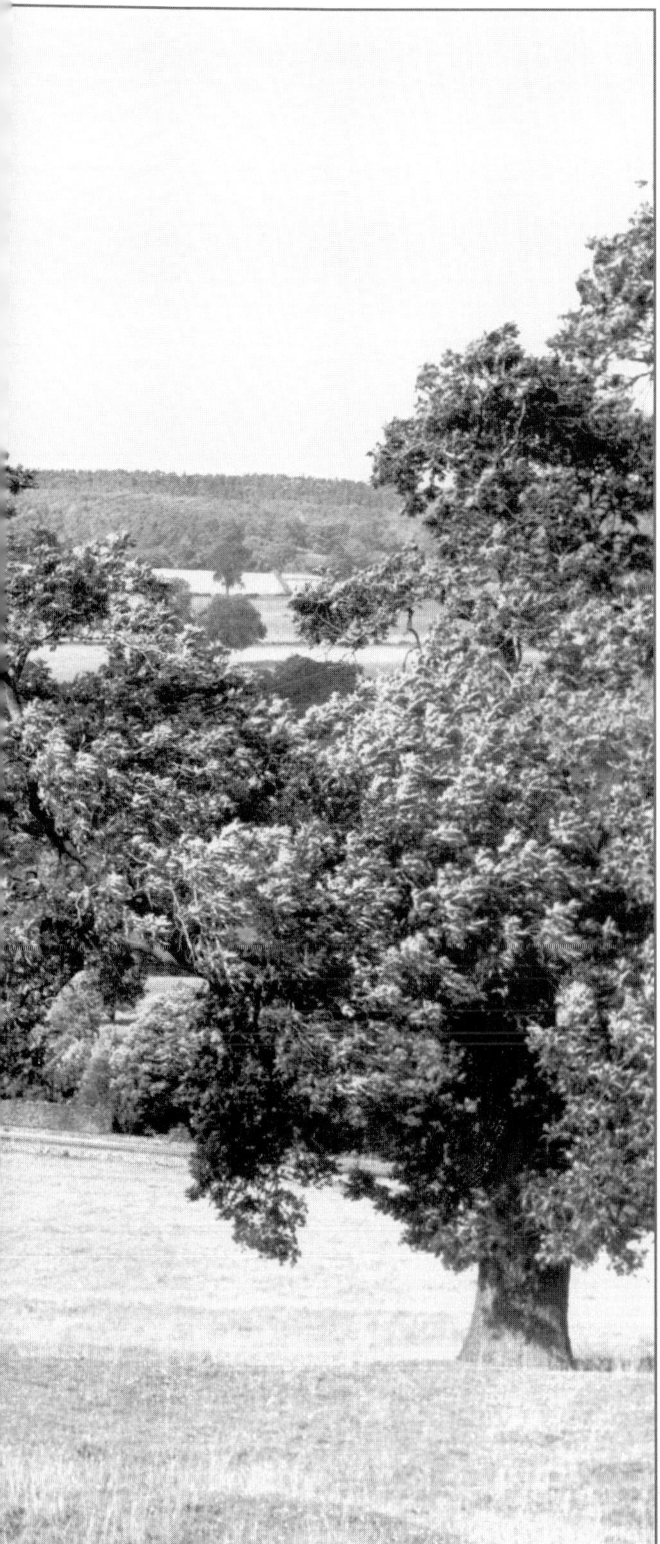

East Midlands

BAKEWELL, HADDON HALL C1955 B6037
The land on which Haddon Hall stands was once owned by William the Conqueror, who gave it to his illegitimate son Peveril. It was acquired by the de Vernon family in 1155, and it subsequently passed to the Dukes of Rutland when Dorothy Vernon eloped with Sir John Manners.

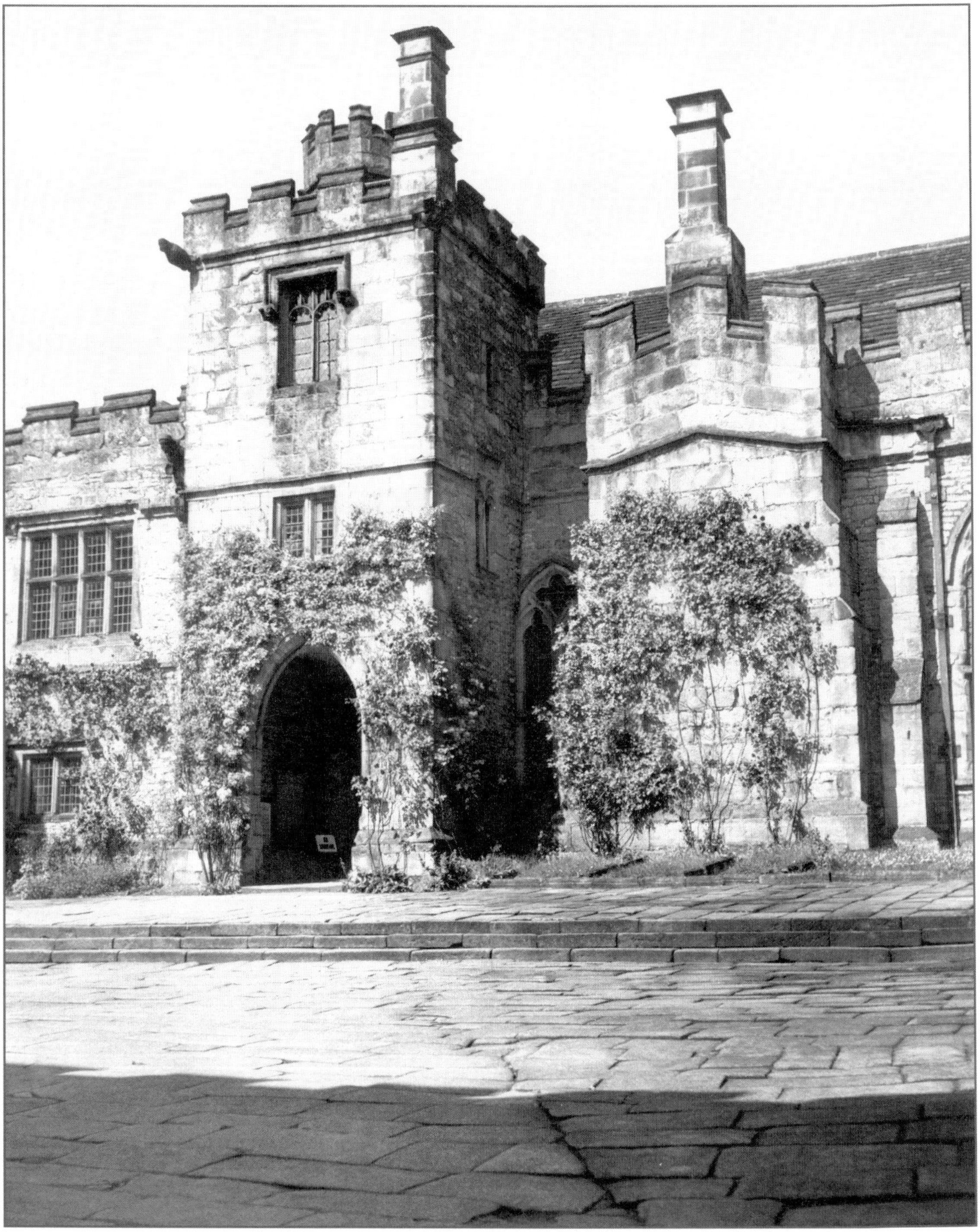

Bakewell, Haddon Hall c1955 B6030

Along with Cotehele in Cornwall, Haddon Hall is one of the few remaining fortified medieval manor houses in England. Unlike Cotehele, Haddon is largely a 20th-century restoration, completed in the 1930s, although parts date from the 13th century, such as the galleried banqueting hall.

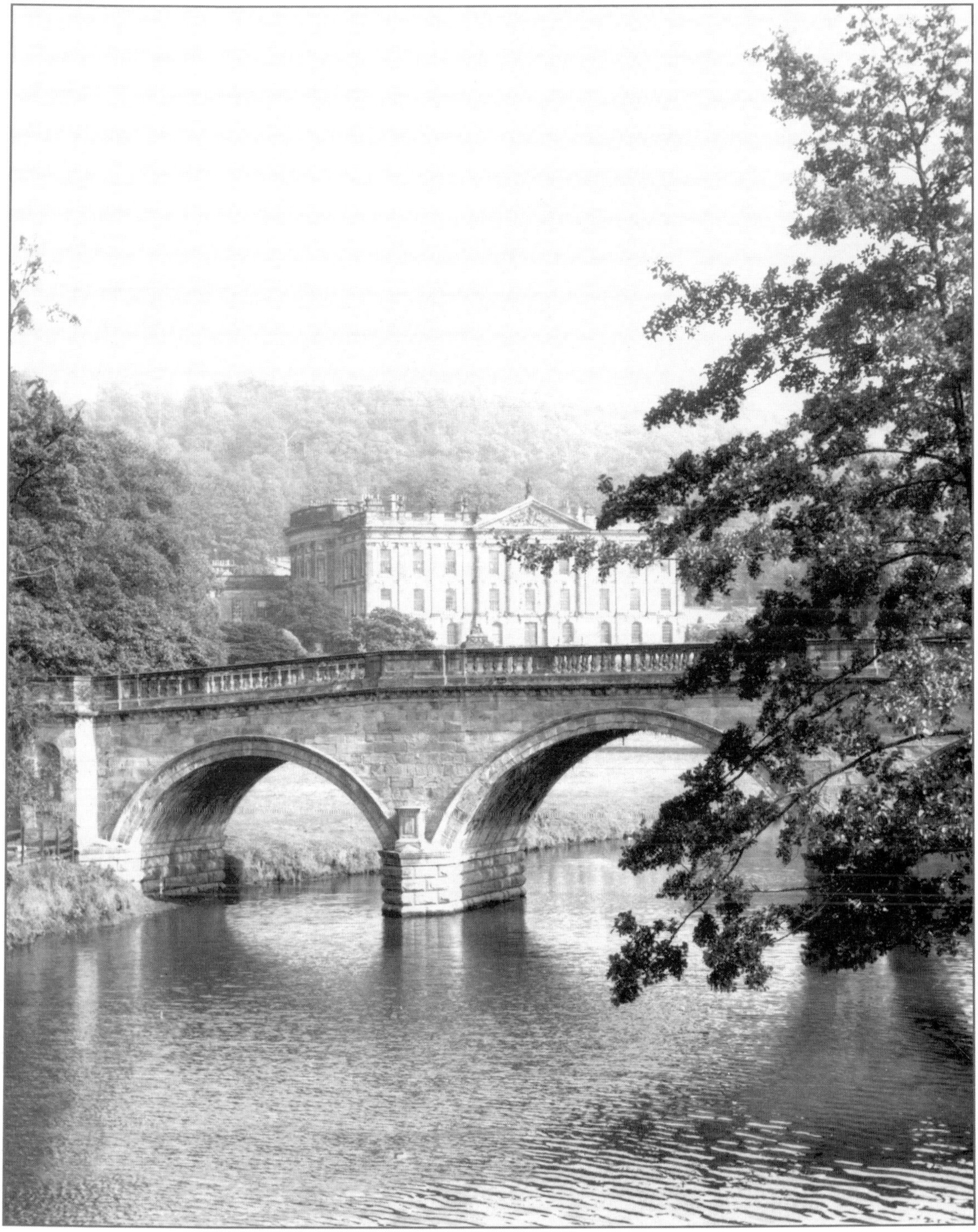

BAKEWELL, CHATSWORTH HOUSE c1955 B6121
The home of the Dukes of Devonshire, Chatsworth was built by William Talman in 1687-1707. Over the centuries, Chatsworth has received the attentions of many of the leading architects and garden designers: James Paine, Sir Jeffrey Wyattville, George London, Thomas Archer, Capability Brown and Joseph Paxton.

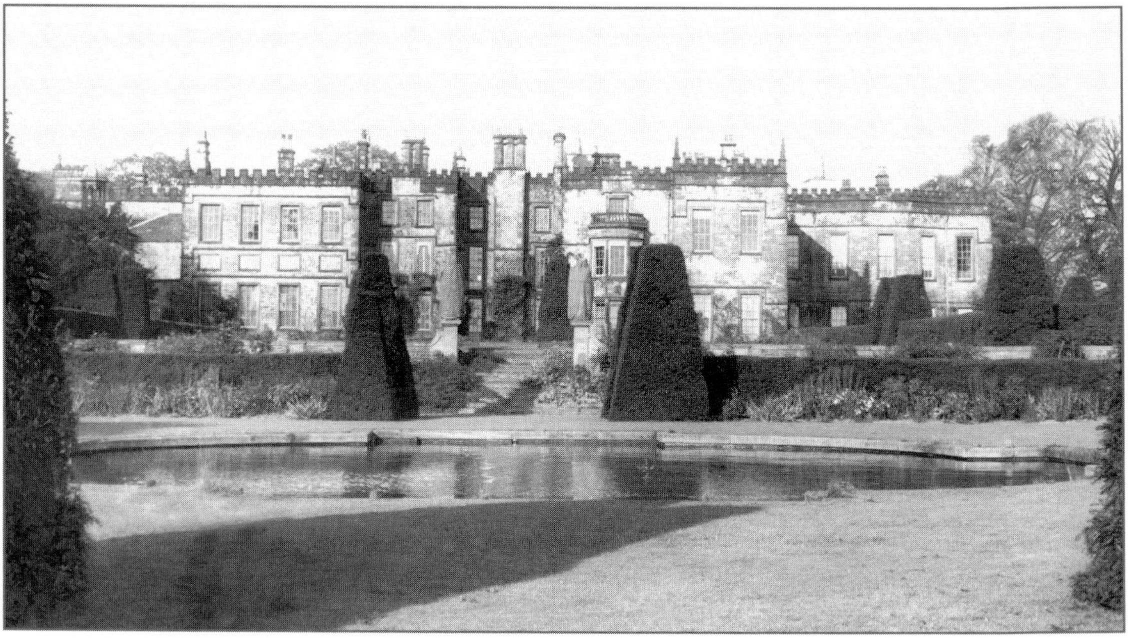

ECKINGTON, RENISHAW HALL c1955 E226007
George Sitwell built Renishaw Hall in 1625 with profits from his Renishaw Iron Works, and it was later modified by the first Baronet Sir Sitwell Sitwell. The house, which has the country's most northerly vineyard, has several ghosts, including the Kissing Ghost - a little boy in pink who haunts people by kissing them.

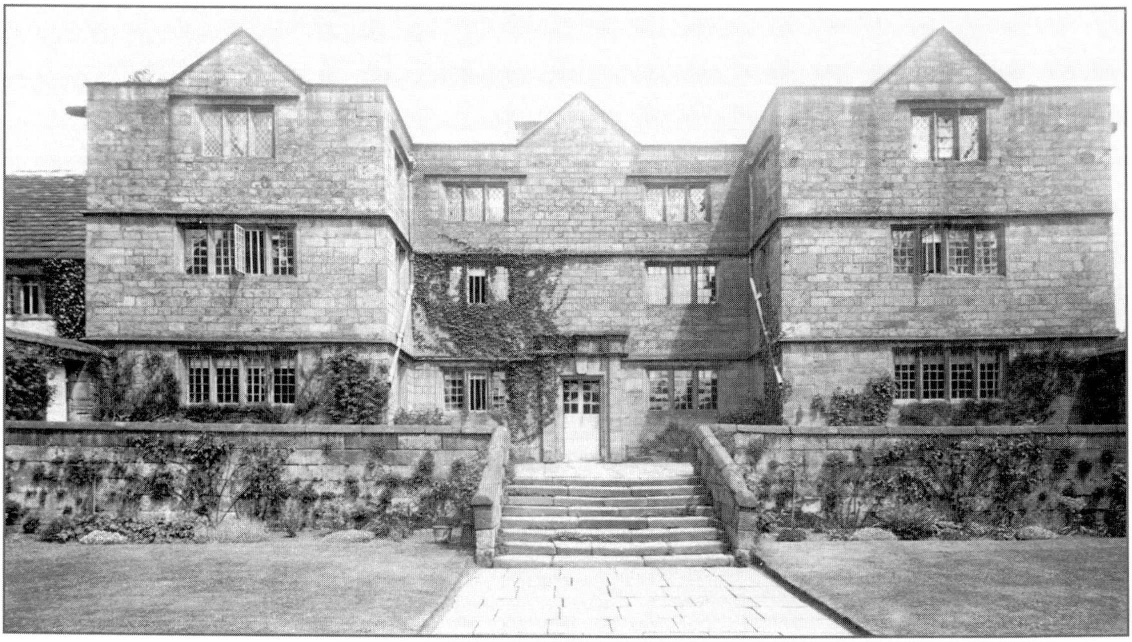

EYAM, THE HALL 1896 37816
A 16th-century staircase in Eyam Hall is thought to have first adorned Bradshaw Hall, the original building on this site, of which a only a barn now exists. Eyam Hall is an unspoilt 17th-century manor and has been the home of the Wright family for over 300 years.

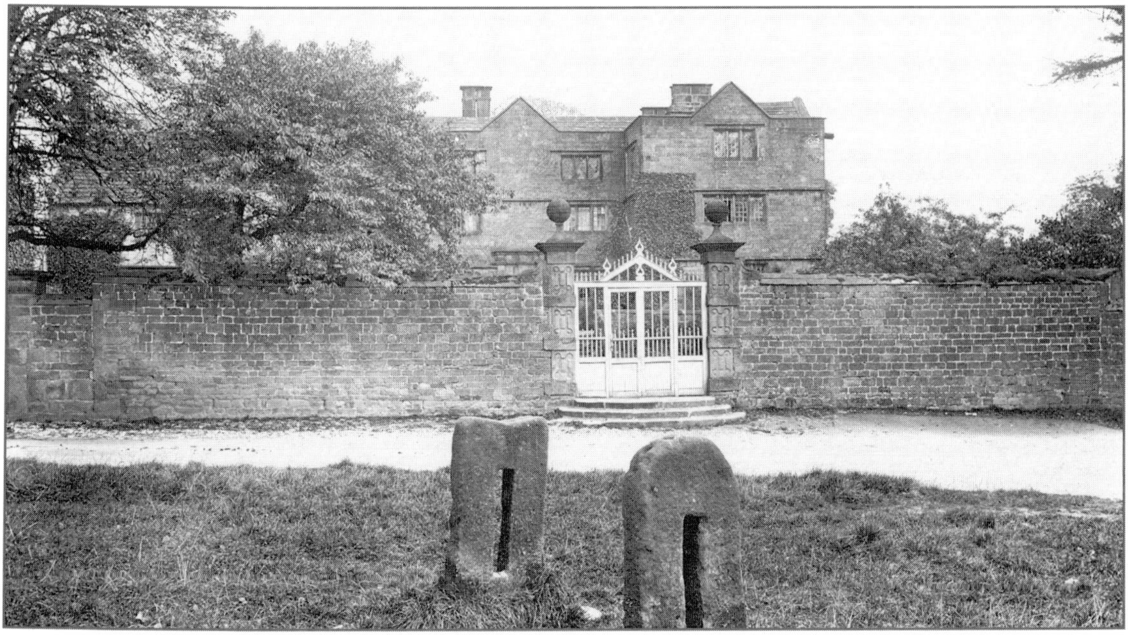

Eyam, The Hall and the Stocks 1919 69210
A decade before the Hall was built, Eyam secured its place in history when a parcel of clothes delivered to village tailor George Viccars brought the plague with it. To prevent the plague spreading, the village voluntarily isolated itself; 262 out of 350 villagers had died by the time the epidemic ended a year later.

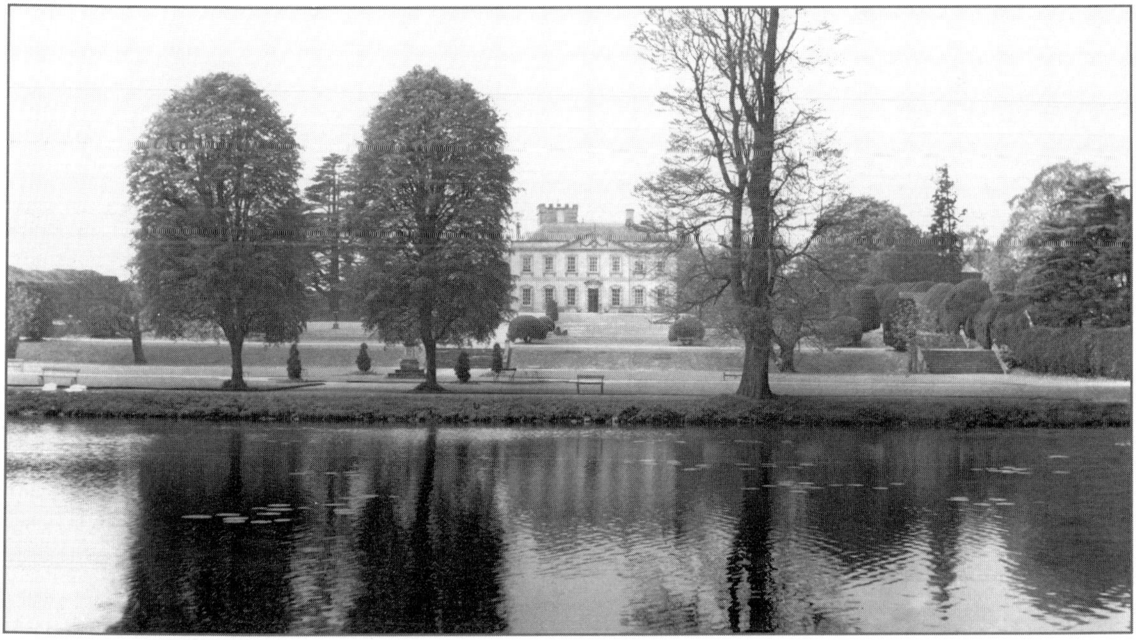

Melbourne Hall, From the Lake c1955 M243279
Birthplace of the Victorian statesman who gave his name to the Australian city, Melbourne Hall occupies the site of the manor of the Bishops of Carlisle. The house was built in the 17th century by Sir John Coke, and was developed further by Sir Thomas Coke in the 18th century.

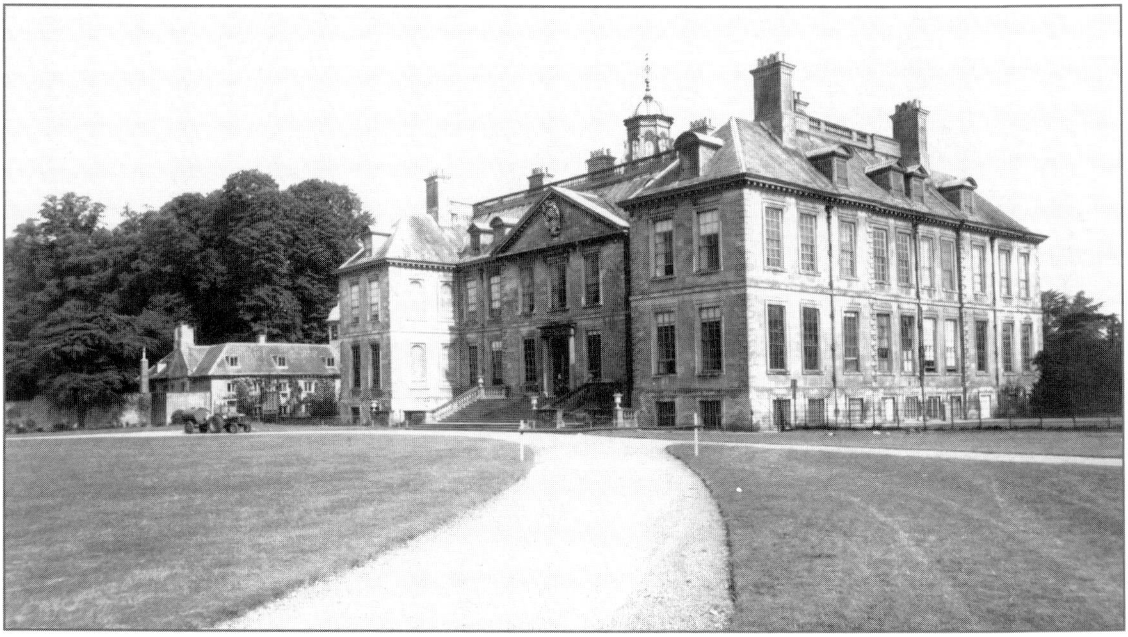

GRANTHAM, BELTON HOUSE c1960 G43072
Belton House is one of the finest surviving examples of a Restoration country house, and was built in the style of Christopher Wren by an unknown architect in 1685-8. It is the home of the Brownlow family, whose coat of arms can be seen on the pediment above the broad flight of steps.

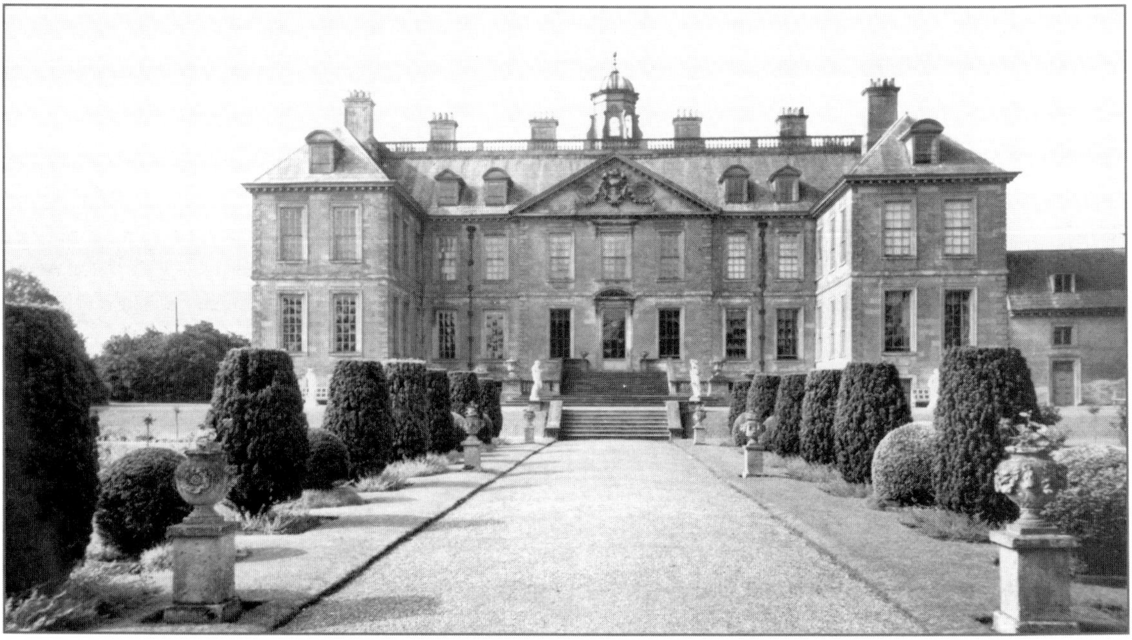

GRANTHAM, BELTON HOUSE c1960 G43094
The house, which was built on an H-plan, was altered by James Wyatt in 1776. It has magnificent interiors with fine plasterwork and wood-carving, and collections of paintings, furniture, and silverware. In the collection devoted to the Duke of Windsor is the only known painting of him as Edward VIII.

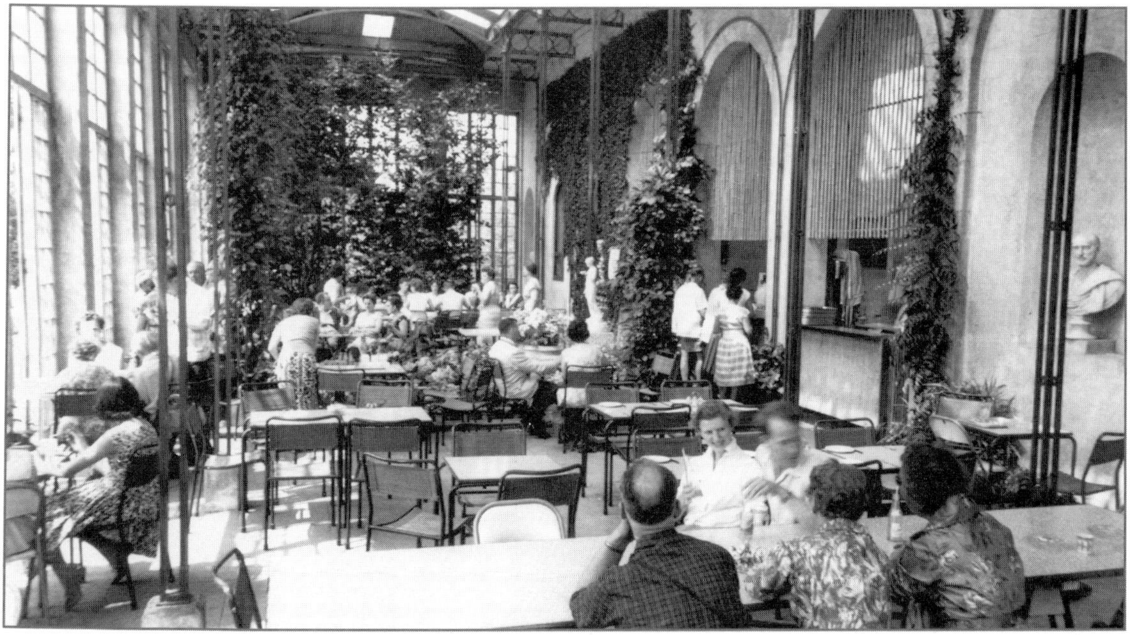

Grantham, Belton House, The Orangery Restaurant c1960 G43087

Orangeries made their first appearance in the 17th century when the fruit was popularised by the likes of Nell Gwynne. Built to protect orange trees from the English climate, they characteristically face south and have high windows to let in the maximum of light. This one was designed by Sir Jeffry Wyattville, nephew of James Wyatt.

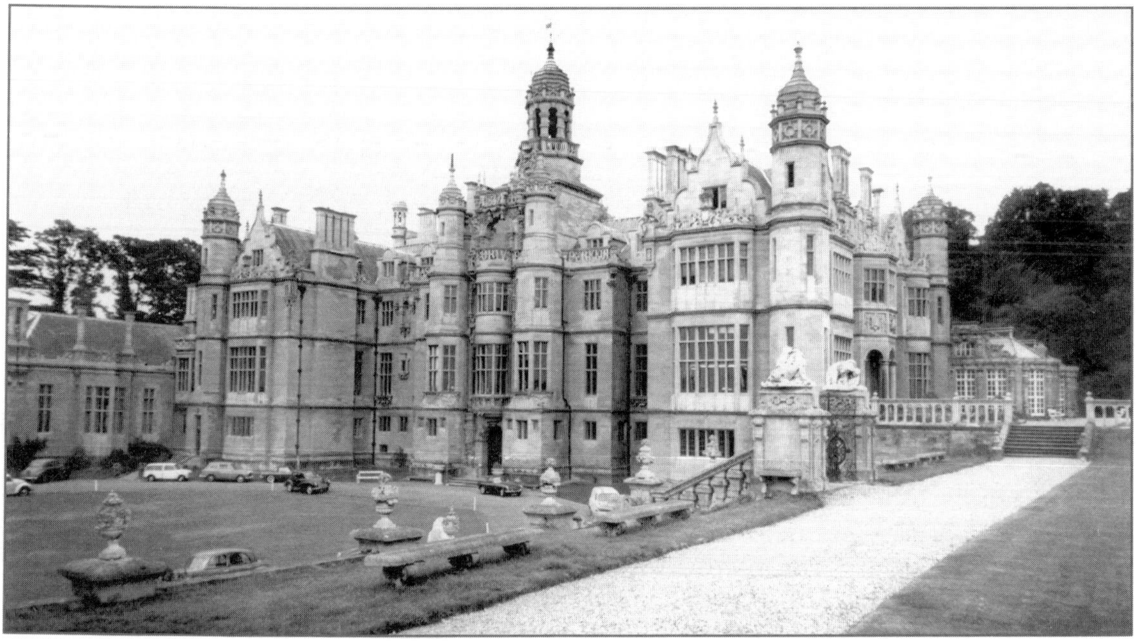

Grantham, Harlaxton Manor c1960 G43133

Anthony Salvin built Harlaxton Manor in the 1830s for George de Ligne Gregory, who needed a suitably extravagant edifice to house his huge art collection. The baroque interior was completed by William Burne, and includes a hall and staircase with extraordinarily ornate plasterwork.

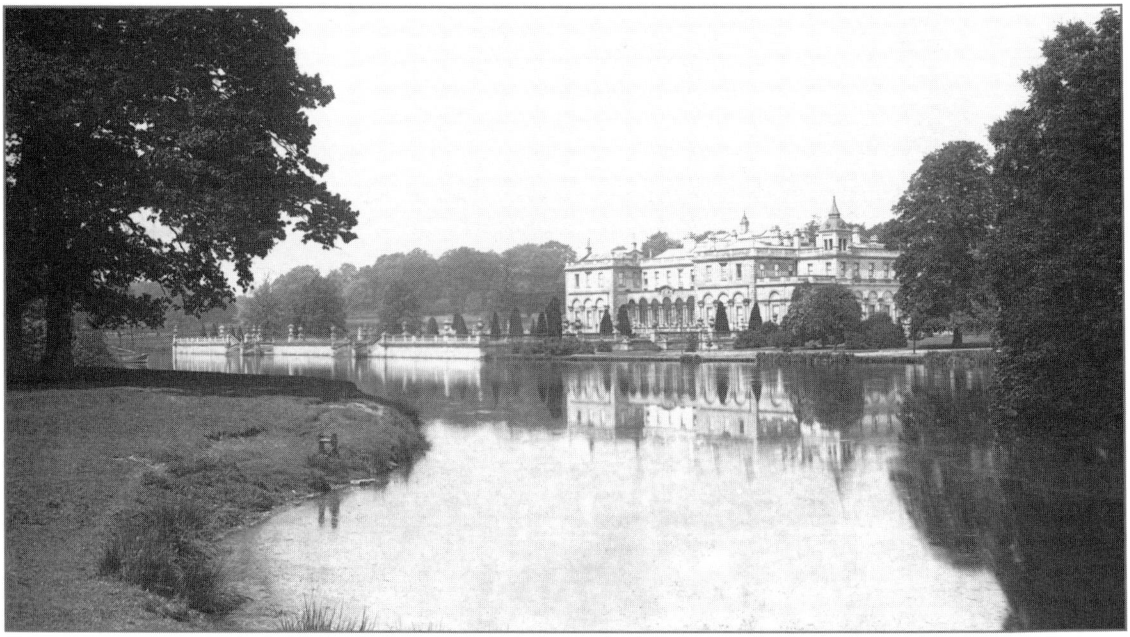

Clumber Park, The House c1873 6628
The Deer Park was created in 1707 for the Duke of Newcastle, and the house was built in 1770. It was demolished in 1938, and all that is now left are the stables and chapel. The park survives, however, and one of its glories is Duke's Drive - a three-mile avenue of lime trees.

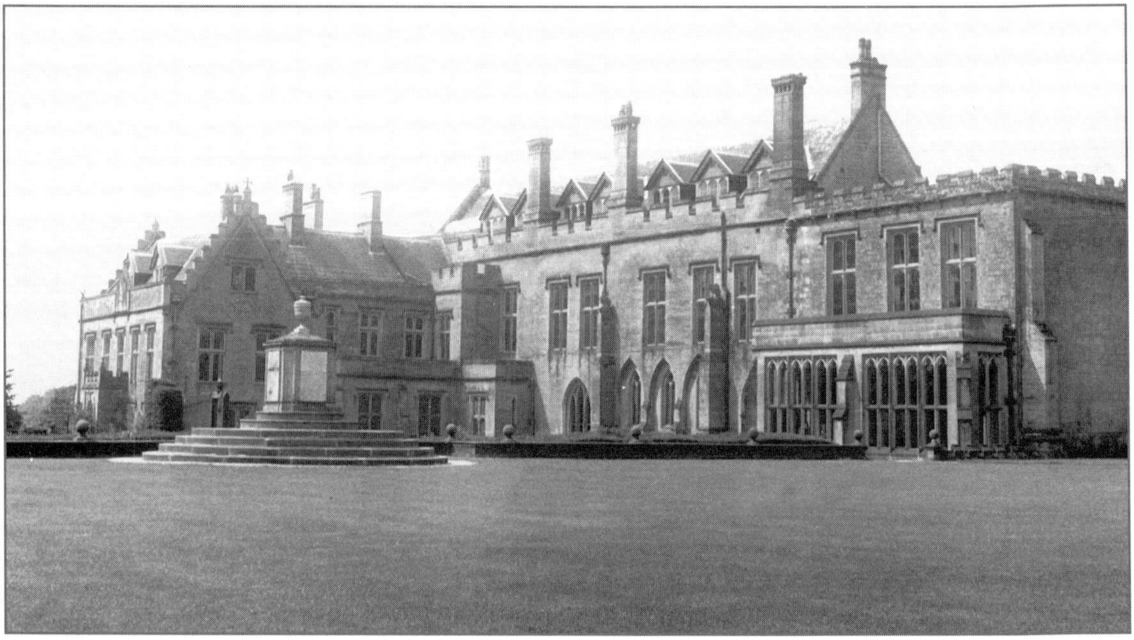

Nottingham, Newstead Abbey, East Side c1955 N29018
The Augustinian priory that once stood here was reputedly founded in 1170 by Henry II as an act of atonement for the killing of Thomas a Becket. In 1540 Sir John Byron bought the priory from Henry VIII and converted it into a house, which was remodelled in the 19th century.

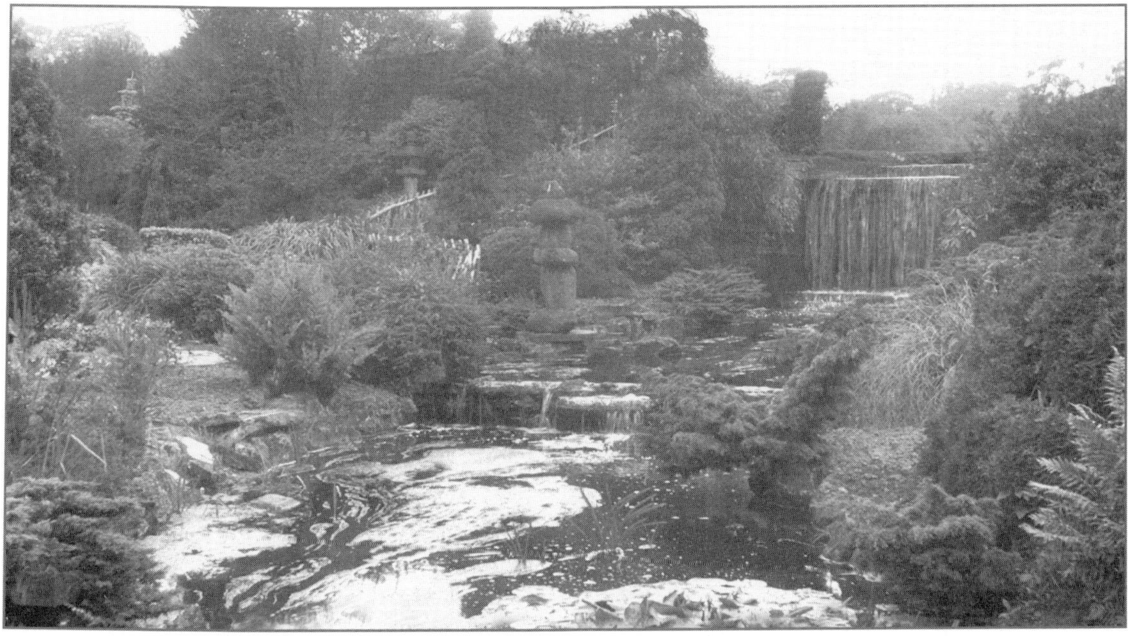

NOTTINGHAM, NEWSTEAD ABBEY, JAPANESE WATER GARDENS c1955 N29020
The most famous occupant of Newstead Abbey was the poet Lord Byron, who inherited it in 1798. He spent little time here, preferring a Bohemian life of dissipation which eventually led to the family selling the Abbey in 1818 to pay off his debts.

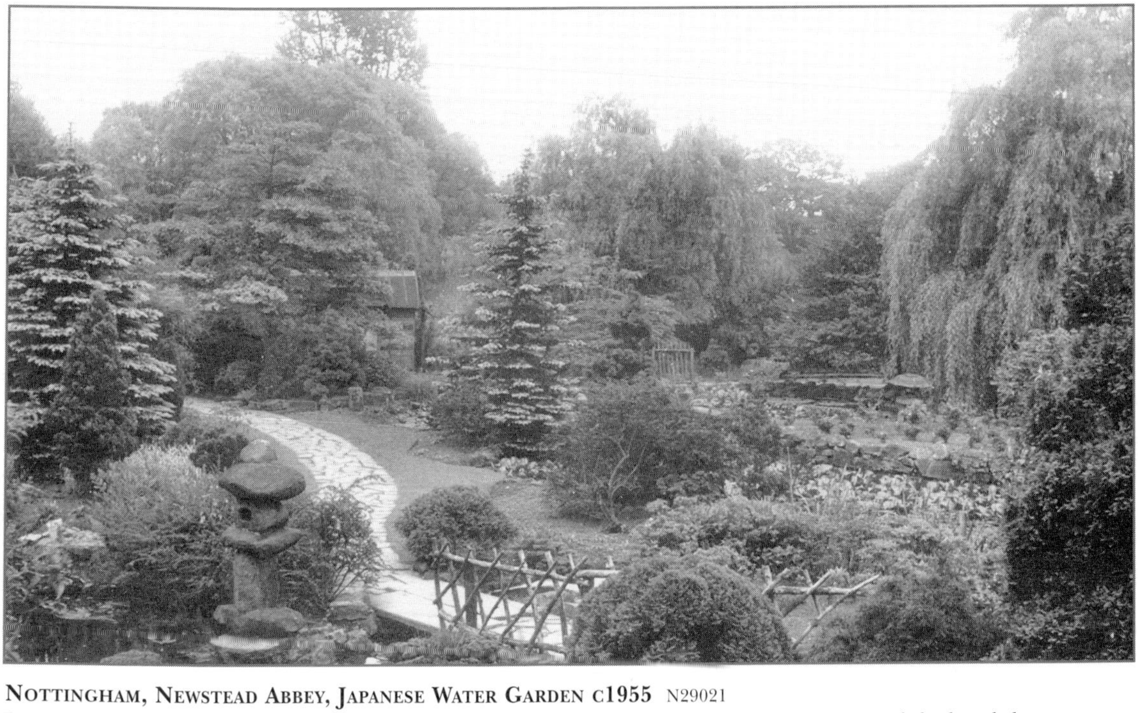

NOTTINGHAM, NEWSTEAD ABBEY, JAPANESE WATER GARDEN c1955 N29021
Lady Caroline Lamb (not exactly a shrinking violet herself) described Lord Byron as 'mad, bad and dangerous to know' - a sentiment quite possibly shared by Byron's family. The house contains a number of Byron's relics.

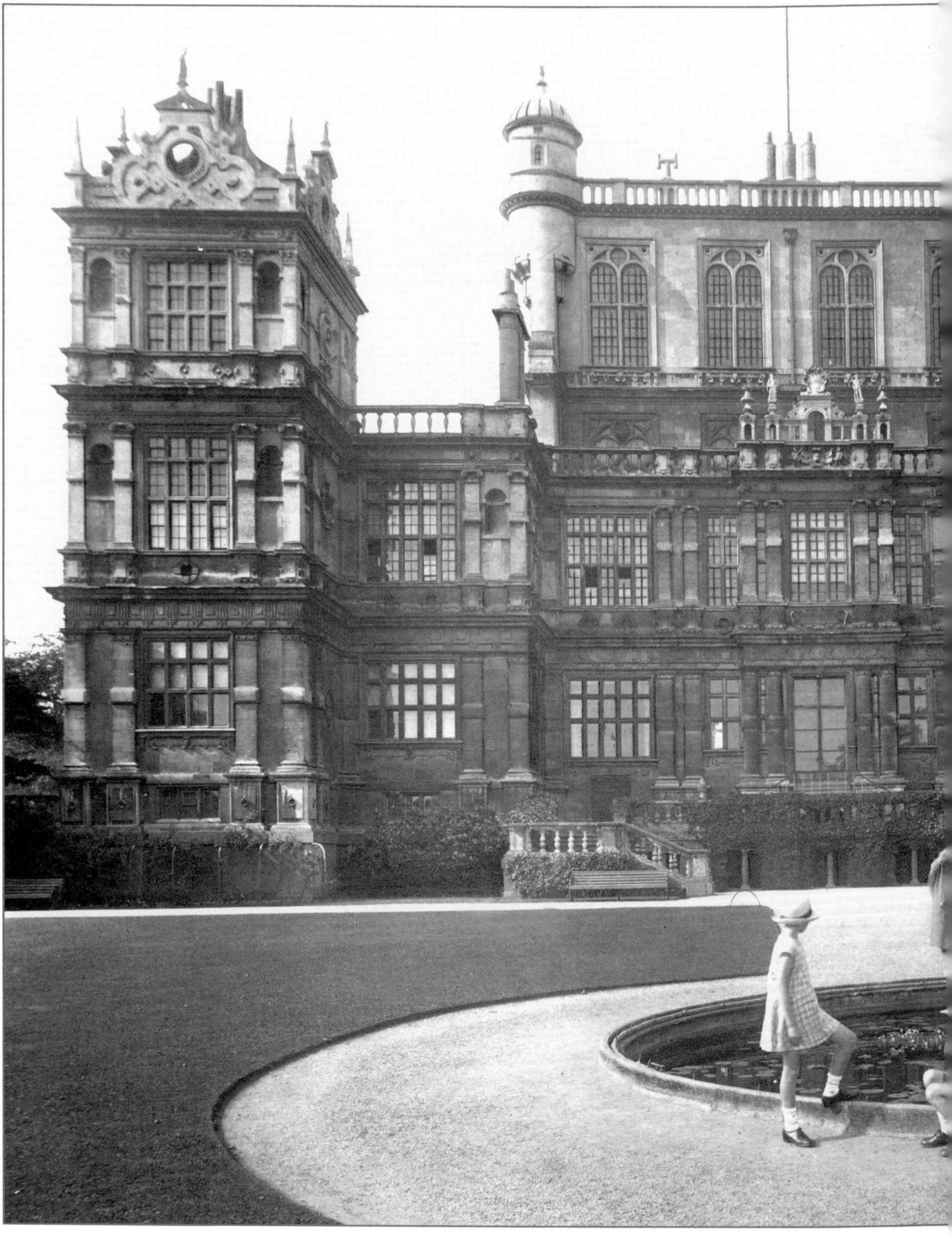

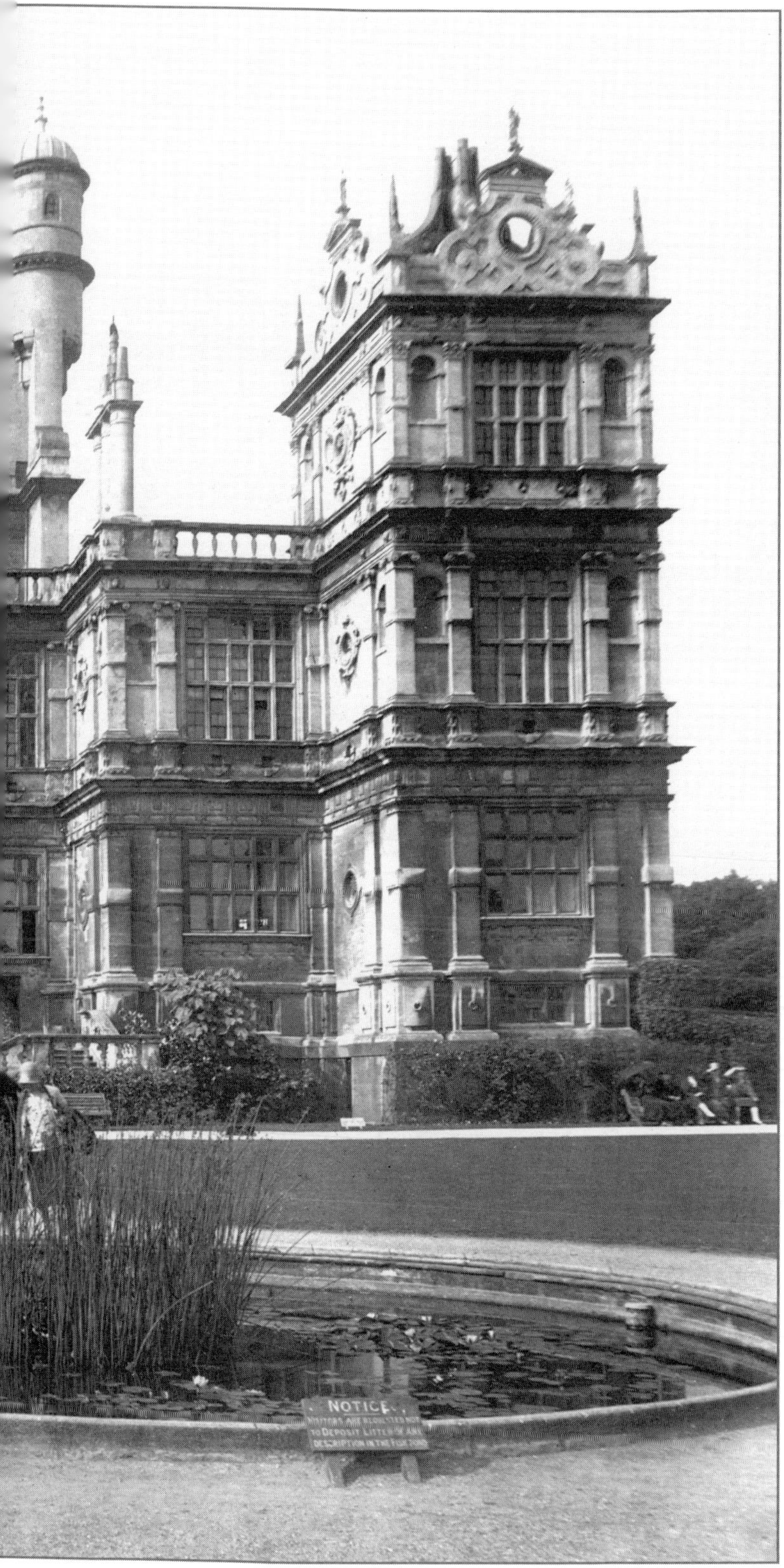

NOTTINGHAM
WOLLATON HALL 1928 81579
Designed by Robert Smythson, who also designed Longleat, Wollaton Hall is one of the best examples of Elizabethan Renaissance architecture. It was built in 1580-8, and now houses the Nottingham Natural History Museum.

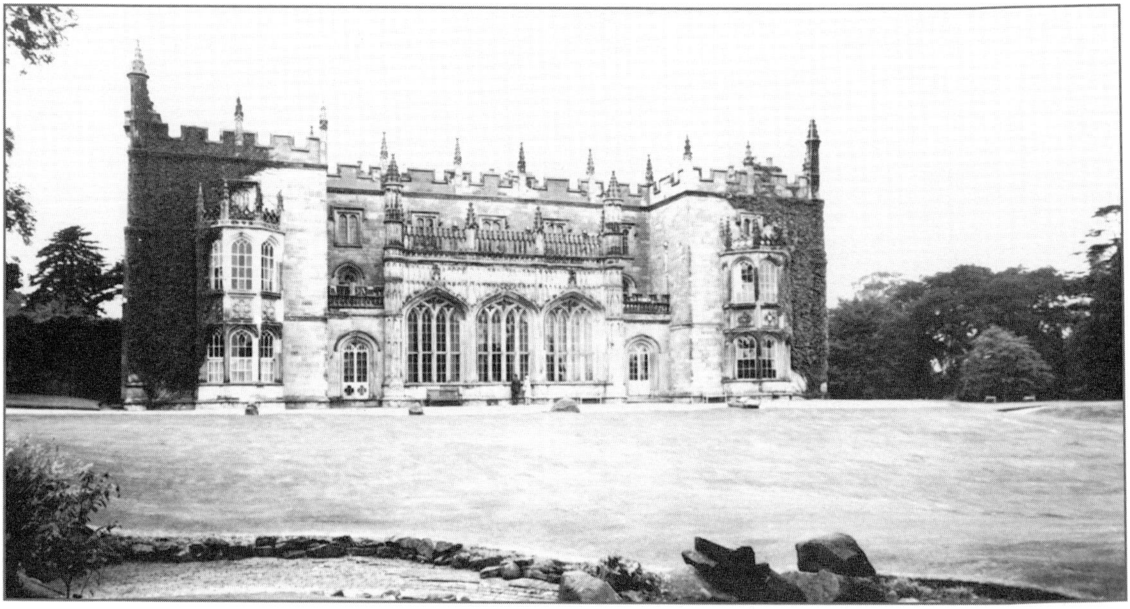

Nuneaton, Arbury Hall c1960 N89119
First an Augustinian priory, then a Tudor manor, Arbury House was converted to the Gothic Revival mansion in this picture by Sir Roger Newdegate in 1750-1805. It has stables by Wren and a magnificent plaster ceiling by Edward Martin in the chapel. Mary Fitton, sister-in-law of one of the early Newdegates, is thought to have been the 'dark lady' of Shakespeare's sonnets.

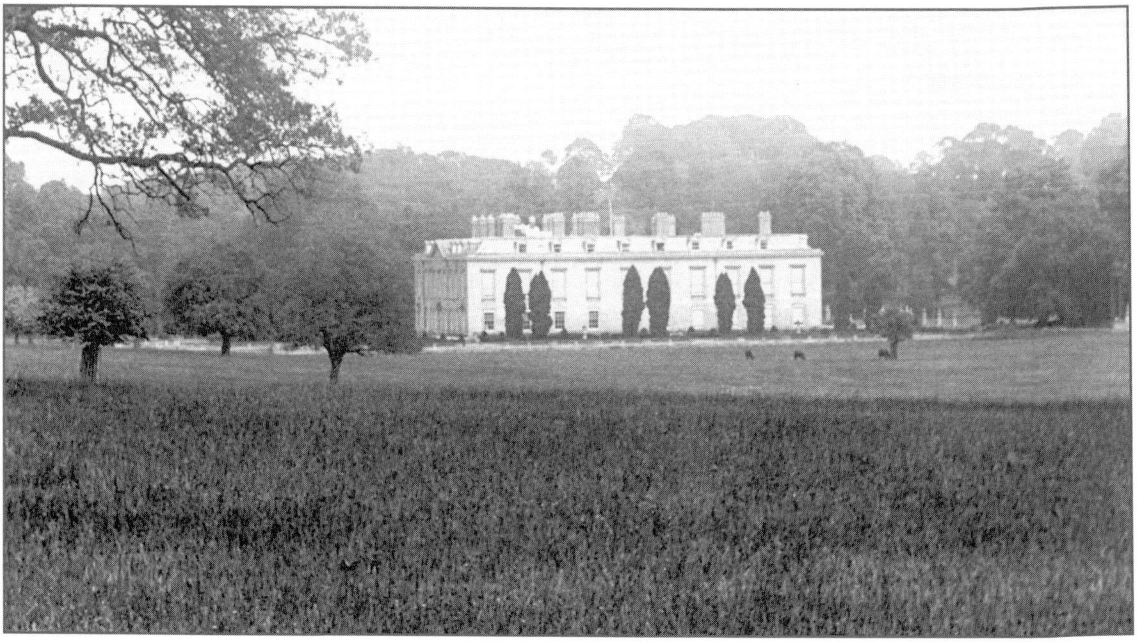

Althorp House 1922 72211
Wealthy sheep farmer John Spencer bought Althorp in 1508, and it has remained in the Spencer family ever since. In 1603 Queen Anne stayed here on her way to join her husband who was shortly to be crowned James I of England, and in 1647 Charles I played bowls here while in the custody of Parliamentarian forces.

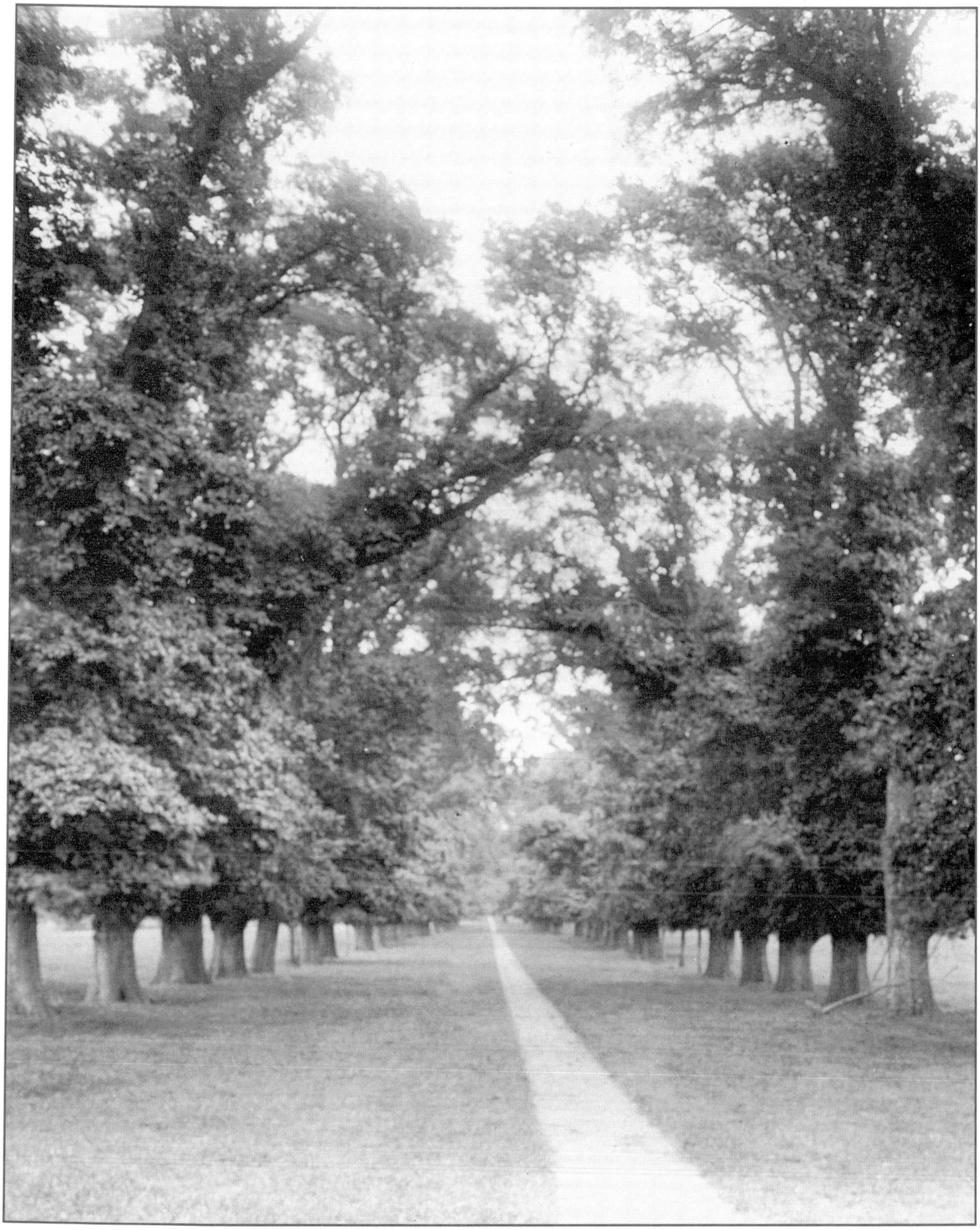

Althorp Park, Church Avenue 1922 72212
The first Earl Spencer was created in 1765, and his descendants went on to a variety of fame and fortune. The third Earl was responsible for the Reform Bill and Factory Act, and in the 20th century one of the daughters of the family married into royalty.

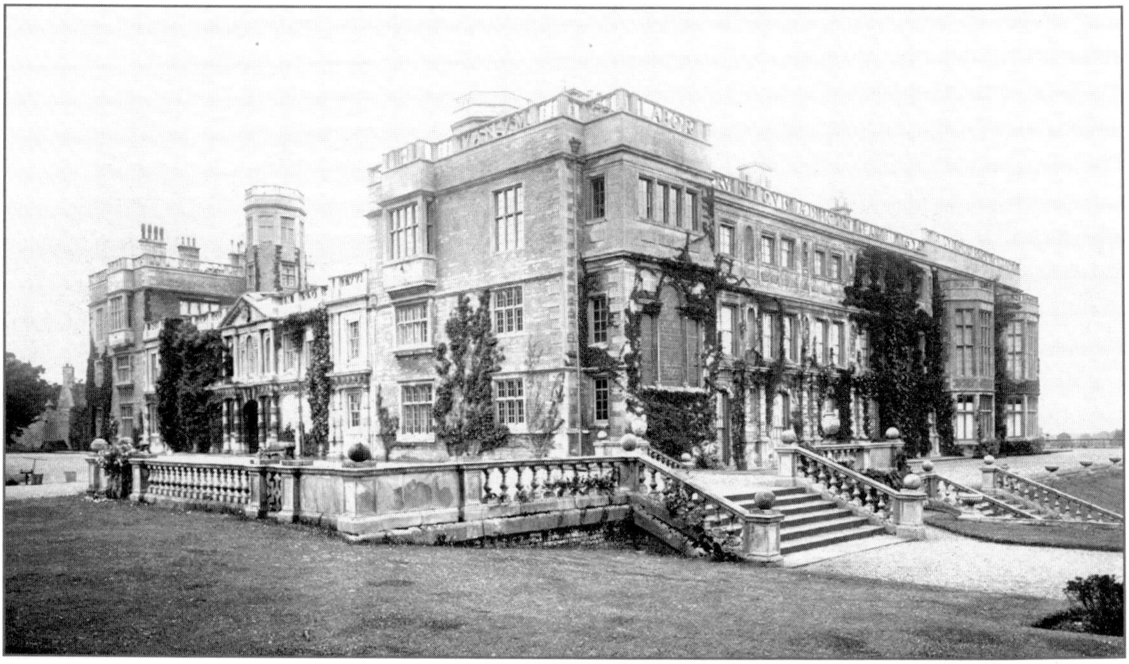

Castle Ashby, The House 1922 72221
Originally built to the Elizabethan E-plan in 1574 by the Compton family, Castle Ashby was modified in the 17th century by Inigo Jones, who added the south wing. The parkland was landscaped by Capability Brown.

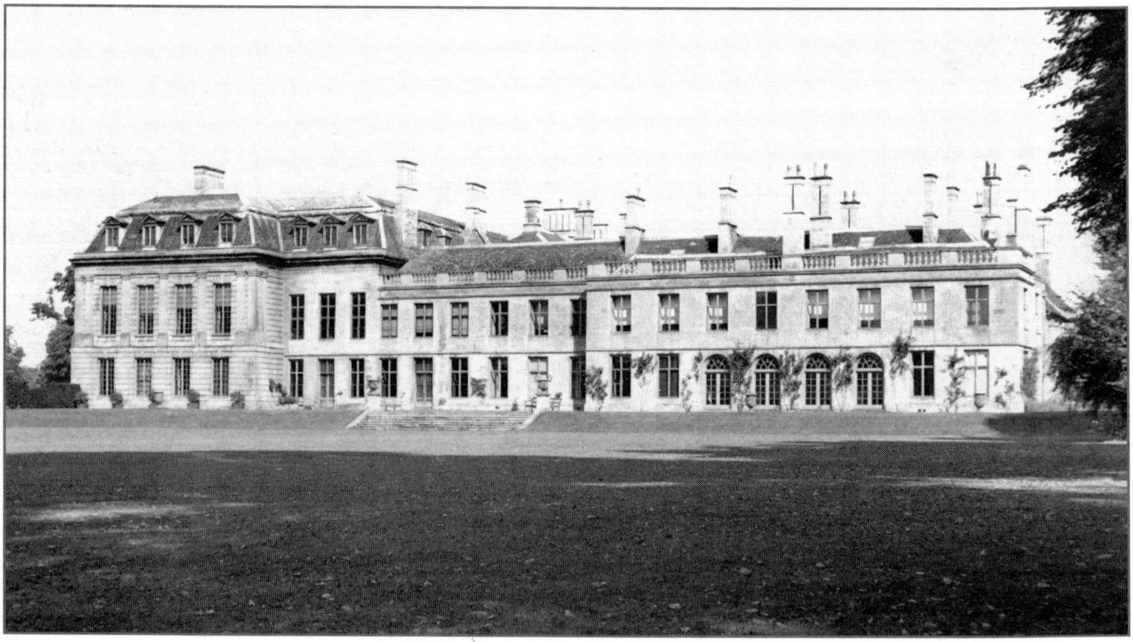

Geddington, Boughton House c1955 G84023
Built around the theme of time, with seven courtyards, 52 chimney stacks and 365 windows, Boughton House was begun in 1530 by Sir Edward Montagu. The house was extended several times, culminating in the building of the north front in the late 17th century by the first Duke of Montagu.

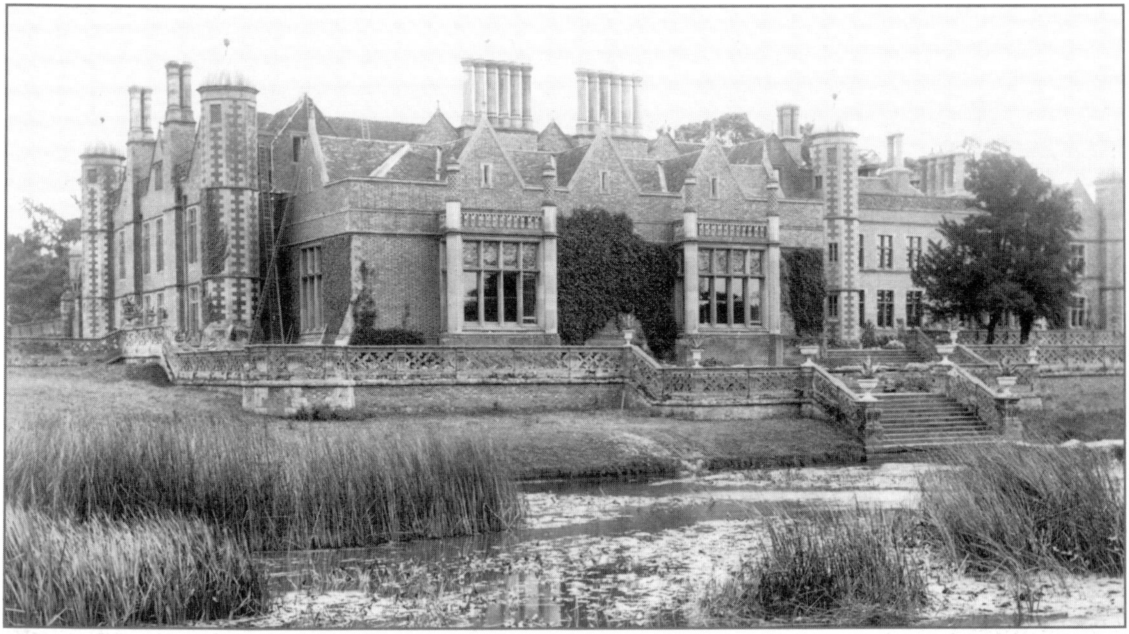

Charlecote Hall c1955 C25101
Much altered in the 19th century, Charlecote Hall was built in 1588 by Sir Thomas Lucy. The young William Shakespeare was caught poaching by Sir Thomas, but Shakespeare had his revenge when he used Sir Thomas as the model for the character of Justice Shallow in 'The Merry Wives of Windsor'.

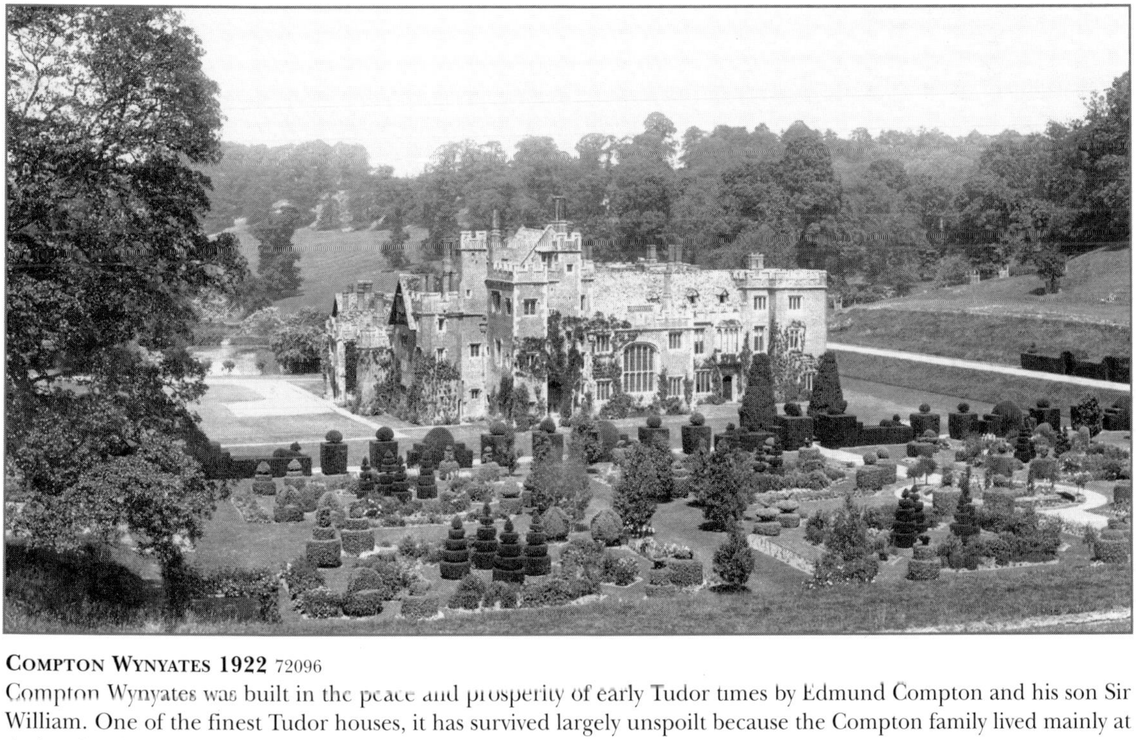

Compton Wynyates 1922 72096
Compton Wynyates was built in the peace and prosperity of early Tudor times by Edmund Compton and his son Sir William. One of the finest Tudor houses, it has survived largely unspoilt because the Compton family lived mainly at their other house, Castle Ashby, after the Civil War.

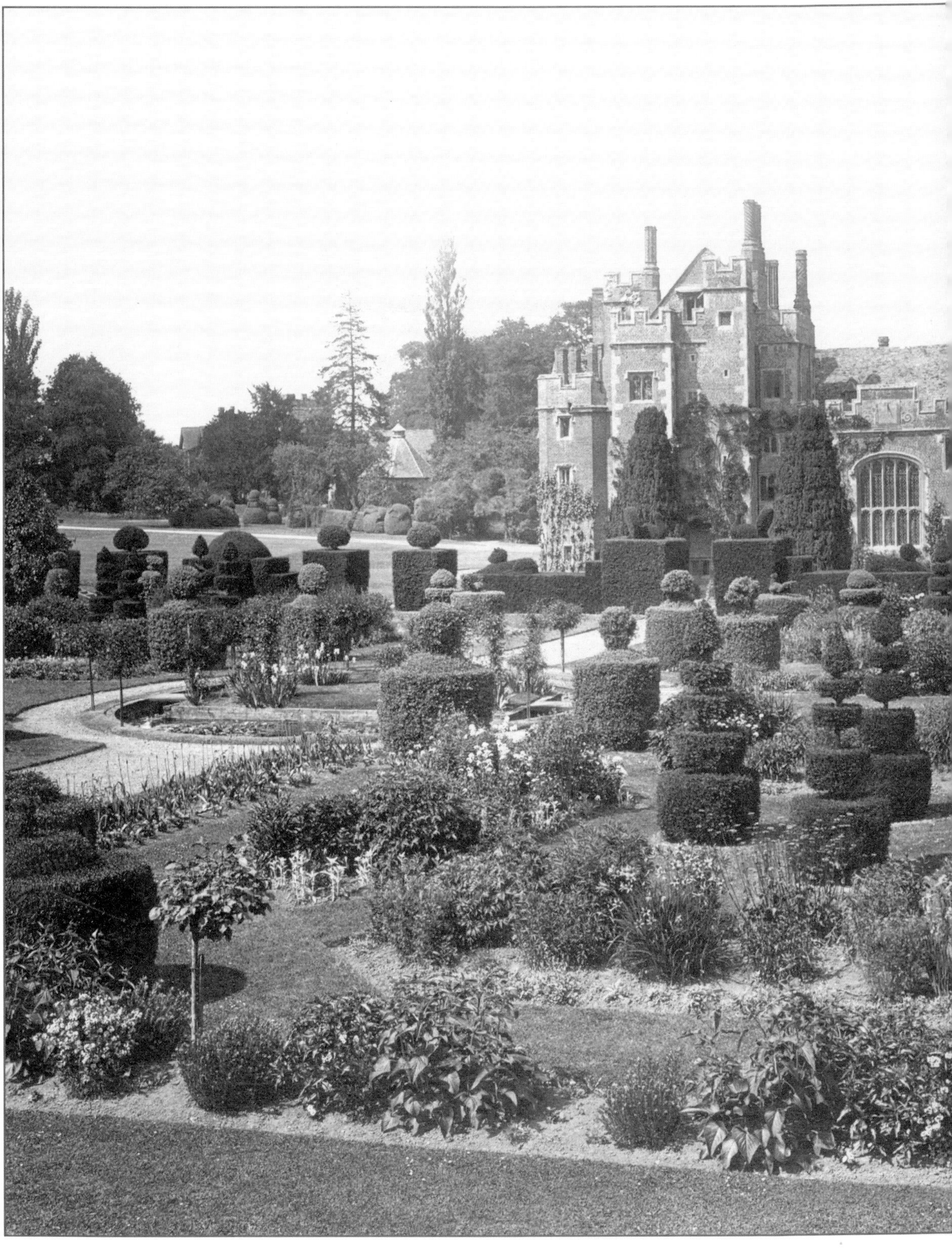

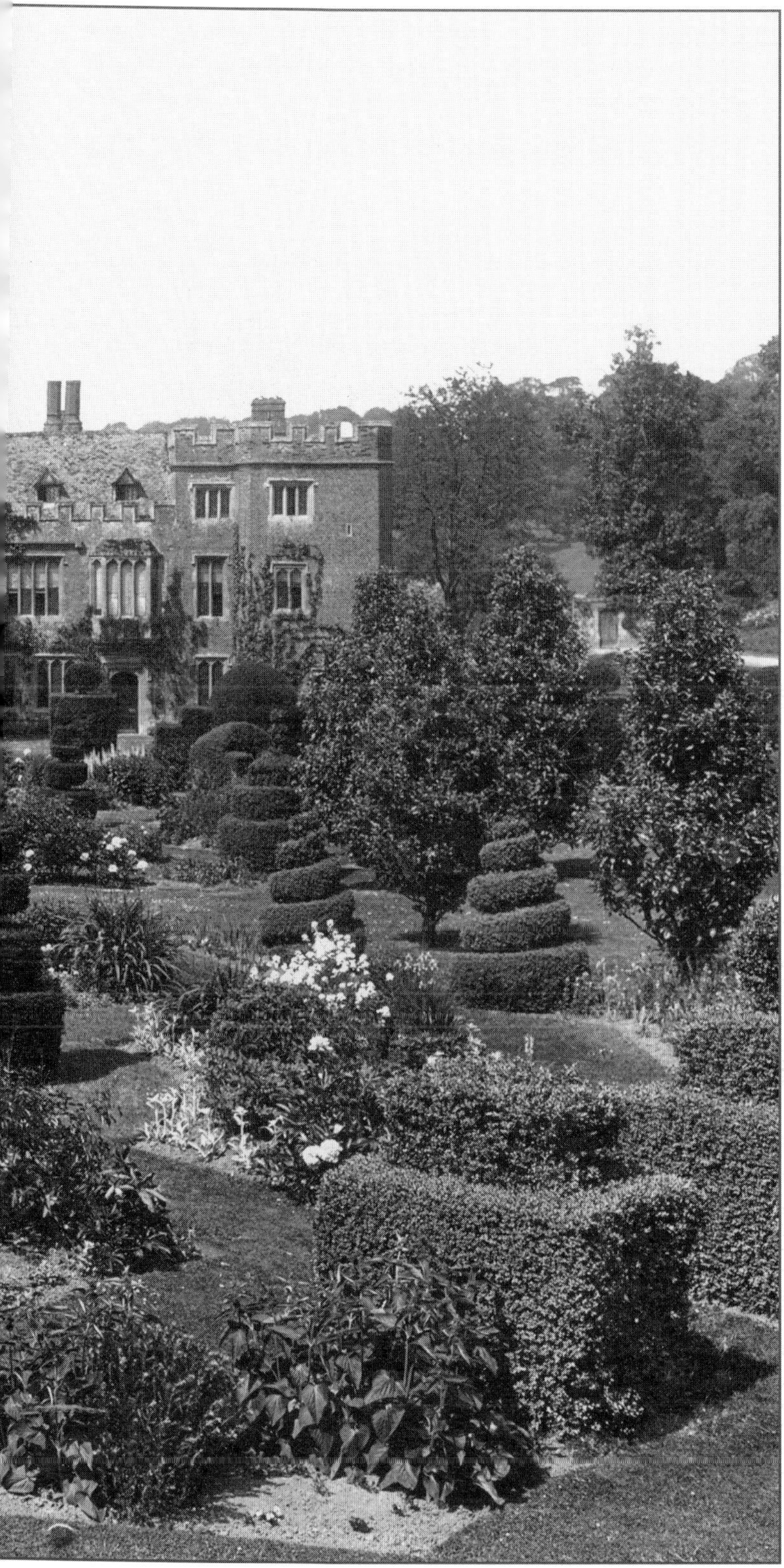

Compton Wynyates 1922 72098
The large arched window is that of the chapel, which was finished in 1515. Sir William was courtier and friend to Henry VIII; the king often stayed at Compton Wynyates, including one occasion with the doomed Katherine of Aragon.

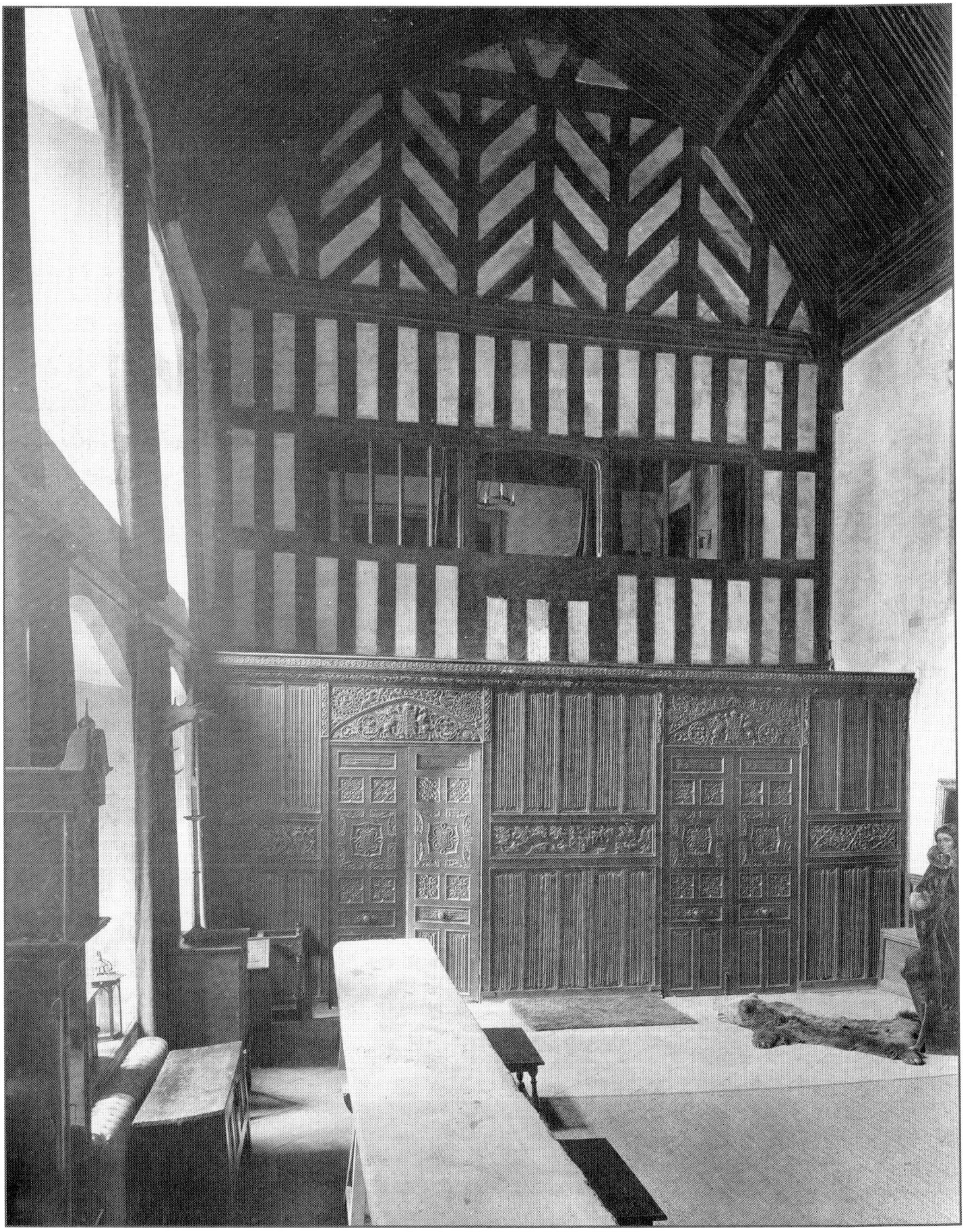

COMPTON WYNYATES, THE MINSTRELS' GALLERY 1922 72106
The Comptons' royal connections caused them a lot of trouble in the Civil War. In 1644 the house was besieged and captured by Parliamentarian troops, and was only returned to the family two years later upon payment of a £20,000 fine.

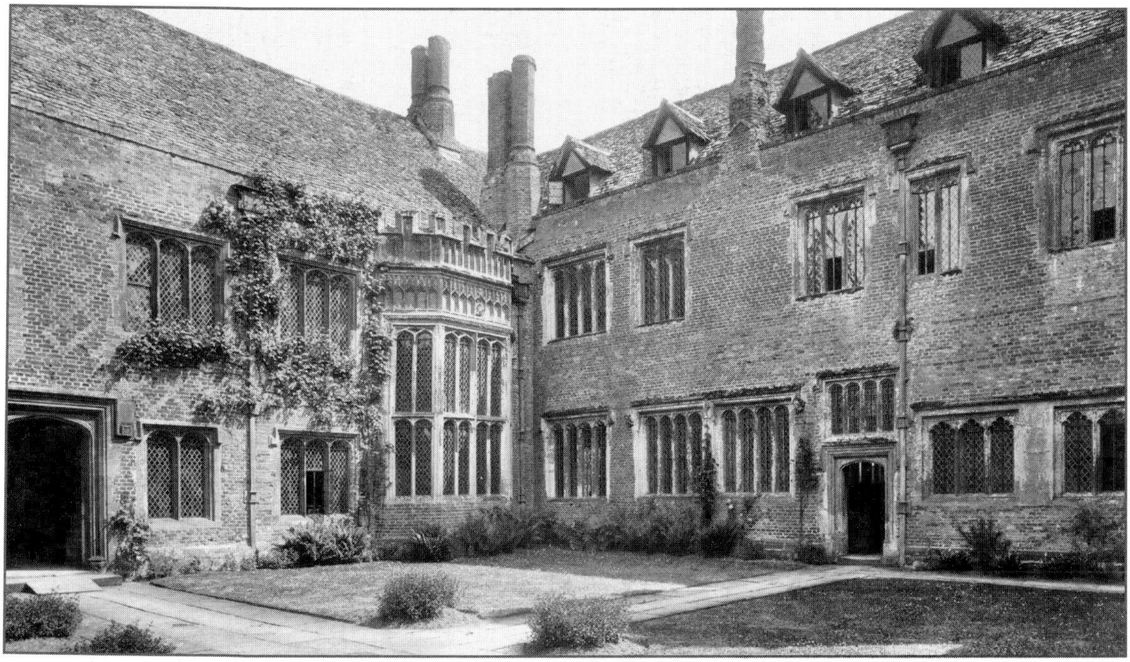

COMPTON WYNYATES, THE COURTYARD 1922 72104
Another royal visitor was Queen Elizabeth I, who in 1572 brought her entire court to Compton Wynyates, causing vast expense to Sir Henry Compton. James I and Charles I also stayed here.

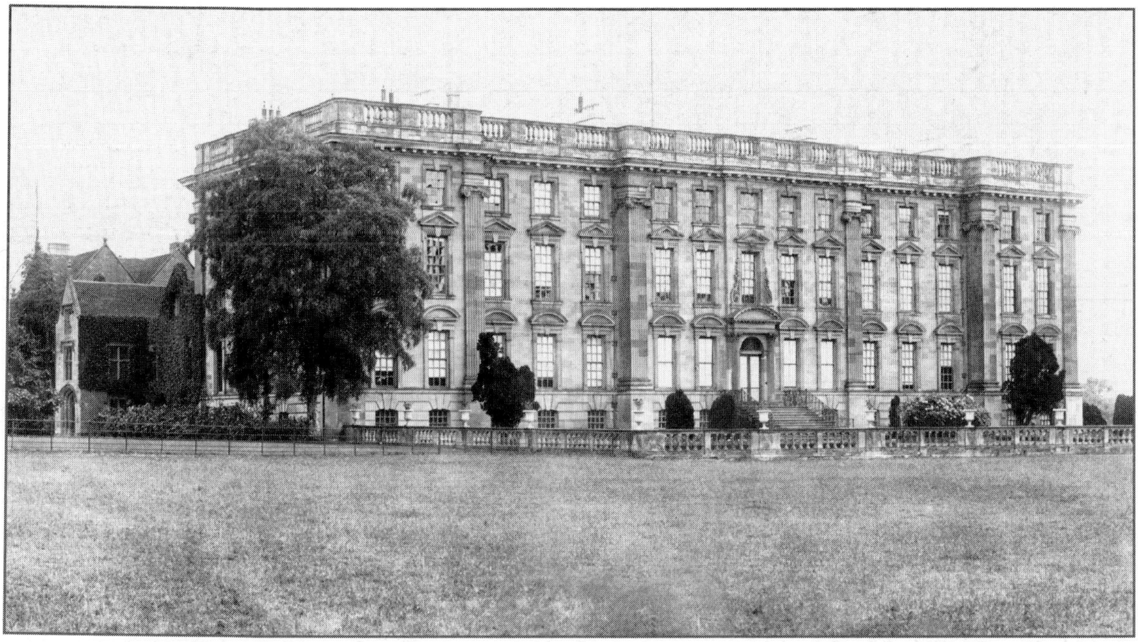

STONELEIGH ABBEY 1892 30993
The little gabled wing on the left is the 14th-century monastery gatehouse, all that remains of the abbey that once stood on the site. Behind the gatehouse is the Elizabethan wing. The grand Italianate mansion of the main house was completed in 1726.

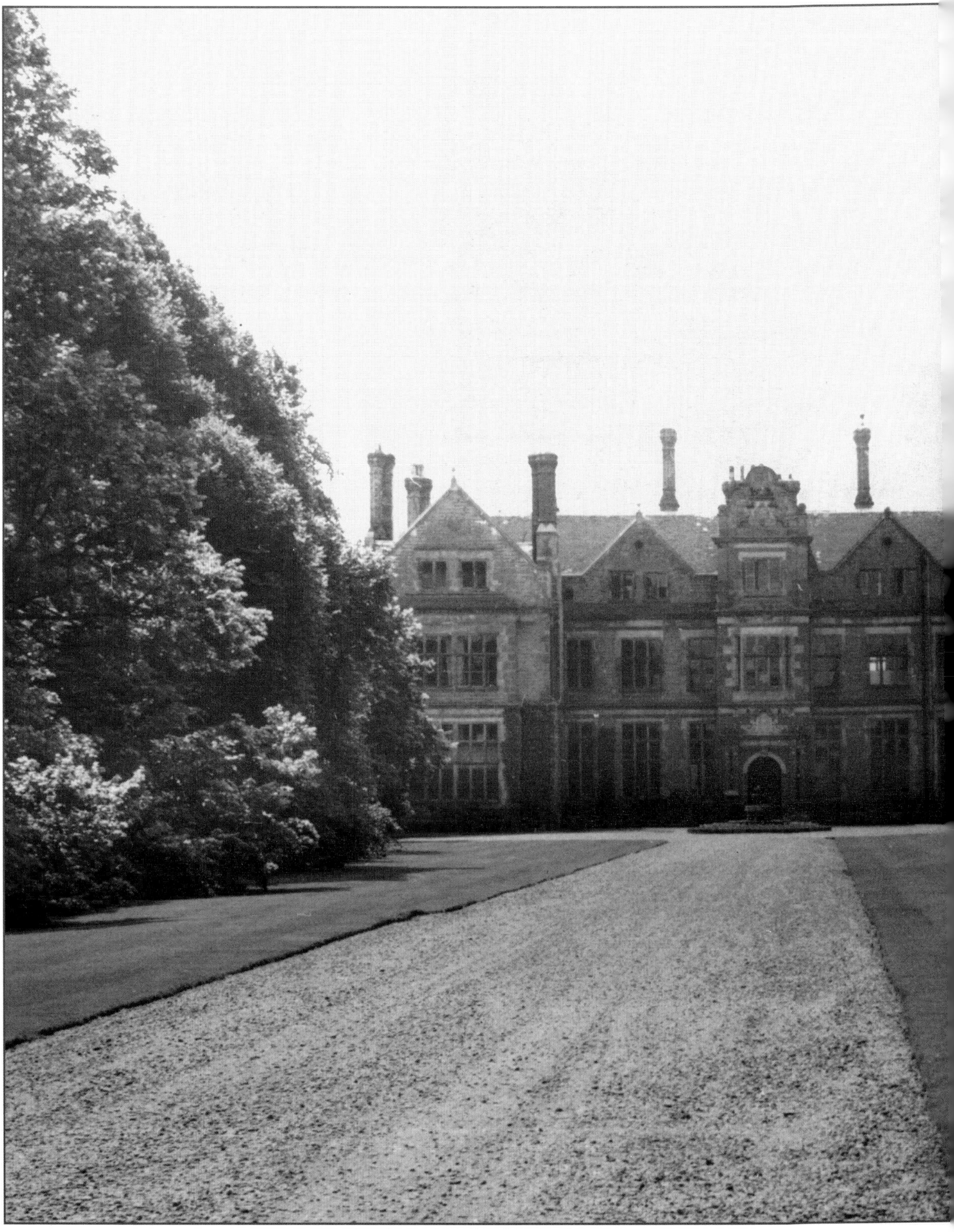

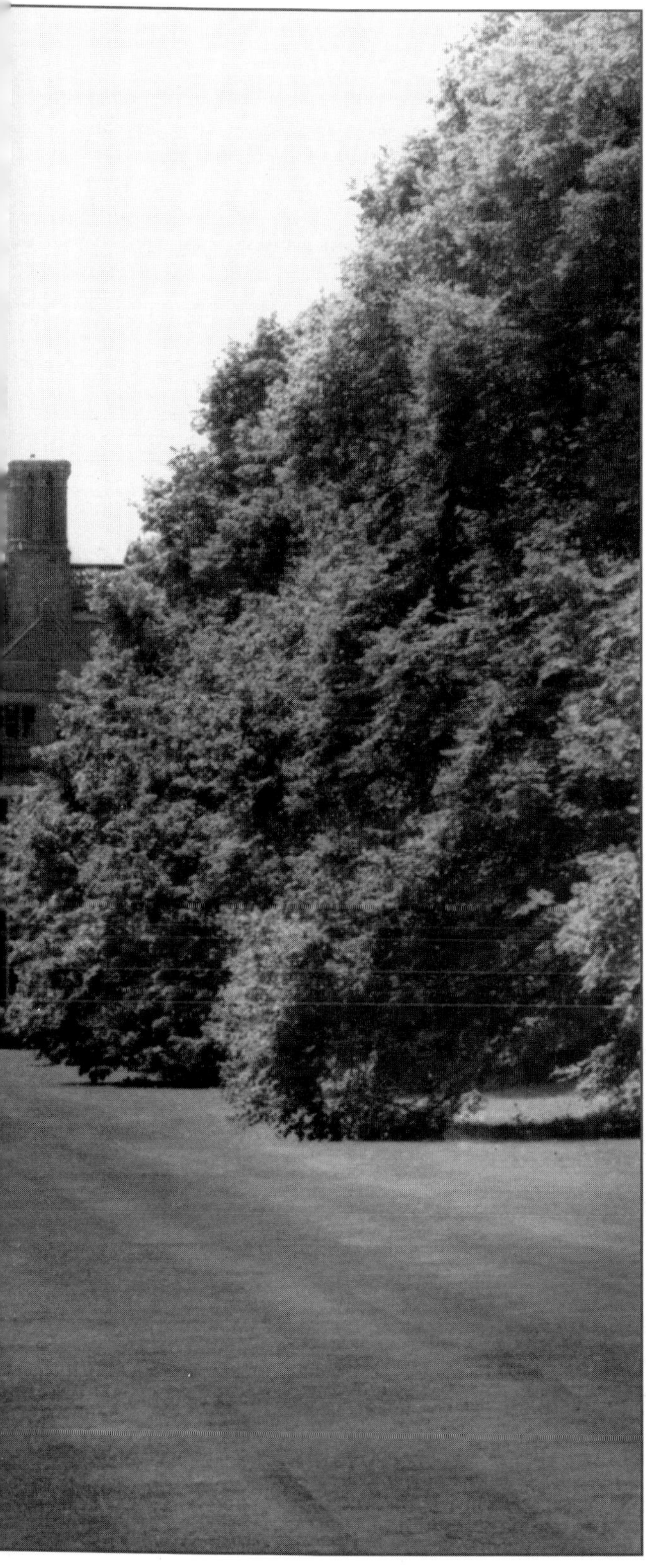

West Midlands

Market Drayton, Hodnet Hall c1960 H379031
Although the chimneys and gables of this red-brick mansion shout 'Tudor', Hodnet Hall was actually built in the 19th century. It was designed by Anthony Salvin, an expert on medieval architecture; he restored many castles, including Warwick and Windsor.

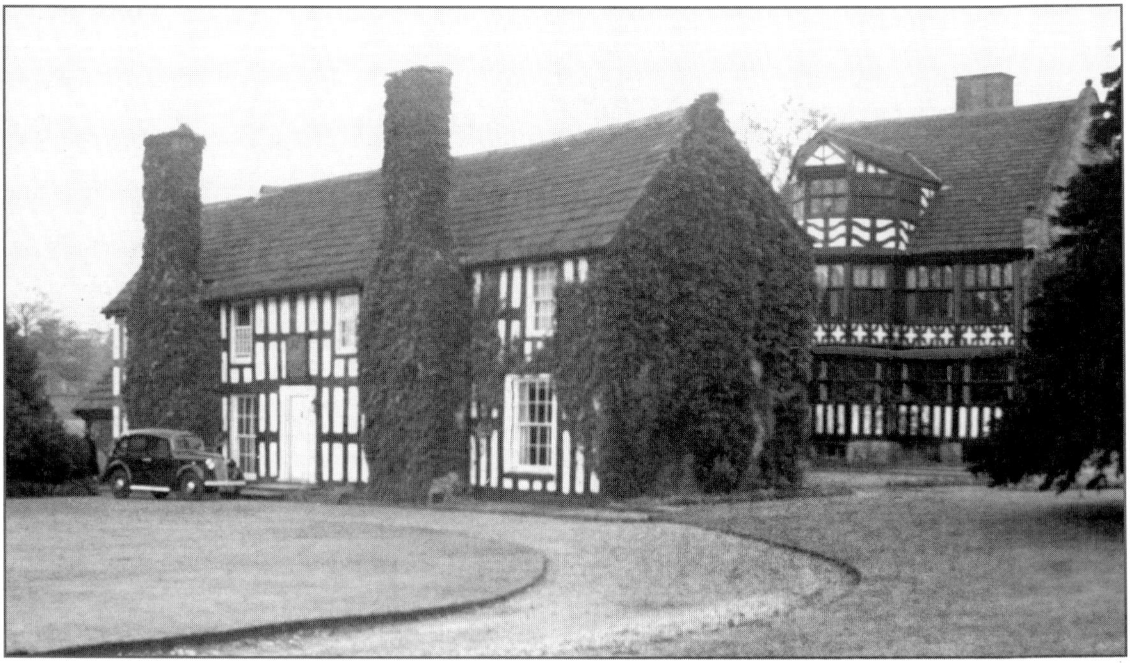

GAWSWORTH, THE OLD HALL C1955 G5024
This fine half-timbered Elizabethan manor house has a medieval jousting ground in its park. It was the birthplace of Mary and Anne Fitton, either of whom, it is thought, could have been the 'dark lady' of Shakespeare's sonnets.

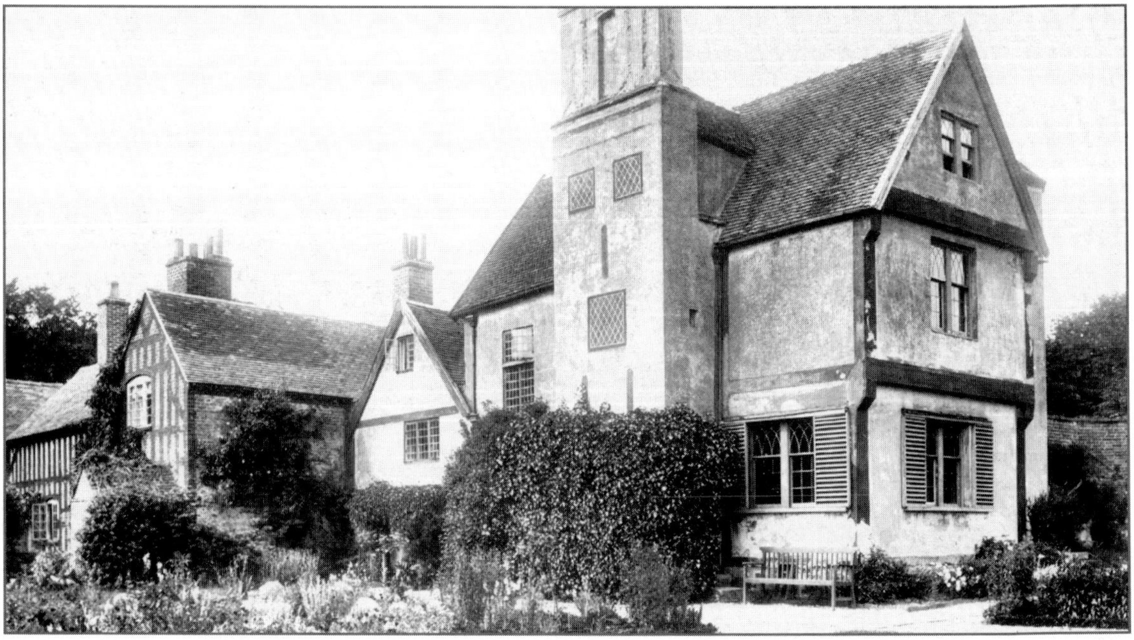

BOSCOBEL, THE HOUSE 1898 41885
Boscobel House was built around 1600 by John Giffard as a hunting lodge, and was often used as a hideout for Catholics. Charles II hid here after the Battle of Worcester in 1651, concealing himself by day in an oak tree in the grounds. A Royal Oak still stands on the spot - grown, it is said, from an acorn of the original tree.

ALTON TOWERS
The Yew Arches c1955
Originally farmland and wild hillside, the large ornamental park at Alton Towers was created between 1814 and 1827 by Charles Talbot, fifteenth Earl of Shrewsbury. His nephew John built the Gothic mansion, of which only the shell remains, in 1831.

ALTON TOWERS
The Rose Garden and the Grand Conservatory c1955
Charles Talbot gave his imagination free rein when it came to designing the gardens at Alton Towers: a Roman bath and colonnade, a Chinese temple and a Swiss cottage are among the features. There is a memorial to Talbot in the gardens bearing the inscription 'he made the desert smile'.

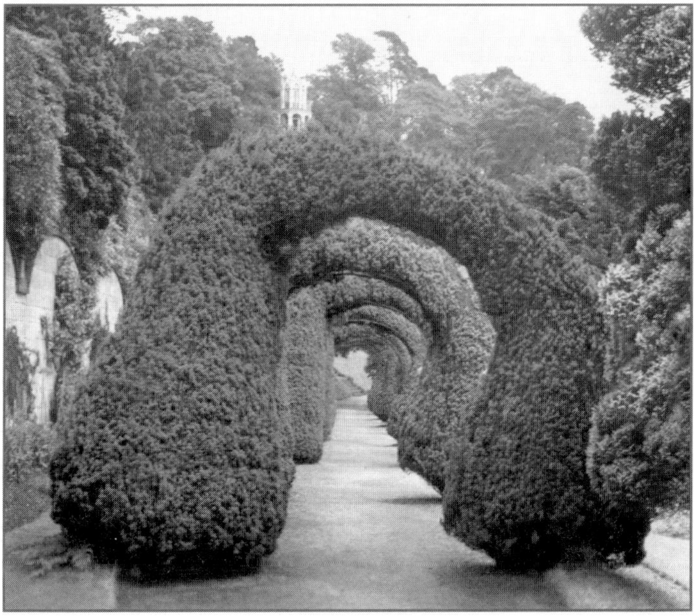
ALTON TOWERS, THE YEW ARCHES c1955 A216153

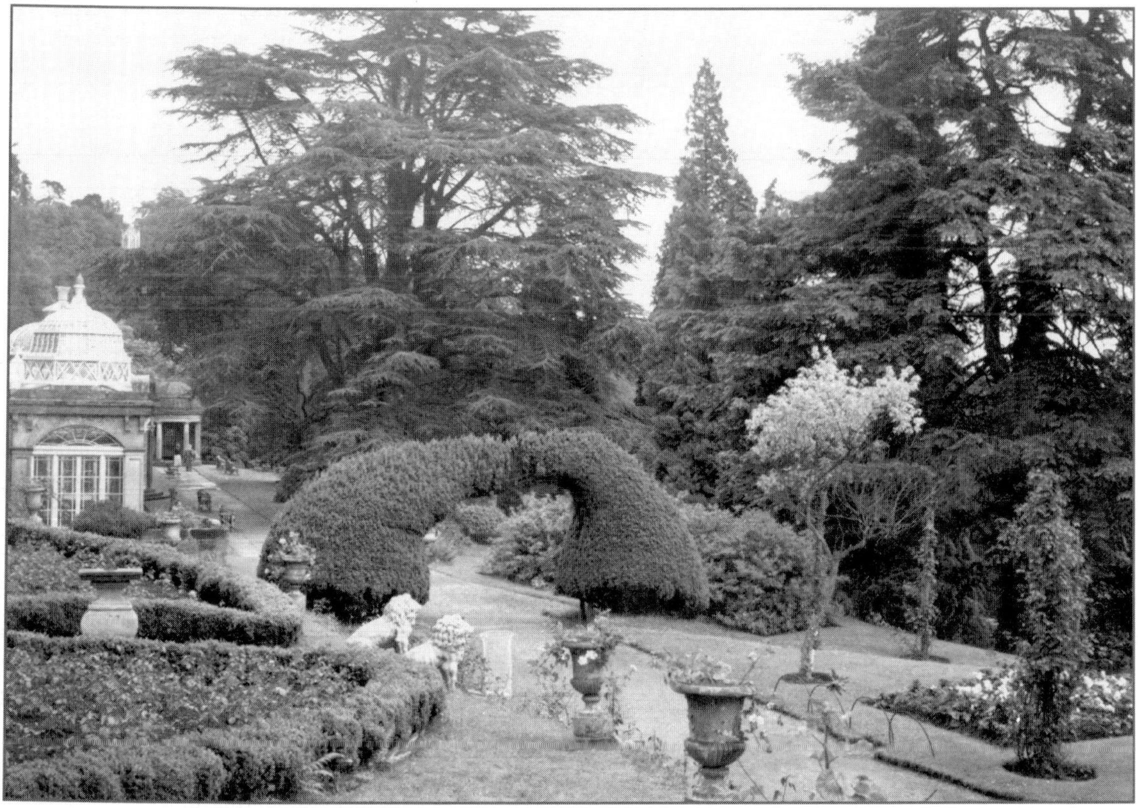
ALTON TOWERS, THE ROSE GARDEN AND THE GRAND CONSERVATORY c1955 A216152

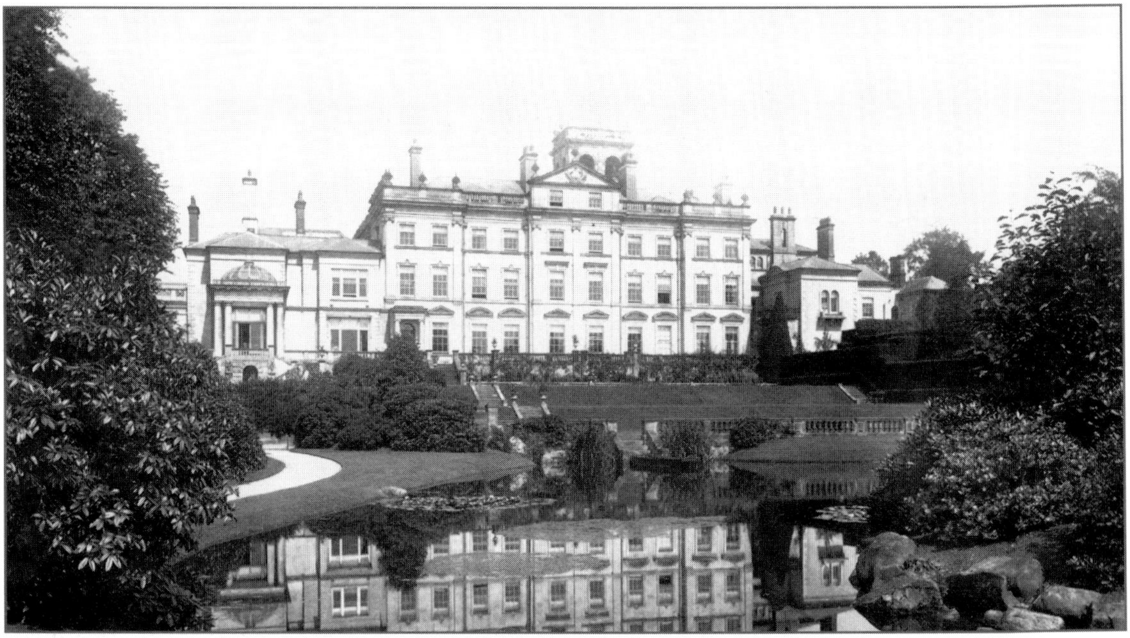

Biddulph, The Grange 1902 48668
This is another house where the garden designer's imagination ran riot. James Bateman designed the garden in the mid 19th century to show off his collection of plants in a series of connected compartments which take the visitor on a tour of the world - including the Great Wall of China and the Egyptian Court.

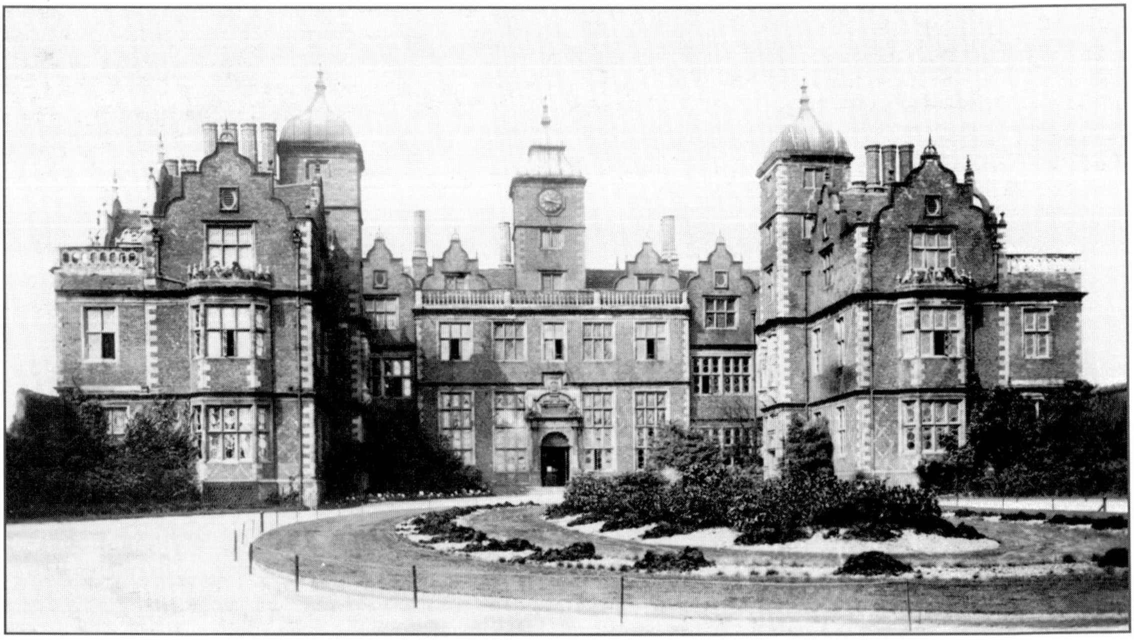

Birmingham, Aston Hall 1896 37295
Aston Hall was built in 1618-35 by Sir Thomas Holte; as a result of entertaining Charles I in 1642, Sir Thomas was imprisoned by the Parliamentarians. However, the Holte family managed to keep Aston Hall until 1818, when it was let to James Watt, son of the famous engineer and inventor.

Yorkshire & The North East

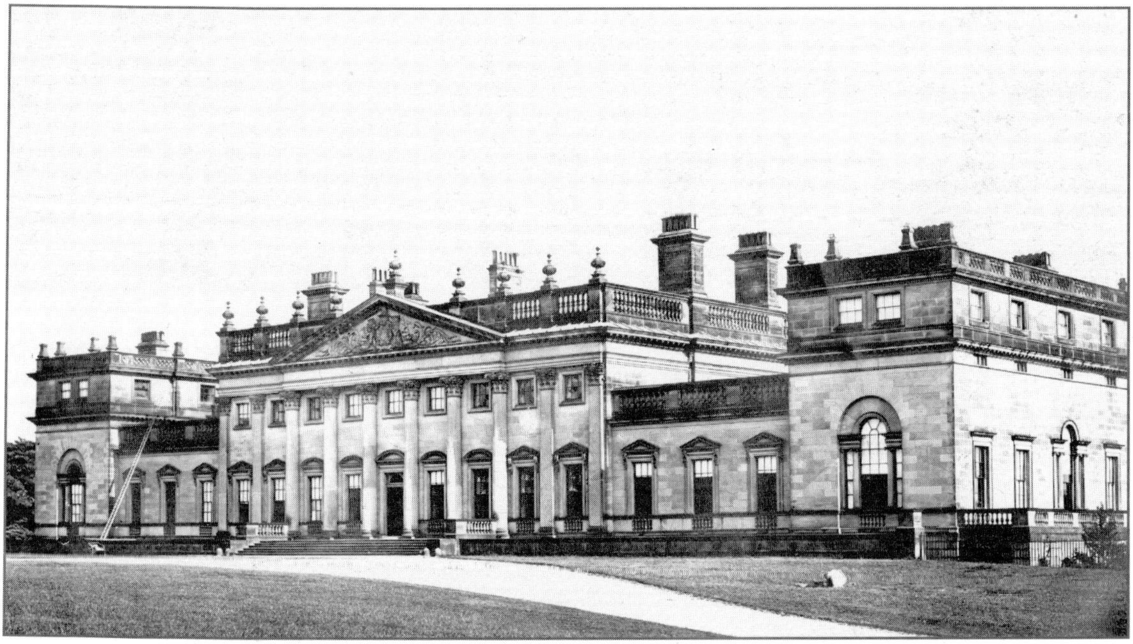

Harrogate

Harewood House c1886 7364

Harewood House is the result of a happy conjunction of some of the greatest talent in design and architecture. Edwin Lascelles (later the first Earl of Harewood) employed John Carr to design the house, Robert Adam to decorate it, and Capability Brown to lay out the park.

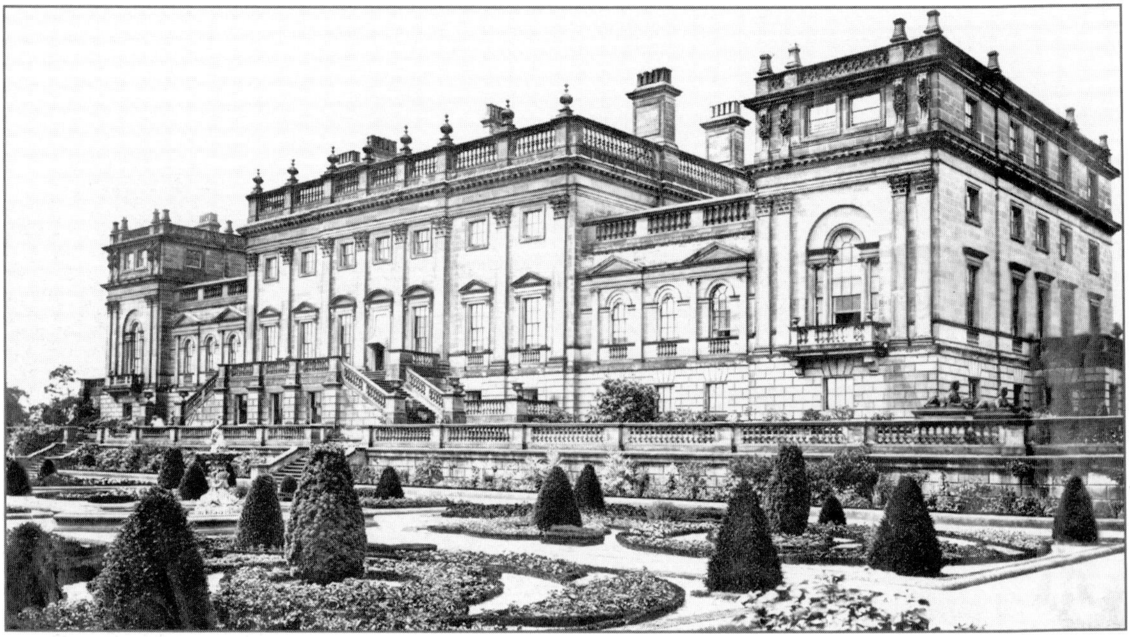

Harrogate, Harewood House c1886 7365
The north front of Harewood was remodelled in 1843 by the great Victorian architect Sir Charles Barry, who also designed the Houses of Parliament. Barry was much influenced by classic Greek and Italian architecture; he flew the flag for his style while all around were going Gothic.

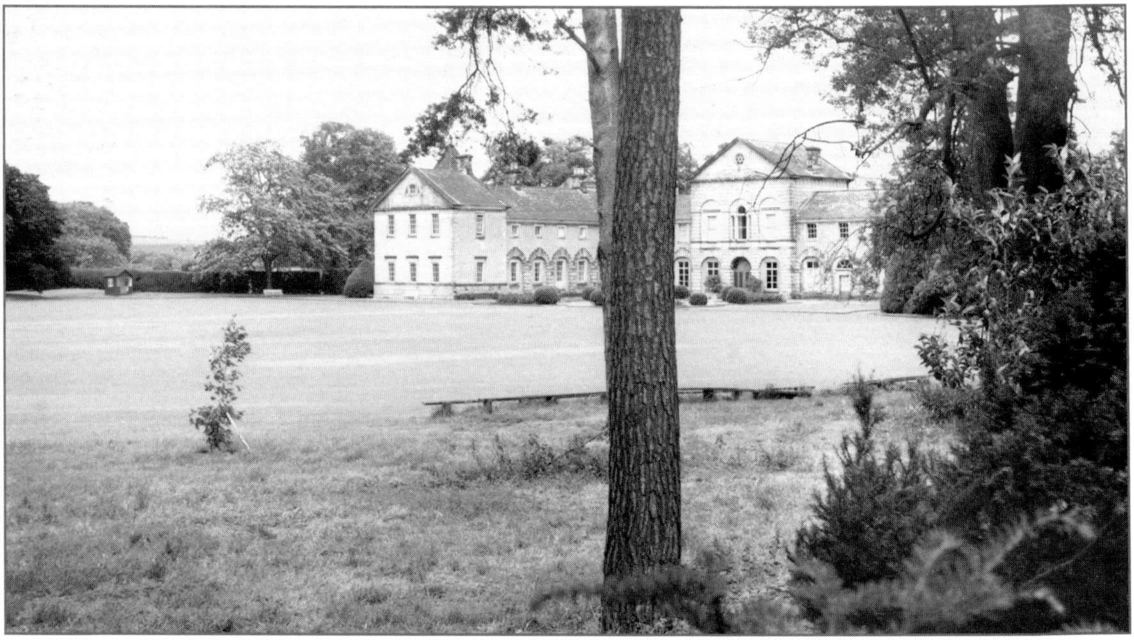

Hovingham, The Hall c1965 H217026
It appears that Sir Thomas Worsley was horse-mad, for the house is built around a central riding school, approached through a vaulted tunnel archway. Even the ballroom is on an upper floor to allow more space on the ground floor for horses.

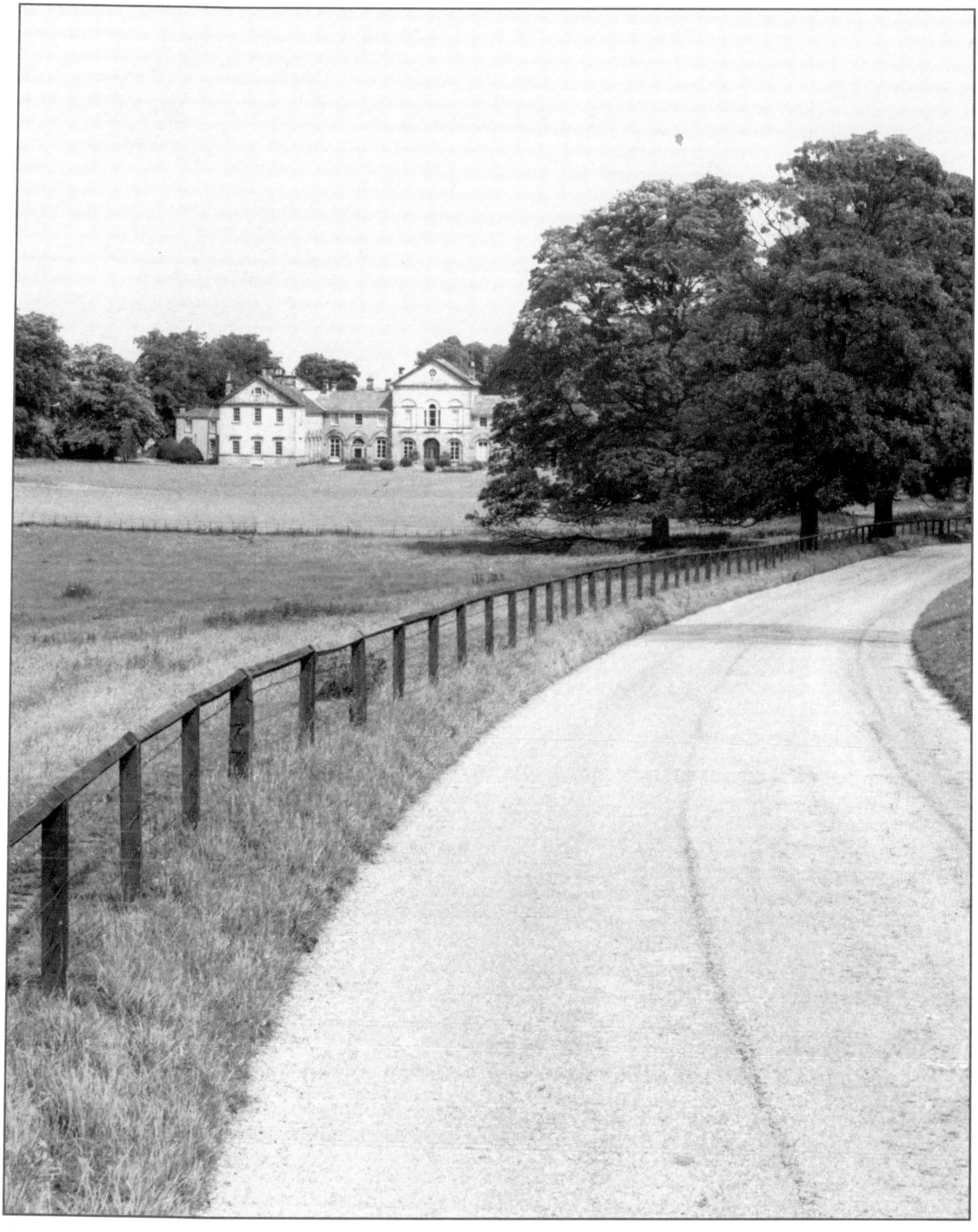

Hovingham, The Hall c1965 H217024
The beautiful parkland on which Hovingham Hall stands was once a Roman site. A Roman bath house and pavements were discovered during the building of the Hall, which was carried out in 1745-55 by Sir Thomas Worsley, the Surveyor-General.

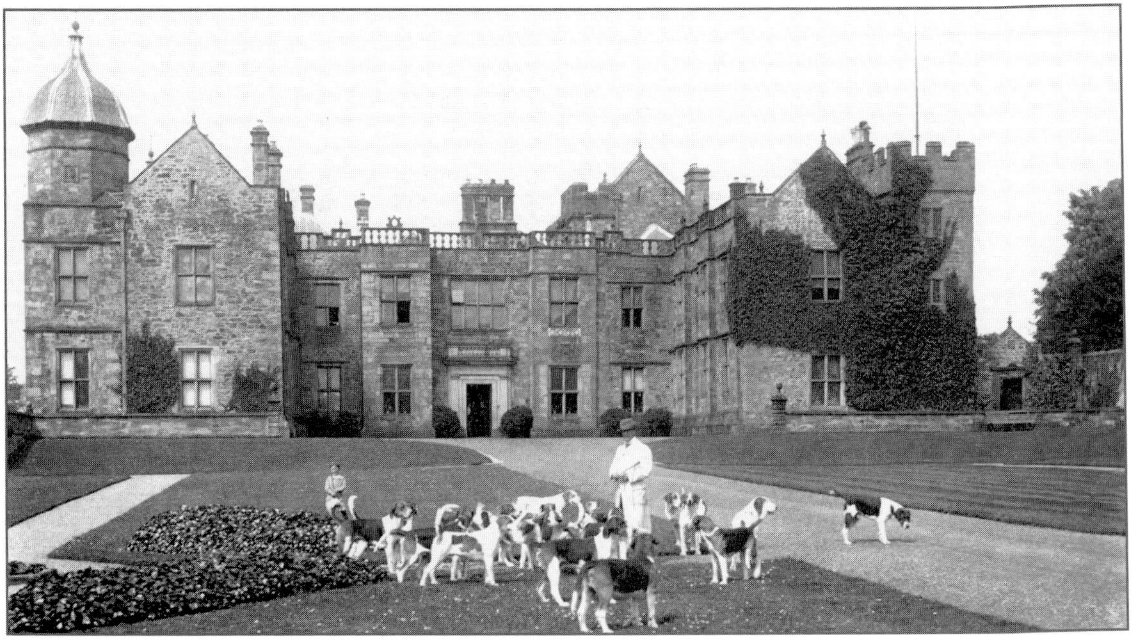

Middleham, Danby Hall 1906 55995
Like many country houses, Danby Hall has evolved in several phases. The north-east tower (right) is a 14th- or 15th-century Pele Tower; the east side was built in the 16th century and remodelled in the 17th century; and the south front (pictured) was built in 1855 by Joseph Hansom for Thornton Steward.

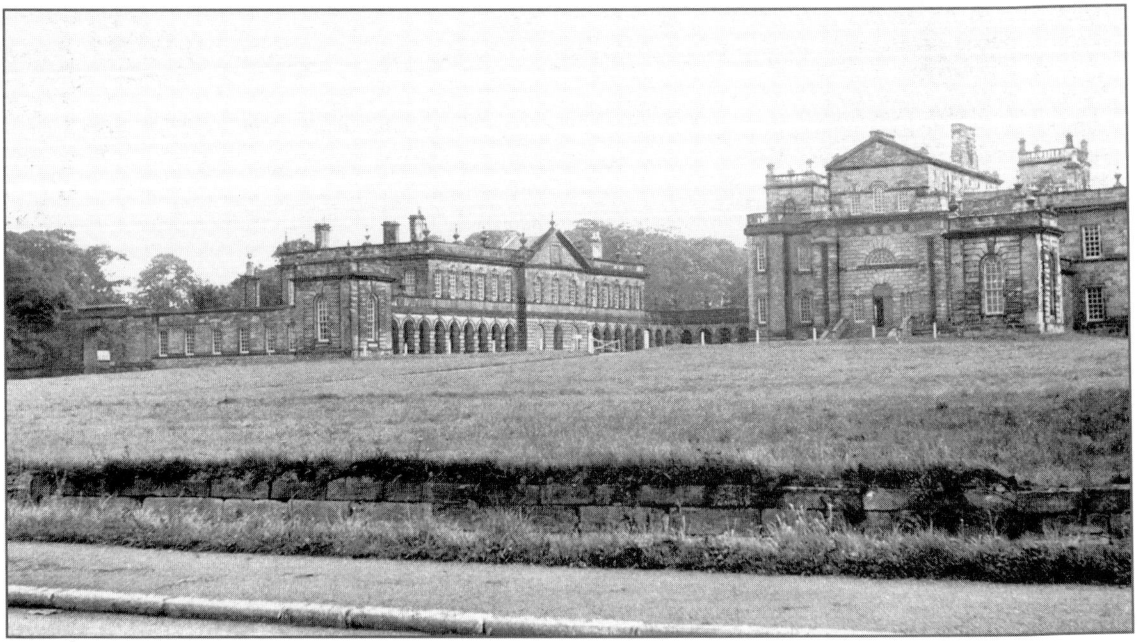

Seaton Delaval, The Hall c1965 S522007
Considered by many to be Sir John Vanbrugh's masterpiece, Seaton Delaval Hall was built between 1718 and 1728 for Admiral George Delaval. Unfortunately, neither architect or owner lived to see this magnificent baroque house completed.

Yorkshire & The North West

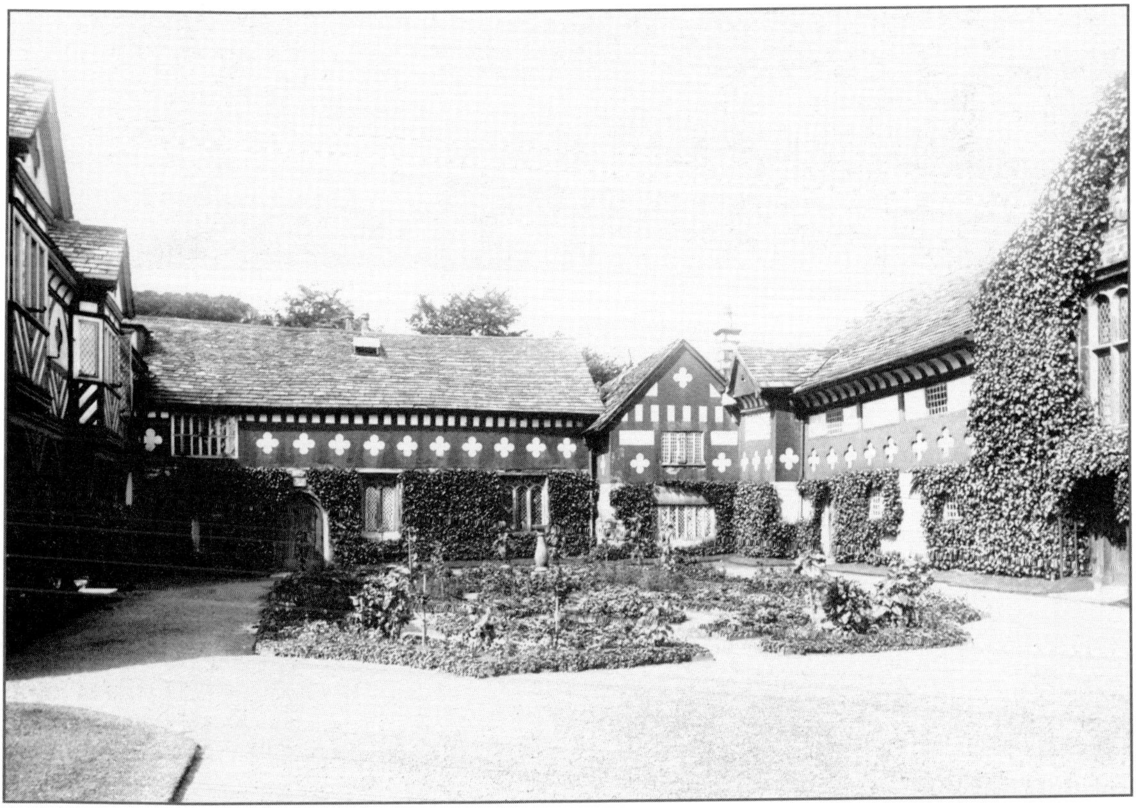

Bolton, Smithill's Hall 1894 34392
One of Lancashire's oldest timbered manor houses, Smithill's Hall was first built in the 14th century. The Great Hall dates from this period, and the rest of the house is Tudor.

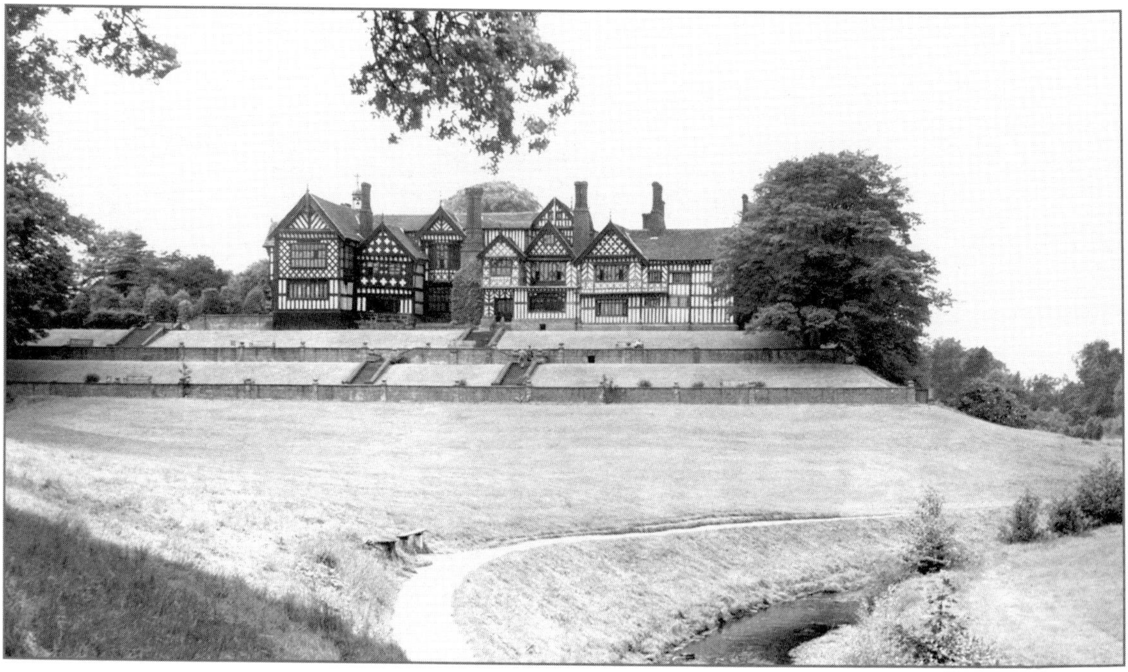

Cheadle Hulme, Bramall Hall c1965 C285013
One of the finest timber-framed houses in the country, with the 'magpie' exterior and gables characteristic of the area, Bramall Hall was built in the 14th century and extended in the 1590s.

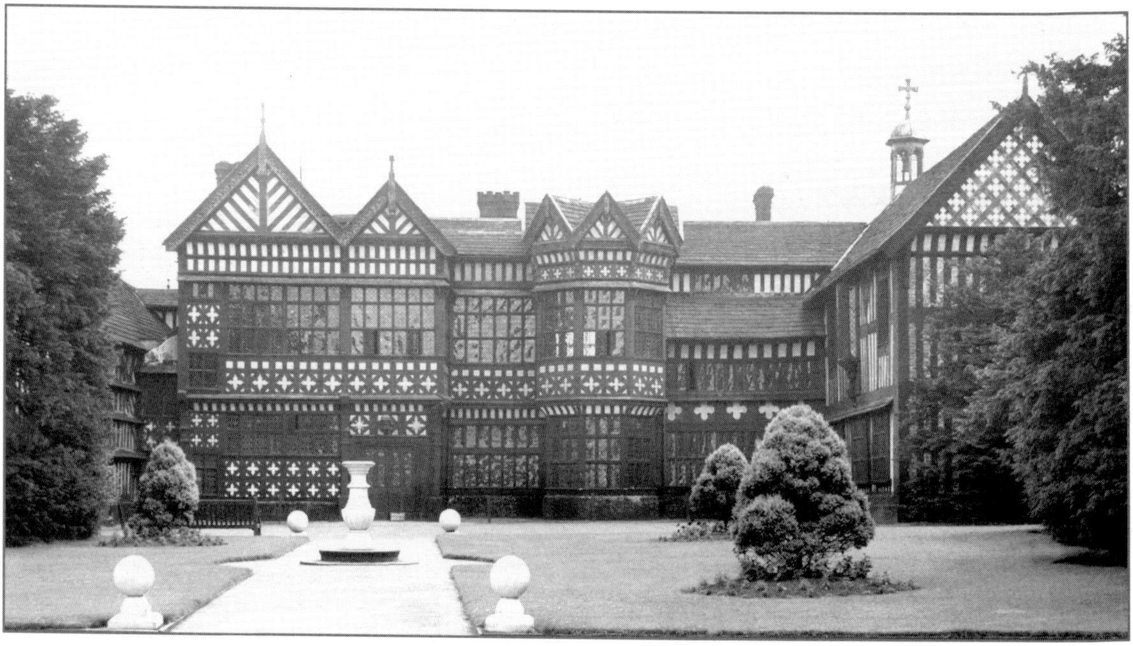

Cheadle Hulme, Bramall Hall c1965 C285026
Bramall Hall was for many years the home of the Davenport family; the master bedroom contains a tapestry by Dame Dorothy Davenport which took her 36 years to complete. The house has a fine collection of Elizabethan and Jacobean furniture, including a spiral staircase and a Flemish travelling bed.

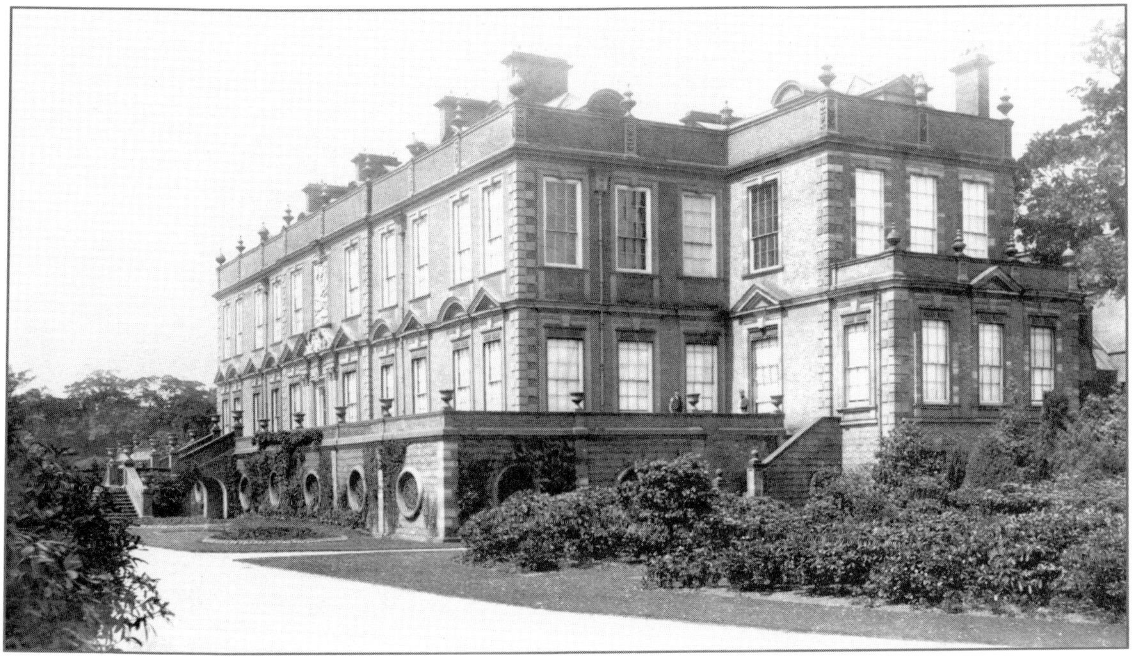

Croxteth Hall 1887 20065
In the picture is the west wing, built in 1702-14. Part of the original Elizabethan house survives at the back, and the stables were built by Caryll Molyneux in 1678-1706.

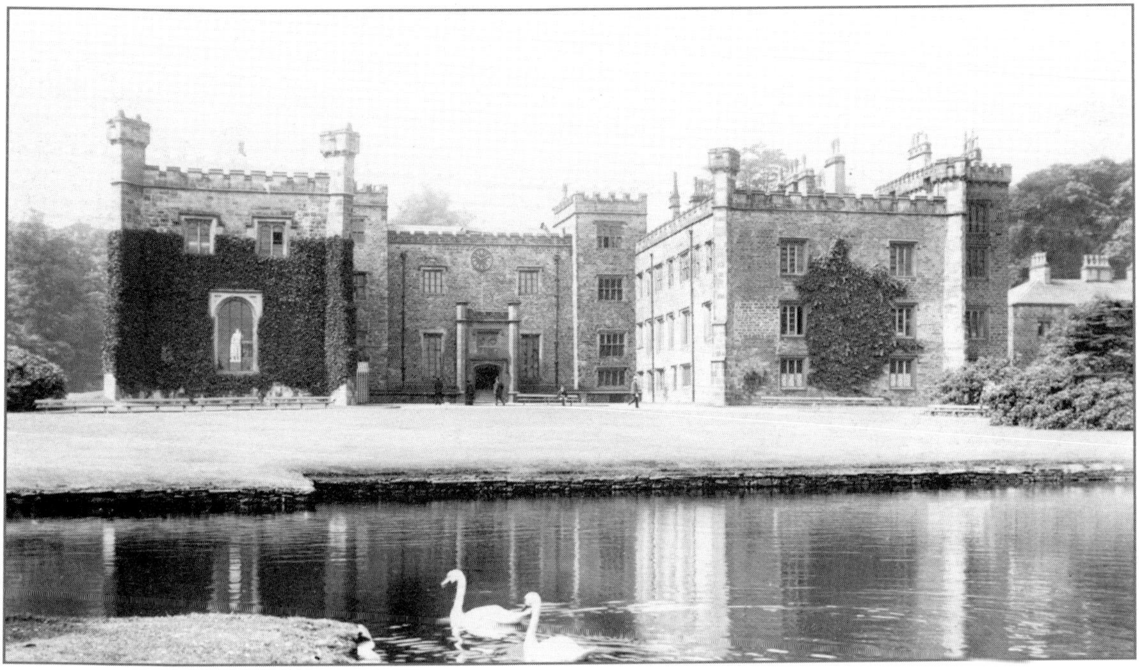

Burnley, Townley Hall 1906 54201
Built by the Townley family in the 13th century, this fortified house underwent constant modification in the 16th, 17th and 19th centuries. It has an Elizabethan gallery and entrance hall, and now houses two museums.

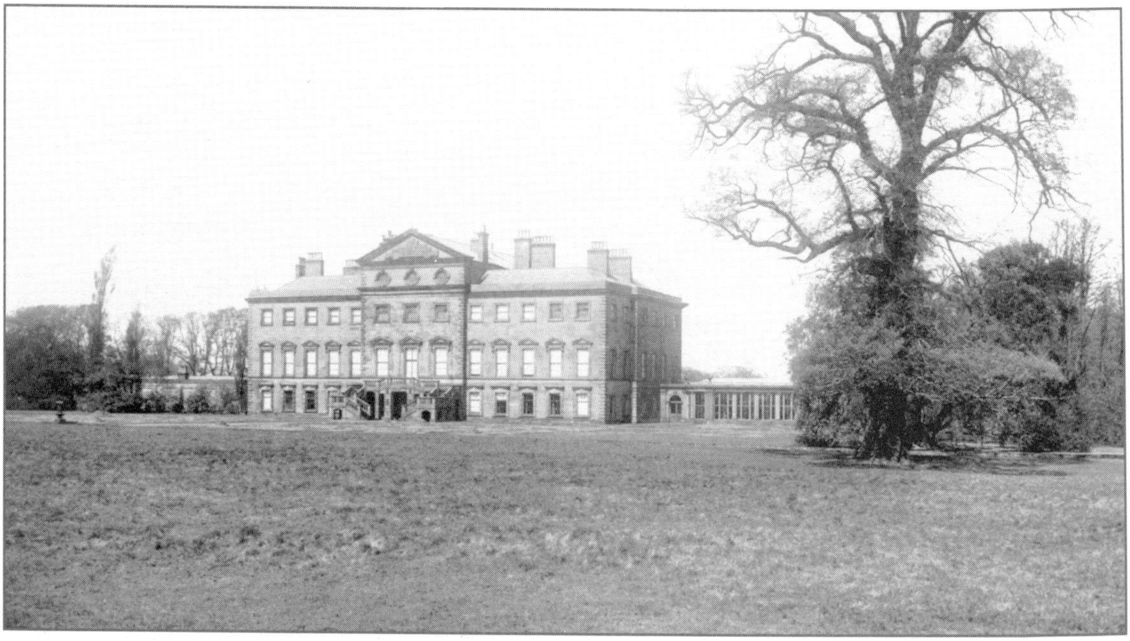

Ormskirk, Lathom House 1896 37418

The first house on this site was built by Lord Stanley, Earl of Derby, and was besieged by Parliamentarian troops in 1644. It was defended bravely by the Countess, Charlotte de Tremoville, but it eventually fell and was destroyed. The only surviving part of the original house is the chapel, consecrated in 1509 and still used as a place of worship today.

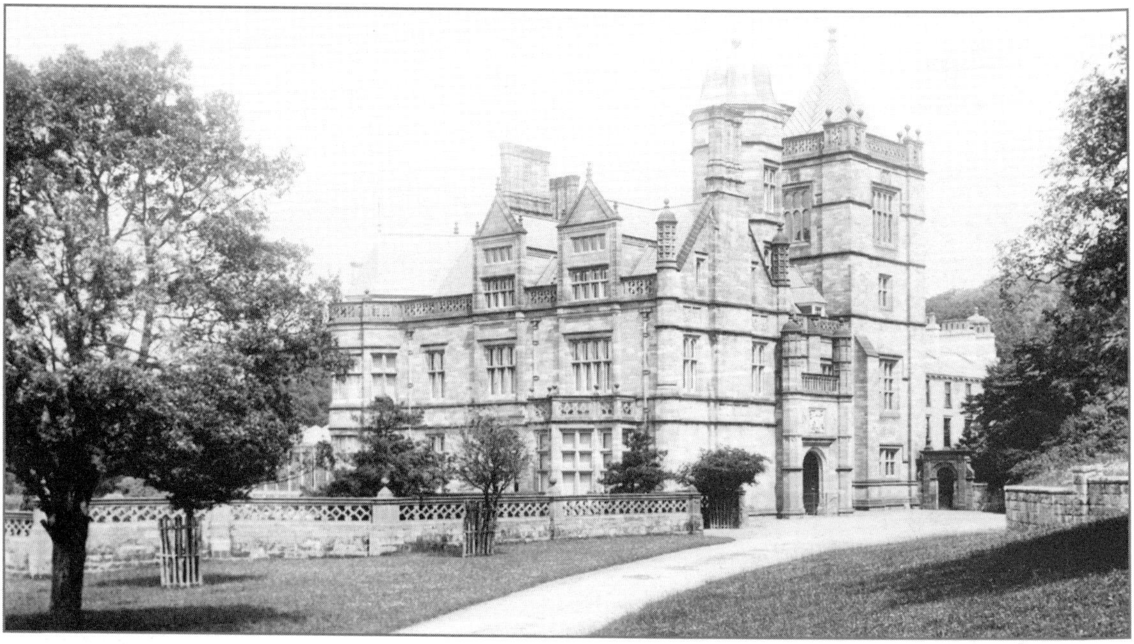

Holker Hall 1894 34106

Home of the Cavendish family since 1756, the 17th-century Holker Hall was rebuilt after a fire in 1871. Luckily, the fire spared the library; it contains 3,500 books, including some by Henry Cavendish, who investigated the properties of hydrogen in 1760.

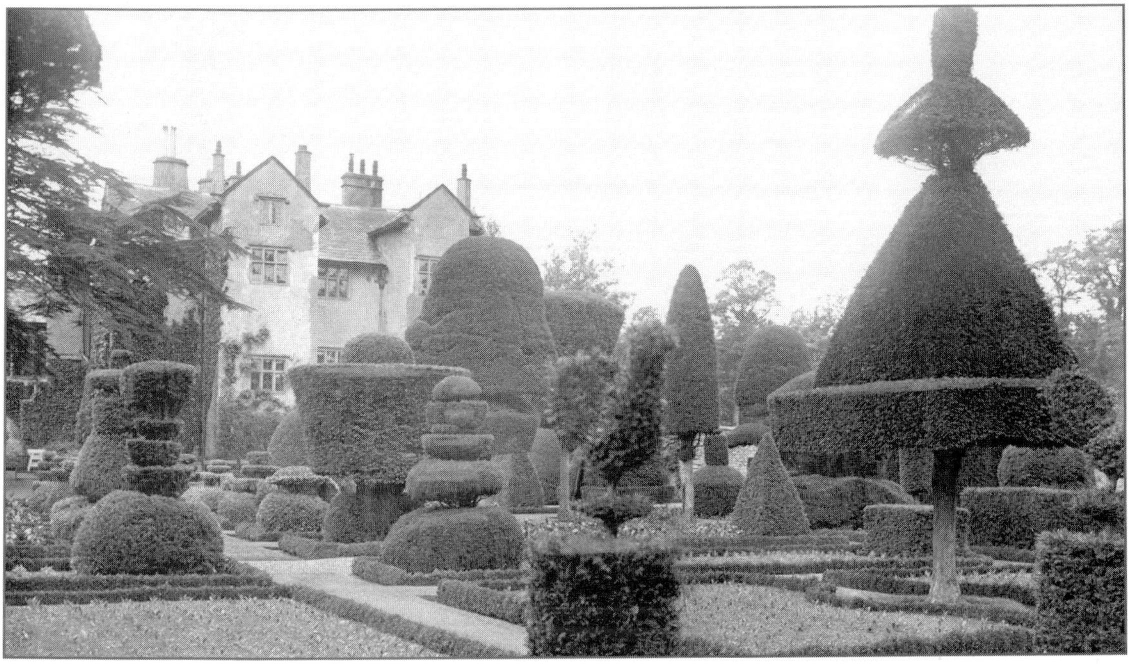

LEVENS HALL AND GARDENS c1955 L447021
The Elizabethan mansion of Levens Hall, completed in 1586, was previously a Pele Tower - a fortified refuge against marauding Scots, who were very keen on cross-border raids.

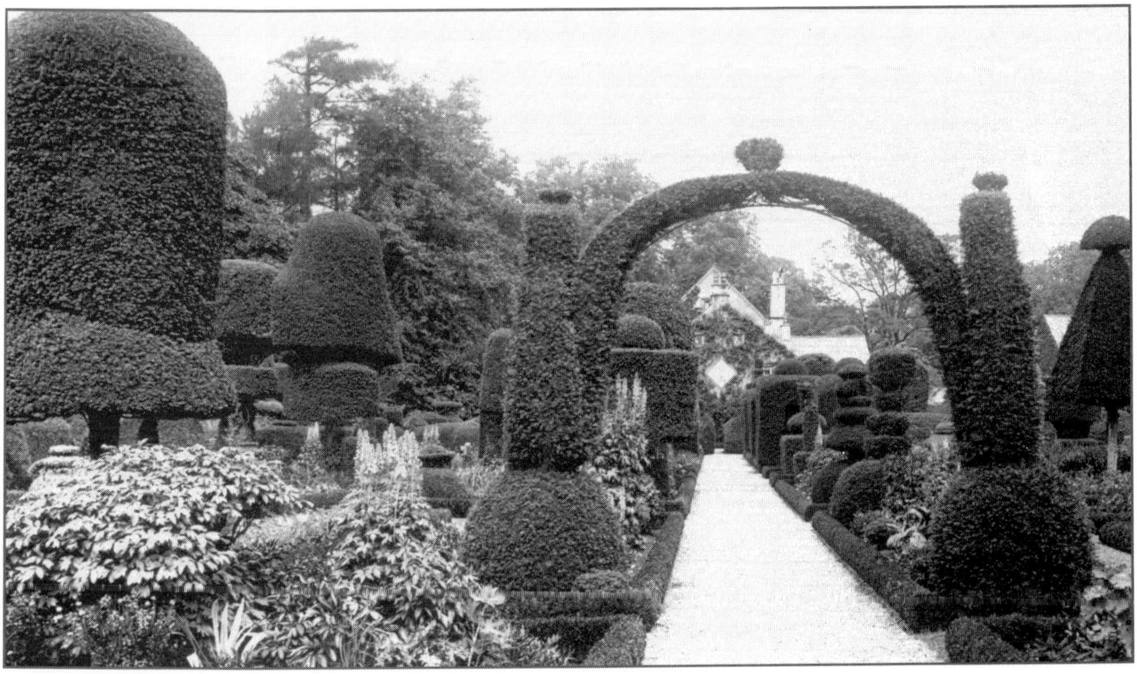

LEVENS HALL 1891 28630
The gardens of Levens Hall, with enough topiary to keep Black and Decker in business, were designed in 1690 by a Frenchman, Guillaume Beaumont; he was trained at Versailles, and died at Levens Hall in 1727.

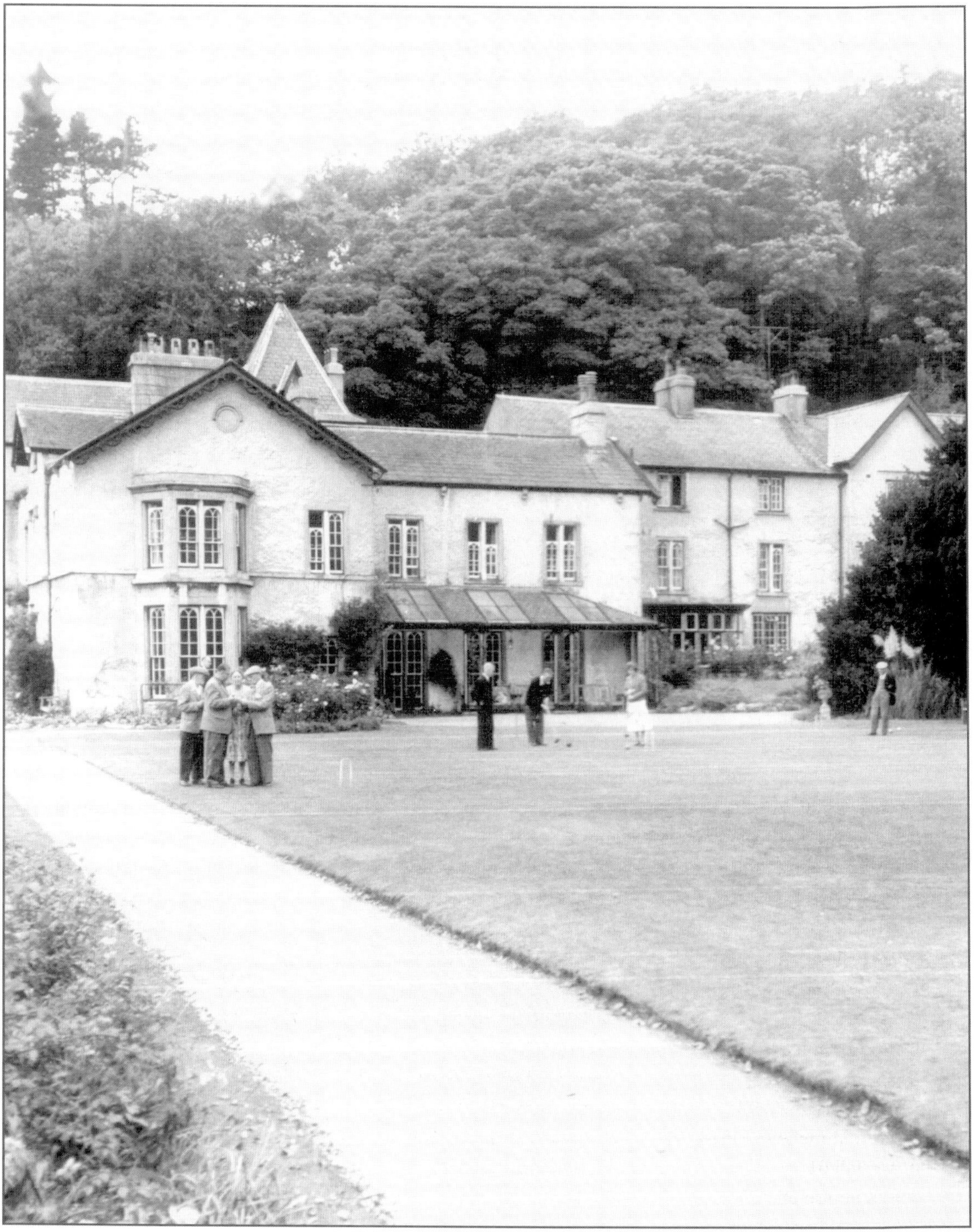

Kents Bank, Abbot Hall c1955 KL47099

The upper floors are now an art gallery, displaying modern paintings and sculpture. Downstairs, the original decoration and period furniture is intact, much as it would have looked in 1759 when the house was designed by John Carr of York. Later in the same year he commenced work on Harewood House.

Index

Frith Book Co Titles

www.frithbook.co.uk

The Frith Book Company publishes over 100 new titles each year. A selection of those currently available are listed below. For latest catalogue please contact Frith Book Co.

Town Books 96pp, 100 photos. County and Themed Books 128pp, 150 photos (unless specified). All titles hardback laminated case and jacket except those indicated pb (paperback)

Around Bakewell	1-85937-113-2	£12.99
Around Barnstaple	1-85937-084-5	£12.99
Around Bath	1-85937-097-7	£12.99
Berkshire (pb)	1-85937-191-4	£9.99
Around Blackpool	1-85937-049-7	£12.99
Around Bognor Regis	1-85937-055-1	£12.99
Around Bournemouth	1-85937-067-5	£12.99
Brighton (pb)	1-85937-192-2	£8.99
British Life A Century Ago	1-85937-103-5	£17.99
Buckinghamshire (pb)	1-85937-200-7	£9.99
Around Cambridge	1-85937-092-6	£12.99
Cambridgeshire	1-85937-086-1	£14.99
Canals and Waterways	1-85937-129-9	£17.99
Cheshire	1-85937-045-4	£14.99
Around Chester	1-85937-090-x	£12.99
Around Chichester	1-85937-089-6	£12.99
Churches of Berkshire	1-85937-170-1	£17.99
Churches of Dorset	1-85937-172-8	£17.99
Colchester (pb)	1-85937-188-4	£8.99
Cornwall	1-85937-054-3	£14.99
Cumbria	1-85937-101-9	£14.99
Dartmoor	1-85937-145-0	£14.99
Around Derby	1-85937-046-2	£12.99
Derbyshire (pb)	1-85937-196-5	£9.99
Devon	1-85937-052-7	£14.99
Dorset	1-85937-075-6	£14.99
Dorset Coast	1-85937-062-4	£14.99
Down the Severn	1-85937-118-3	£14.99
Down the Thames	1-85937-121-3	£14.99
Around Dublin	1-85937-058-6	£12.99
East Sussex	1-85937-130-2	£14.99
Around Eastbourne	1-85937-061-6	£12.99
Edinburgh (pb)	1-85937-193-0	£8.99
English Castles	1-85937-078-0	£14.99
Essex	1-85937-082-9	£14.99
Around Exeter	1-85937-126-4	£12.99
Exmoor	1-85937-132-9	£14.99
Around Falmouth	1-85937-066-7	£12.99
Around Great Yarmouth	1-85937-085-3	£12.99
Around Guildford	1-85937-117-5	£12.99
Hampshire	1-85937-064-0	£14.99
Around Harrogate	1-85937-112-4	£12.99
Around Horsham	1-85937-127-2	£12.99
Around Ipswich	1-85937-133-7	£12.99
Ireland (pb)	1-85937-181-7	£9.99
Isle of Man	1-85937-065-9	£14.99
Isle of Wight	1-85937-114-0	£14.99
Kent (pb)	1-85937-189-2	£9.99
Around Leicester	1-85937-073-x	£12.99
Leicestershire (pb)	1-85937-185-x	£9.99
Around Lincoln	1-85937-111-6	£12.99
Lincolnshire	1-85937-135-3	£14.99
London (pb)	1-85937-183-3	£9.99
Around Maidstone	1-85937-056-x	£12.99
New Forest	1-85937-128-0	£14.99
Around Newark	1-85937-105-1	£12.99
Around Newquay	1-85937-140-x	£12.99
North Devon Coast	1-85937-146-9	£14.99
Northumberland and Tyne & Wear	1-85937-072-1	£14.99
Norwich (pb)	1-85937-194-9	£8.99
Around Nottingham	1-85937-060-8	£12.99
Nottinghamshire (pb)	1-85937-187-6	£9.99
Around Oxford	1-85937-096-9	£12.99
Oxfordshire	1-85937-076-4	£14.99
Peak District	1-85937-100-0	£14.99
Around Penzance	1-85937-069-1	£12.99
Around Plymouth	1-85937-119-1	£12.99
Around St Ives	1-85937-068-3	£12.99
Around Scarborough	1-85937-104-3	£12.99
Scotland (pb)	1-85937-182-5	£9.99
Scottish Castles	1-85937-077-2	£14.99
Around Sevenoaks and Tonbridge	1-85937-057-8	£12.99
Around Southampton	1-85937-088-8	£12.99
Around Southport	1-85937-106-x	£12.99

Available from your local bookshop or from the publisher

Frith Book Co Titles (continued)

Around Shrewsbury	1-85937-110-8	£12.99
Shropshire	1-85937-083-7	£14.99
South Devon Coast	1-85937-107-8	£14.99
South Devon Living Memories	1-85937-168-x	£14.99
Staffordshire (96pp)	1-85937-047-0	£12.99
Stone Circles & Ancient Monuments	1-85937-143-4	£17.99
Around Stratford upon Avon	1-85937-098-5	£12.99
Sussex (pb)	1-85937-184-1	£9.99
Around Torbay	1-85937-063-2	£12.99
Around Truro	1-85937-147-7	£12.99
Victorian & Edwardian Kent	1-85937-149-3	£14.99
Victorian & Edwardian Yorkshire	1-85937-154-x	£14.99
Warwickshire (pb)	1-85937-203-1	£9.99
Welsh Castles	1-85937-120-5	£14.99
West Midlands	1-85937-109-4	£14.99
West Sussex	1-85937-148-5	£14.99
Wiltshire	1-85937-053-5	£14.99
Around Winchester	1-85937-139-6	£12.99

Frith Book Co titles available Autumn 2000

Croydon Living Memories (pb)	1-85937-162-0	£9.99	Aug
Glasgow (pb)	1-85937-190-6	£9.99	Aug
Hertfordshire (pb)	1-85937-247-3	£9.99	Aug
North London	1-85937-206-6	£14.99	Aug
Victorian & Edwardian Maritime Album	1-85937-144-2	£17.99	Aug
Victorian Seaside	1-85937-159-0	£17.99	Aug
Cornish Coast	1-85937-163-9	£14.99	Sep
County Durham	1-85937-123-x	£14.99	Sep
Dorset Living Memories	1-85937-210-4	£14.99	Sep
Herefordshire	1-85937-174-4	£14.99	Sep
Kent Living Memories	1-85937-125-6	£14.99	Sep
Leeds (pb)	1-85937-202-3	£9.99	Sep
Ludlow (pb)	1-85937-176-0	£9.99	Sep
Norfolk (pb)	1-85937-195-7	£9.99	Sep
Somerset	1-85937-153-1	£14.99	Sep
Tees Valley & Cleveland	1-85937-211-2	£14.99	Sep
Thanet (pb)	1-85937-116-7	£9.99	Sep
Tiverton (pb)	1-85937-178-7	£9.99	Sep
Victorian and Edwardian Sussex	1-85937-157-4	£14.99	Sep
Weymouth (pb)	1-85937-209-0	£9.99	Sep
Worcestershire	1-85937-152-3	£14.99	Sep
Yorkshire Living Memories	1-85937-166-3	£14.99	Sep
British Life A Century Ago (pb)	1-85937-213-9	£9.99	Oct
Camberley (pb)	1-85937-222-8	£9.99	Oct
Cardiff (pb)	1-85937-093-4	£9.99	Oct
Carmarthenshire	1-85937-216-3	£14.99	Oct
Cornwall (pb)	1-85937-229-5	£9.99	Oct
English Country Houses	1-85937-161-2	£17.99	Oct
Gloucestershire	1-85937-102-7	£14.99	Oct
Humberside	1-85937-215-5	£14.99	Oct
Manchester (pb)	1-85937-198-1	£9.99	Oct
Middlesex	1-85937-158-2	£14.99	Oct
Norfolk Living Memories	1-85937-217-1	£14.99	Oct
Preston (pb)	1-85937-212-0	£9.99	Oct
South Hams	1-85937-220-1	£14.99	Oct
Suffolk	1-85937-221-x	£9.99	Oct
Swansea (pb)	1-85937-167-1	£9.99	Oct
West Yorkshire (pb)	1-85937-201-5	£9.99	Oct

See Frith books on the internet www.frithbook.co.uk

FRITH PRODUCTS & SERVICES

Francis Frith would doubtless be pleased to know that the pioneering publishing venture he started in 1860 still continues today. A hundred and forty years later, The Francis Frith Collection continues in the same innovative tradition and is now one of the foremost publishers of vintage photographs in the world. Some of the current activities include:

Interior Decoration

Today Frith's photographs can be seen framed and as giant wall murals in thousands of pubs, restaurants, hotels, banks, retail stores and other public buildings throughout the country. In every case they enhance the unique local atmosphere of the places they depict and provide reminders of gentler days in an increasingly busy and frenetic world.

Product Promotions

Frith products are used by many major companies to promote the sales of their own products or to reinforce their own history and heritage. Frith promotions have been used by Hovis bread, Courage beers, Scots Porage Oats, Colman's mustard, Cadbury's foods, Mellow Birds coffee, Dunhill pipe tobacco, Guinness, and Bulmer's Cider.

Genealogy and Family History

As the interest in family history and roots grows world-wide, more and more people are turning to Frith's photographs of Great Britain for images of the towns, villages and streets where their ancestors lived; and, of course, photographs of the churches and chapels where their ancestors were christened, married and buried are an essential part of every genealogy tree and family album.

Frith Products

All Frith photographs are available Framed or just as Mounted Prints and Posters (size 23 x 16 inches). These may be ordered from the address below. From time to time other products - Address Books, Calendars, Table Mats, etc - are available.

The Internet

Already twenty thousand Frith photographs can be viewed and purchased on the internet. By the end of the year 2000 some 60,000 Frith photographs will be available on the internet. The number of sites is constantly expanding, each focussing on different products and services from the Collection.
The main Frith sites are listed below.

www.francisfrith.co.uk
www.frithbook.co.uk

See the complete list of Frith Books at:
www.frithbook.co.uk
This web site is regularly updated with the latest list of publications from the Frith Book Company. If you wish to buy books relating to another part of the country that your local bookshop does not stock, you may purchase on-line.

For further information, trade, or author enquiries please contact us at the address below:
The Francis Frith Collection, Frith's Barn, Teffont, Salisbury, Wiltshire, England SP3 5QP.
Tel: +44 (0)1722 716 376 Fax: +44 (0)1722 716 881 Email: uksales@francisfrith.com

See Frith books on the internet www.frithbook.co.uk

To receive your FREE Mounted Print

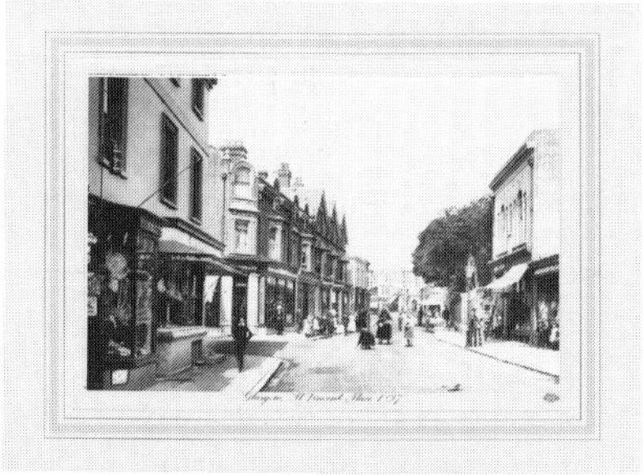

Mounted Print
Overall size 14 x 11 inches

Cut out this Voucher and return it with your remittance for £1.50 to cover postage and handling, to UK addresses. For overseas addresses please include £4.00 post and handling.
Choose any photograph included in this book. Your SEPIA print will be A4 in size, and mounted in a cream mount with burgundy rule lines, overall size 14 x 11 inches.

Order additional Mounted Prints at HALF PRICE (only £7.49 each*)
If there are further pictures you would like to order, possibly as gifts for friends and family, purchase them at half price (no additional postage and handling required).

Have your Mounted Prints framed*
For an additional £14.95 per print you can have your chosen Mounted Print framed in an elegant polished wood and gilt moulding, overall size 16 x 13 inches (no additional postage and handling required).

*** IMPORTANT!**
These special prices are only available if ordered using the original voucher on this page (no copies permitted) and at the same time as your free Mounted Print, for delivery to the same address

Frith Collectors' Guild

From time to time we publish a magazine of news and stories about Frith photographs and further special offers of Frith products. If you would like 12 months FREE membership, please return this form.

Send completed forms to:
The Francis Frith Collection, Frith's Barn, Teffont, Salisbury, Wiltshire SP3 5QP

Voucher for FREE and Reduced Price Frith Prints

Picture no.	Page number	Qty	Mounted @ £7.49	Framed + £14.95	Total Cost
		1	**Free of charge***	£	£
			£7.49	£	£
			£7.49	£	£
			£7.49	£	£
			£7.49	£	£
			£7.49	£	£

Please allow 28 days for delivery *** Post & handling** **£1.50**

Book Title . . . . **Total Order Cost** **£**

Please do not photocopy this voucher. Only the original is valid, so please cut it out and return it to us.

I enclose a cheque / postal order for £ . . . .
made payable to 'The Francis Frith Collection'
OR please debit my Mastercard / Visa / Switch / Amex card
Number . . . .
Issue No (Switch only) . . . . Valid from (Amex/Switch) . . . .
Expires . . . . Signature . . . .
Name Mr/Mrs/Ms ....
Address ....
....
....
....
.... Postcode ....
Daytime Tel No .... Valid to 31/12/02

The Francis Frith Collectors' Guild

Please enrol me as a member for 12 months free of charge.

Name Mr/Mrs/Ms ....
Address ....
....
....
.... Postcode ....